THE NEW GROVE
TWENTIETH-CENTURY
FRENCH MASTERS

THE NEW GROVE®

Twentieth-century French Masters

**FAURÉ DEBUSSY SATIE
RAVEL POULENC
MESSIAEN BOULEZ**

Jean-Michel Nectoux

Roger Nichols

Patrick Gowers

G. W. Hopkins

Paul Griffiths

W. W. NORTON & COMPANY
NEW YORK   LONDON

First published in
The New Grove Dictionary of Music and Musicians®,
edited by Stanley Sadie, 1980

The New Grove and *The New Grove Dictionary of Music and Musicians*
are registered trademarks of Macmillan Publishers Limited, London

First published in UK in paperback with additions 1986 by
PAPERMAC
a division of Macmillan Publishers Limited
London and Basingstoke

First published in UK in hardback with additions 1986 by
MACMILLAN LONDON LIMITED
4 Little Essex Street London WC2R 3LF
and Basingstoke

British Library Cataloguing in Publication Data

French 20th-century Masters: Fauré, Debussy
Satie, Ravel, Poulenc, Messiaen, Boulez.——
(The Composer biography series)
1. Composers——France   2. Music——France——
20th century——History and criticism
I. Nectoux, Jean-Michel   II. The new Grove dictionary
of music and musicians   III. Series
780′.92′2   ML270.5

ISBN 0-333-40239-1 (hardback)
ISBN 0-333-40240-5 (paperback)

First American edition in book form with additions 1986 by
W. W. NORTON & COMPANY
500 Fifth Avenue, New York NY 10110

ISBN 0-393-02284-6 (hardback)
ISBN 0-393-30350-0 (paperback)

Printed in Great Britain by
Redwood Burn Limited, Trowbridge, Wiltshire,
and bound by Pegasus Bookbinding, Melksham, Wiltshire.

Contents

List of illustrations

Cover: detail from Leon Bakst's design for the first tableau of Ravel's 'Daphnis et Chloé' [see fig.16]

Illustration acknowledgments

We are grateful to the following for permission to reproduce illustrative material: Photodécor, Paris (fig.1); Bibliothèque Nationale, Paris (figs.2, 4, 5, 12 [photo], 13); Editions Durand & Cie, Paris (figs.3, 12, 18); SPADEM and Madame de Tinan Collection, Paris (figs.6, 11); Pierpont Morgan Library, New York (Mary Flager Cary Music Collection, fig.7; Robert O. Lehman Collection, fig.18); H. Roger-Viollet, Paris (fig.8); BBC Hulton Picture Library, London (fig.9); Madame Alexandre Taverne, Rougement, Switzerland (fig.15); Musée des Arts Décoratifs, Paris (fig.16, cover); photo Editions du Seuil, Paris (fig.17); Luciana Frassati, Turin: from L. Frassati, *Il maestro: Arturo Toscanini e il suo mondo* (Turin, 1967) (fig.19); Popperfoto, London (fig.20); Editions Alphonse Leduc, Paris (figs.20, 21); Bibliothèque et Musée de l'Opéra, Paris/photo Jacques Moatti (fig.23); photo Clive Barda, London (fig.24); Universal Edition (London) Ltd (fig.25)

Music example acknowledgments

We are grateful to the following music publishers for permission to reproduce copyright material: Editions Alphonse Leduc et Cie, Paris (*Messiaen* 1–3); Editions Amphion, Paris/United Music Publishers Ltd, London [UMP] (*Boulez* 1–3); Editions Arima Ltd and Durand S. A. Editions Musicales, Paris/UMP (*Ravel* 1–4); Durand S. A. Editions Musicales/UMP (*Poulenc* 1); Editions Heugel et Cie, Paris/UMP (*Poulenc* 2); Universal Edition (London) Ltd (*Boulez* 4, 5).

General abbreviations

A	alto, contralto [voice]	inc.	incomplete
a	alto [instrument]	inst	instrument, instrumental
acc.	accompaniment, accompanied by	IRCAM	Institut de Recherche et de Coordination Acoustique/Musique (France)
B	bass [voice]		
b	bass [instrument]		
b	born	K	Köchel catalogue [Mozart]
Bar	baritone [voice]		
BBC	British Broadcasting Corporation		
bn	bassoon	mar	marimba
BWV	Bach-Werke-Verzeichnis [Schmieder, catalogue of J. S. Bach's works]	Mez	mezzo-soprano
		movt	movement
		n.d.	no date of publication
c	circa [about]		
CBS	Columbia Broadcasting System (USA)	ob	oboe
		orch	orchestra, orchestral
cel	celesta	orchd	orchestrated (by)
cl	clarinet	org	organ
CNRS	Centre National de la Recherche Scientifique (France)	ORTF	Office de Radiodiffusion-Télévision Française
collab.	in collaboration with		
conc.	concerto	perc	percussion
cond.	conductor, conducted by	perf.	performance, performed (by)
		pic	piccolo
d	died	PO	Philharmonic Orchestra
db	double bass	posth.	posthumous(ly)
		prol	prologue
edn.	edition	pubd	published
elec	electric, electronic		
ens	ensemble	qnt	quintet
		qt	quartet
facs.	facsimile		
fl	flute	*R*	photographic reprint
		red.	reduction, reduced for
gui	guitar	rev.	revision, revised (by/for)
		RSO	Radio Symphony Orchestra
hn	horn		
hpd	harpsichord		

S	soprano [voice]	transcr.	transcription, transcribed by/for
sax	saxophone		
SO	Symphony Orchestra	trbn	trombone
str	string(s)		
sum.	summer	U.	University
sym.	symphony, symphonic		
		v, vv	voice, voices
		va	viola
T	tenor [voice]	vc	cello
timp.	timpani	vib	vibraphone
tpt	trumpet	vn	violin

Symbols for the library sources of works, printed in *italic*, correspond to those used in *Répertoire International des Sources Musicales*, Ser. A.

Bibliographical abbreviations

AMw	*Archiv für Musikwissenschaft*
BSIM	*Bulletin français de la S*[*ociété*] *I*[*nternationale de*] *M*[*usique*] [previously *Le Mercure musical*; also other titles]
CMc	*Current Musicology*
FAM	*Fontes artis musicae*
IMSCR	*International Musicological Society Congress Report*
Mf	*Die Musikforschung*
ML	*Music and Letters*
MMR	*The Monthly Musical Record*
MO	*Musical Opinion*
MQ	*The Musical Quarterly*
MR	*The Music Review*
MT	*The Musical Times*
Mw	Das Musikwerk
NRMI	*Nuova rivista musicale italiana*
NZM	*Neue Zeitschrift für Musik*
PNM	*Perspectives of New Music*
PRMA	*Proceedings of the Royal Musical Association*
RBM	*Revue belge de musicologie*
RdM	*Revue de musicologie*
ReM	*La revue musicale*
RIM	*Rivista italiana di musicologia*
SMz	*Schweizerische Musikzeitung/Revue musicale suisse*
ZMw	*Zeitschrift für Musikwissenschaft*

Preface

This volume is one of a series of short biographies derived from *The New Grove Dictionary of Music and Musicians* (London, 1980). In their original form, the texts were written in the mid-1970s, and finalized at the end of that decade. For this reprint, they have been re-read and brought up to date, mostly by their original authors; the exceptions are the sections contributed by the late G. W. Hopkins, on Ravel and Boulez—which have been kindly prepared by Roger Nichols and Paul Griffiths respectively—and the essay on Messiaen, where Paul Griffiths has contributed a new study to replace the earlier one.

The fact that the texts of the books in the series originated as dictionary articles inevitably gives them a character somewhat different from that of books conceived as such. They are designed, first of all, to accommodate a very great deal of information in a manner that makes reference quick and easy. Their first concern is with fact rather than opinion, and this leads to a larger than usual proportion of the texts being devoted to biography than to critical discussion. The nature of a reference work gives it a particular obligation to convey received knowledge and to treat of composers' lives and works in an encyclopedic fashion, with proper acknowledgment of sources and due care to reflect different standpoints, rather than to embody imaginative or speculative writing about a composer's character or his music. It is hoped that the comprehensive work-lists and extended bibliographies, indicative of the origins of the books in a reference work, will be valuable to the reader who is eager for full and accurate reference information and who may not have ready access to *The New Grove Dictionary* or who may prefer to have it in this more compact form.

S.S.

GABRIEL FAURÉ

Jean-Michel Nectoux

CHAPTER ONE

Life

Gabriel Urbain Fauré was born in Pamiers, Ariège, on 12
May 1845. He was the youngest of six children (one a
daughter), born to Toussaint-Honoré Fauré (1810–85)
and Marie-Antoinette-Hélène Lalène-Laprade (1809–
87), a member of the minor aristocracy. Gabriel was
sent to a foster-nurse in the village of Verniolle for four
years. In 1849 his father was appointed director of the
Ecole Normale at Montgauzy, near Foix; Fauré later
recalled that from his early childhood he spent hours
playing the harmonium in the chapel adjoining the
school. An old blind lady, who came to listen and give
advice, told his father about his gift for music. During
summer 1853 de Saubiac, archivist at the Paris
Assemblée, heard Fauré and advised his father to send
him to the Ecole de Musique Classique et Religieuse
which Louis Niedermeyer had just established in Paris.
After a year's reflection, Toussaint-Honoré decided that
the Ecole Niedermeyer, as it was later called, could
prepare his son for the profession of choirmaster while
cultivating his natural gifts. He took Gabriel to Paris (a
three-day journey) in October 1854.

Fauré remained a boarder at the Ecole Niedermeyer
for 11 years, during which he was helped by a scholar-
ship from the Bishop of Pamiers. His studies, which had
a crucial influence on his style, were chiefly of church
music (plainsong, the organ and Renaissance

1

1. Gabriel Fauré, aged 19, in the uniform of the Ecole Niedermeyer

polyphonic works) since the pupils were to become organists and choirmasters; the musical training was supplemented by serious literary studies. Fauré was taught the organ by Clément Loret, harmony by Louis Dietsch, counterpoint and fugue by Joseph Wackenthaler and the piano, plainsong and composition by Niedermeyer himself. Niedermeyer's death (March 1861) led to Fauré's fortunate encounter with Saint-Saëns, who now took the piano class. He introduced his pupils to contemporary music, which was not part of the school syllabus, including that of Schumann, Liszt and Wagner, and his teaching soon extended beyond the piano to composition. Fauré's first surviving works, *romances* for voice and piano on verses by Hugo, and *Trois romances sans paroles* for piano, date from this period. His student career at the Ecole Niedermeyer was completed on 28 July 1865: he gained *premiers prix* in composition (for the *Cantique de Jean Racine* op.11), and in fugue and counterpoint. He had previously been awarded prizes for solfège (1857), harmony (1860) and piano (1860, with a special prize in 1862).

Fauré's first appointment was as organist of St Sauveur at Rennes, where he remained from January 1866 to March 1870. Austere provincial life did not suit him, and he scandalized the local priest by accompanying the church scene of Gounod's *Faust* at the theatre. Nevertheless he found some friendly families to whom he gave lessons. The chronology of his output to 1875 is imprecise. His years in Rennes were apparently a period of intensive composition, when he wrote some piano pieces, his first attempts in symphonic form, church music and his first songs, in which he was clearly searching for a personal style.

3

On returning to Paris Fauré was immediately appointed assistant organist at the church of Notre Dame
in Clignancourt, near Paris, where he remained for only
a few months. During the Franco-Prussian War he
enlisted (16 August 1870) in the first light infantry
regiment of the Imperial Guard, from which he went to
the 28th temporary regiment; he took part in the action
to raise the siege of Paris. On being discharged (9
March 1871) he was appointed organist at the church of
the Parisian St Honoré d'Eylau. During the period of
the Commune he stayed at Rambouillet and he spent the
whole summer in Switzerland, where he taught composition at the Ecole Niedermeyer, which had taken refuge
in Cours-sous-Lausanne. On his return to Paris he was
appointed assistant organist at St Sulpice (October
1871) and became a regular visitor at Saint-Saëns'
salon, where he met all the members of Parisian musical
society. His friends included d'Indy, Lalo, Duparc and
Chabrier, with whom he formed the Société Nationale
de Musique on 25 February 1871. The subsequent
meetings of this society were the occasions of many of
his works' first performances.

In January 1874 Fauré left St Sulpice to deputize for
Saint-Saëns at the Madeleine during his absences. When
Saint-Saëns resigned in April 1877 Théodore Dubois
succeeded him as organist and Fauré became choirmaster. In July he became engaged to Marianne Viardot
(daughter of the singer Pauline Viardot) with whom he
had been in love for five years, but the engagement was
broken off in October by the girl, who felt only affection
mixed with fear for her fiancé. Fauré's friends the Clerc
family helped him to recover. It was about this time that
he composed the three masterpieces of his youth, the

First Violin Sonata, the First Piano Quartet and the Ballade for piano. A period of musical travels followed. In Weimar (December 1877) he met Liszt, who was performing Saint-Saëns' *Samson et Dalila*; he presented him with his Ballade op.19, which Liszt said he found too difficult to play. But his main concern was to see Wagner productions and this led him to Cologne (April 1879) for *Das Rheingold* and *Die Walküre*, and to Munich for the *Ring* (September 1879), *Tannhäuser* (July 1880), *Die Meistersinger* (July 1880 and September 1881), *Lohengrin* and *Tristan* (September 1881) and to London for the *Ring* (May 1882). He was fascinated by Wagner but, almost alone among his contemporaries, did not come under his influence. He met Liszt again in July 1882 in Zurich.

On 27 March 1883 Fauré married Marie Fremiet, the daughter of a highly regarded sculptor. Although he always retained great affection for his wife, her withdrawn, bitter and difficult character, coupled with Fauré's keen sensuality and desire to please, explain his infidelities. They had two sons, Emmanuel (*b* 29 Dec 1883; *d* 6 Nov 1971) and Philippe (*b* 28 July 1889; *d* 19 Nov 1954). To support his family Fauré spent most of his time in tedious and futile activities, such as organizing the daily service at the Madeleine (which he called his 'mercenary job'), and giving piano and harmony lessons. His music brought him almost nothing because his publisher bought his songs, with full copyright, for 50 francs each. Throughout his life Fauré was able to compose only during the summer holidays.

Fauré's principal compositions of this period were piano pieces and numerous songs, including the 20 songs in the second collection written between 1878 and

5

1887. He also attempted some large-scale compositions, but disowned them after a few performances, keeping manuscript copies of certain movements from which he later re-used the themes. The works involved were the Symphony in D minor op.40 (his second symphony, taking into account that in F op.20, written in early youth and also rejected), and the Violin Concerto op.14, of which he completed only two movements. Such severe self-criticism is regrettable in that Fauré's wider reputation has suffered from the lack of large-scale works in his published output, despite the existence and enormous popularity of his Requiem op.48. The success of this work cannot be explained without reference to the religious works which preceded it, the *Cantique de Jean Racine* (1865), some motets and (particularly) the touching *Messe basse* for female voices, written in 1881 during a holiday at Villerville on the Normandy coast. The Requiem was not composed to the memory of a specific person but, in Fauré's words, 'for the pleasure of it'; it was long unknown that the work took over 20 years to assume its present form, the composition extending from 1877 to about 1890, and the orchestration being completed only in 1900. A restoration of the version evolved between 1888 and 1892, for small orchestra (without violins and woodwind), has been attempted with some success. The other important work of this period is the Second Piano Quartet op.45. And for the Odéon Fauré composed two sets of incidental music: *Caligula* op.52 (1888) for the tragedy by Dumas *père*, and *Shylock* op.57 (1889) for a play by Edmond de Haraucourt after Shakespeare. He valued incidental music as a form, writing to Saint-Saëns in 1893 that it was 'the only [form] which is suited to my meagre talents'. The symphonic suite from *Shylock* is seldom played, despite the scarcity of symphonic works by Fauré.

Until he was about 40 Fauré retained his youthful liveliness and gaiety, was easily satisfied and happy with his friends and was without any marked ambition or self-importance. The breaking of his engagement to Marianne Viardot, however, brought out a certain violence in his temperament in spite of his apparent good nature. In the years 1880–90 he often suffered severe depression, which he himself called 'spleen'. Too many occupations prevented him from concentrating on composition; he was disturbed about writing too slowly and dreamt of vast works – concertos, symphonies and innumerable operatic projects in collaboration with Verlaine, Bouchor, Samain, Maeterlinck and Mendès. As the years passed he despaired of ever reaching the public and was angry with performers who played 'always the same eight or ten pieces'. His jealousy (quickly forgotten) was aroused by the popularity of Théodore Dubois, Charles Lenepveu, Charles-Marie Widor and Massenet and his taste for musical purity and sobriety of expression made him condemn the Italian *verismo*.

The 1890s were a turning-point in Fauré's life and work; he began to realize some of his ambitions: in May and June 1891 he was received in Venice, with a group of friends, by the Princesse Edmond de Polignac, then Princess of Scey-Montbéliard. This delightful visit, prolonged by a brief stay in Florence, occasioned the *Cinq mélodies* op.58 on poems by Verlaine; these directly anticipate *La bonne chanson*. It was also the period of his happy liaison with Emma Bardac, the future

Mme Debussy, to whom he dedicated *La bonne chanson* and the *Salve regina*; to her daughter he dedicated *Dolly* (1894–7), the collection for piano duet. In May 1892 he succeeded Ernest Guiraud as inspector of the national conservatories in the provinces; this post relieved him of his teaching but obliged him to make tedious journeys across the whole of France. On 2 June 1896 he became chief organist at the Madeleine, and in October he succeeded Massenet as teacher of the composition class at the Conservatoire. For Fauré this was an act of retribution, as he had been refused the post four years earlier when the director, Ambroise Thomas, thought him too revolutionary even though the Institut had awarded him the Chartier Prize for chamber music in 1885; he had won it again in 1893. His pupils at the Conservatoire included Ravel, Florent Schmitt, Koechlin, Louis Aubert, Roger-Ducasse, Enescu, Paul Ladmirault, Nadia Boulanger and Emile Vuillermoz.

At over 50 Fauré was becoming known. He had previously been esteemed only by a restricted group of friends and musicians in the Société Nationale; and this was not fame, for his music was too modern to appear in a concert where even Wagner was considered advanced. He was not, however, a stereotype of the rejected artist, for he was much fêted in the grand salons, such as those of Mme de Saint-Marceaux and of the Princesse Edmond de Polignac, which were then the stronghold of the avant garde. Music was important to a society passionately interested in 'art' and its fashions. Proust, who knew Fauré, was, as he once wrote to him, 'intoxicated' by his music, and drew his inspiration for the descriptions of Vinteuil's music from it. Both Proust and Fauré have been criticized for the brilliant but superficial company they kept. But Fauré was not snobbish, and moved in these circles through friendship and also out of necessity, since the salons offered the best means of making his music known. Most of his friends probably admired his personality more than his music, which was considered too severe. Fauré was always so unsure of the real value of his compositions that he submitted them to the judgment of colleagues before publication; and he needed this private recognition to encourage him to continue. As a pianist Fauré was not a virtuoso like his friend Saint-Saëns, but he was an admirable performer of his works, as is shown by a dozen player-piano rolls that he recorded for the firms Hupfeld and Welte & Söhne between 1904 and 1913. The rolls of the third *Romance sans paroles*, the first Barcarolle, the third prelude, the *Pavane*, the third nocturne, the *Sicilienne*, *Thème et variations* and the *Valses-caprices* nos.1, 3 and 4 survive and several rolls have been re-recorded on LP records.

Fauré often went to London for private festivals organized by loyal friends like the Maddisons, Frank Schuster and John Sargent (who painted his portrait); he returned almost every year between 1892 and 1900, and so acquired the commission to write incidental music for the English translation of Maeterlinck's *Pelléas et Mélisande* (1898). The original version for small orchestra was orchestrated by Koechlin as Fauré was too overworked; Fauré drew from it a Suite op.80, which is his symphonic masterpiece. Saint-Saëns, who urged Fauré to write large-scale works, got him a commission for a lyric tragedy for the amphitheatre at Béziers. This work, *Prométhée*, being intended for open-air performance, is scored for three wind bands, 100

9

2. *Members of the founding committee of the Société Musicale Indépendante: (standing, left to right) Louis Aubert, A. Z. Mathot, Maurice Ravel, André Caplet, Charles Koechlin, Emile Vuillermoz, Jean Huré, and (seated) Gabriel Fauré and Jean Roger-Ducasse*

strings and 12 harps, choirs and solo voices. The success of the productions on 27 and 28 August 1900 was immense; the work was revived on 25 and 27 August 1901. With the help of his favourite pupil Roger-Ducasse, Fauré completed a reduction of the original orchestration for normal symphony orchestra.

From 2 March 1903 to 1921 Fauré was music critic of *Le Figaro*. He was not a natural critic and was prompted mainly by need to accept a duty that he fulfilled with some inner torment. His natural kindness and broad-mindedness predisposed him to see the positive aspects of a work, and he had no inclination to polemics. When he disliked a composition, he preferred to remain silent. His criticisms were colourless, and interesting only to those who knew how to read between the lines.

The year 1905 marked a crucial stage in Fauré's career: in October he succeeded Théodore Dubois as director of the Conservatoire, where he initiated a series of important reforms that led to the resignations of certain reactionary professors. In carrying out his aims Fauré showed such astonishing resoluteness that his adversaries nicknamed him 'Robespierre'. The directorship made him better off, though not rich (he had never sought wealth), and it also made him suddenly famous: his works were performed at important concerts, and on 13 March 1909 he was elected to the Institut succeeding Ernest Reyer (he had been passed over in favour of Théodore Dubois in 1894 and Lenepveu in 1896). His official position did not prevent him from breaking with the established Société Nationale de Musique in the same year and accepting the presidency of a dissident society founded by the young musicians evicted by the

Société Nationale, nearly all of whom were his pupils. Fauré's late recognition, however, was overshadowed by growing deafness and, still worse, the general weakening of his hearing was compounded by a systematic distortion that produced, he said, a 'veritable cacophony' – high sounds were heard a 3rd lower, low sounds a 3rd higher, while the middle of the range remained correct.

The responsibilities of the Conservatoire left Fauré too little time to compose, and it took him five summers to finish the lyric drama *Pénélope*, which the singer Lucienne Bréval had persuaded him to write in collaboration with René Fauchois. It was begun in 1907, set aside in 1910 and finished just in time for the première (inadequately rehearsed by Raoul Gunsbourg) in Monte Carlo on 4 March 1913. The Paris première on 10 May 1913 was a triumph, but the run was terminated by the bankruptcy of the Théâtre des Champs-Elysées the following October and the revival at the Opéra-Comique was delayed for five years by the war. The work never recovered from this unhappy beginning, despite its musical qualities. The period of *Pénélope* was also that of great piano pieces (Nocturnes nos.9–11, Barcarolles nos.7–11) and songs (the cycle *La chanson d'Eve* op.95, to verses by Van Lerberghe). In autumn 1910 Fauré undertook his most extended journey. Concerts were organized at St Petersburg, where he had a triumphant reception, Helsinki and Moscow. But for his composing holidays he generally returned to Switzerland where he found the calm atmosphere he needed. *Pénélope* was composed at Lausanne and Lugano, while the gardens of the Italian lakes inspired *Paradis*, the first song of *La chanson d'Eve*, written at Stresa.

12

During World War I Fauré remained in Paris as head of the Conservatoire, giving up his visits to Switzerland in favour of Evian or the south of France, which he loved. The years of the war, with the years 1894–1900, were the most productive of his life. His compositions of this period are among the most powerful in French music, having unusual force and even violence; they include the second sonata for violin (op.108) and the first for cello (op.109), the *Fantaisie* for piano and orchestra op.111 and a second song cycle on poems by Van Lerberghe, *Le jardin clos*. During this productive period, which continued without interruption until 1921, he revised for the Durand editions the complete piano works of Schumann (one of his favourite composers) and, in collaboration with Joseph Bonnet, the organ works of Bach.

In October 1920 Fauré retired from the Conservatoire. Having reached the age of 75, he could at last devote himself entirely to composition, and produced a series of works that crown his whole output – the Second Cello Sonata, the Second Piano Quintet, the song cycle *L'horizon chimérique* and the 13th nocturne for piano. He had by now become a celebrity: in 1920 he was awarded the Grand Croix of the Légion d'honneur (exceptional for a musician) and on 20 June 1922 his friend Fernand Maillot organized a national tribute at the Sorbonne, where noted performers of his music played to an enthusiastic gathering in the presence of the president of the republic. His last two years were overshadowed by declining health, with increasing symptoms of sclerosis, poor breathing (due to heavy smoking) and deafness. In 1922 and 1923 he spent long months in his room while his work was acclaimed everywhere; *Pénélope* was staged in Antwerp and at the Théâtre Antique d'Orange, and *Prométhée* at the Théâtre des Champs-Elysées, where Mengelberg had just conducted the Requiem. To the end, however, he made himself available to others, particularly to such young musicians as Arthur Honegger, who with the other members of Les Six fervently admired him. His creative faculties remained intact, but were easily tired; however, the two works he wrote between 1922 and 1924 – the Piano Trio and the String Quartet, his first attempt in that form – were masterpieces. He died in Paris on 4 November 1924.

All witnesses agree that Fauré was extraordinarily attractive; he had a dark complexion (which contrasted with his white hair), a somewhat distant expression of the eyes, a soft voice and gentle manner of speech that retained the rolled provincial 'r', and a simple and charming bearing. His eventual fame did not modify his simple habits; he remained sympathetic towards others and clearsighted in his judgments. In old age he attained a kind of serenity, without losing any of his remarkable spiritual vitality, but rather removed from the sensualism and the passion of the works he wrote between 1875 and 1895.

CHAPTER TWO

Style and works

Fauré's stylistic development links the last years of
Romanticism with the second quarter of the 20th century, and covers a period in which the evolution of
musical language was particularly rapid. When Fauré
was born, Berlioz was writing *La damnation de Faust*;
when he died Berg had finished *Wozzeck* three years
previously and Messiaen was composing his first works.
Fauré nevertheless remained the most advanced figure
in French music until the appearance of Debussy's
Pelléas et Mélisande. As early as 1877–9 he used some
elements of the whole-tone scale (the *Sérénade toscane*)
and anticipated impressionism (Ballade op.19).
Furthermore he developed an immediately identifiable
style and (even rarer) created a personal musical language.

Fauré's music may be divided into four styles,
roughly corresponding to four chronological periods
which represent his responses to the musical problems
of his time. The first shows him assimilating the language and the aesthetics of Romanticism; he initially set
poems by Hugo and Gautier, but he also set Baudelaire;
his best pages are either sombre (*La chanson du pêcheur, L'absent, Elégie*) or express rapt emotion (*Le voyageur, Automne*, the chorus *Les djinns*). Fauré's second
period was that of the Parnassian poets, and coincided
with his discovery of Verlaine, as in *Clair de lune*

(1887), which accorded with his sprightly yet melancholy temper. He also sometimes yielded to the gracefulness of the '1880s style' – melodious, tortuous and languid – which he used in certain piano pieces and the works for women's chorus (such as *Caligula*). The success this music achieved in its own time has since damaged his reputation. In the 1890s his third style matured with an accession of bold and forceful expressiveness; the great piano works and *La bonne chanson* have real breadth. This is particularly evident in the lyric tragedy *Prométhée*, which sums up all the facets of his style at the turn of the century – delicacy and profundity, but also measured force. In the style of his last period Fauré pursued a solitary and confident course, ignoring the attractive innovations of younger composers and the beguiling elements of his 1880s style. The increasing economy of expression, boldness of harmony and enrichment of polyphony give his work of this period an authentic place in 20th-century composition; the expressive dissonances of the 11th Nocturne (ex.1), the whole-tone writing in the Fifth Impromptu (ex.2) and such highly chromatic music as the Scherzo of the Second Piano Quintet are representative.

In spite of Fauré's continuous stylistic development, certain traits characterize nearly all his music. Much of his individuality comes from his handling of harmony and tonality. Without completely destroying the sense of tonality, and with a sure intuitive awareness of what limits ought to be retained, he freed himself from its restrictions. Attention has frequently been drawn to the rapidity of his modulations: these appear less numerous if they are viewed according to the precepts of Fauré's

Ex.1 Nocturne no.11, op.104 no.1

Ex.2 Impromptu no.5, op.102

Allegro vivo ♩ = 168

harmonic training, contained in the famous *Traité d'harmonie* (Paris, 1889) by Gustave Lefèvre, Niedermeyer's son-in-law and successor. The harmonic theory can be traced back to Gottfried Weber, whose ideas had been disseminated in France by Lefèvre and Pierre de Maleden, the teacher of Saint-Saëns. Their concept of tonality was broader than Rameau's classical theory, since for them foreign notes and altered chords did not necessitate a change in tonality, 7th and 9th chords were no longer considered dissonant and the alteration of the mediant was possible without a change of tonality or even of mode. So a student of Fauré's harmony (with its delicate combination of expanded tonality and modality) must consider entire phrases rather than individual chords. Thus the opening of *Les présents* op.46 no.1 (ex.3) is in F, despite its hints of Ab.

Ex.3 *Les présents*, op.46 no.1

The mobility of the 3rd (Ab to A♮) and the harmonic alternations are typical of Fauré's style. His familiarity with the church modes is reflected in the frequently modal character of his music, particularly in the elision of the leading note (the E is flattened in ex.3) facilitating both modulation to a neighbouring key and the pungent use of the plagal cadence (see ex.4). But the flexibility of the modulations to remote keys and the sudden short cuts back to the original key are unprecedented aspects of Fauré's originality.

Fauré's harmonic richness is matched by his melodic invention. He was a consummate master of the art of unfolding a melody: from a harmonic and rhythmic cell he constructed chains of sequences that convey, despite their constant variety, inventiveness and unexpected turns, an impression of inevitability. The long entreaty of the 'In paradisum' in the Requiem is a perfect example of such coherence: its 30 bars form one continuous sentence. In Fauré's music the relationship between harmony and melody is complex; often the melody seems to be the linear expression of the harmony, as in ex.4.

Ex.4 *Les présents,* op.46 no.1

Je te di-rai___pour t'é-mouvoir, U-ne très an-cien ne bal-

-la - de!

Close study of Fauré's use of rhythm reveals certain constant features of his style, in particular his predilection for fluidity within bars; his association of duple and triple time and subtle use of syncopation link him with Brahms (see ex.5). Yet Fauré never emphasized rhythmic values; once a rhythmic formula was established, he tended to maintain it for long passages, thus incurring

Ex.5 Barcarolle no.9, op.101

Andante moderato ♩ = 76

the charge of monotony. The idea of line was too important to Fauré for him to tolerate sudden interruption in the manner of Beethoven.

Fauré's early chamber works have traditional formal structures and his early songs are in strophic or rondo form, but for the piano Ballade op.19 he invented a new and peculiarly unifying three-theme form. In his last chamber works he moved away from classical schemes and generally adopted a four-section form. The free variations in his finales show great richness of melodic and contrapuntal invention. He also had a liking for the scherzo, not the fantastic nocturnal dance of the German Romantics but a sunny, skipping movement with bursts of pizzicato, whose prototype was established in the First Violin Sonata op.13 (1875). Fauré could be described as the creator of the 'French scherzo' that Debussy and Ravel used in their quartets.

Fauré has been generally regarded as the greatest

20

master of French song. Apart from the important song cycles and some individual songs, his works in this form are grouped in three collections (1879, 1897 and 1908), each containing 20 pieces (the second volume originally contained 25 songs, but a few items were reordered with the publication of the third). The first includes *romances* and songs from his youth. The influence of Niedermeyer and Saint-Saëns is clear although Fauré's association with the Viardots from 1872 to 1877 inclined him temporarily towards an Italian style (*Après un rêve*, *Sérénade toscane*, *Barcarolle*, *Tarentelle* for two sopranos). His most successful works are those in which the music is inspired directly by the form of the poem, as in *L'absent* where the dialogue is as restrained as it is dramatic, or *La chanson du pêcheur*, in which a second theme is introduced, thus foreshadowing later songs. Many of the songs of the second collection use the *ABA* scheme (*Automne*, *Les berceaux*), while the boldest pieces, such as the famous *Clair de lune*, anticipate the formal invention of the third collection. In *Spleen* and *Le parfum impérissable* from the final set, the melodic curve coincides with the unfolding of the poem, while in *Prison* the movement of the music matches that of the poetic syntax and the melody develops continuously, with a consistent forward movement. It is regrettable that the third collection, in which prosody, melody, harmony and polyphony achieve a beautiful balance, is much less known than the second and that a masterpiece such as *Le don silencieux* is rarely performed simply because it was not published in a collection.

The criticism that Fauré composed almost half his songs to rather mediocre poems ignores the fact that he sometimes chose his texts for their pliability, lack of

3. *Autograph MS of the opening of 'Exaucement', the first song in Fauré's cycle 'Le jardin clos' op.106, composed July to November 1914*

reference to sounds and, particularly, lack of visual descriptions that would restrict him (hence his predilection for such poets as Armand Silvestre). He apparently remarked that he aimed to convey the prevailing atmosphere rather than detailed images in poems of this kind. The most 'pliable' poems were most easily adapted to his melodic inspiration, and in setting them, he often took great liberties with the prosody. In *Les berceaux*, for example, he superimposed a strong and varied musical rhythm on the flat rhythm of Sully-Prudhomme's verses, creating contradiction, though a felicitous one. Such settings contrast strikingly with his treatment of such poems as Verlaine's.

From 1891 Fauré broadened the scope of his melodic invention by giving a novel structure to a song cycle. The *Cinq mélodies* op.58, and still more *La bonne chanson* op.61, have a dual organization: a literary organization, by virtue of the selection and arrangement of Verlaine's poems to form a story; and a musical organization based on the use of recurrent themes throughout the cycle. The harmonic and formal novelty of *La bonne chanson* shocked Saint-Saëns, and even daunted the young Debussy; the expressive power, the free and varied vocal style and the importance of the piano part seemed to exceed the proper limits of the song. It was difficult to go beyond the form of *La bonne chanson* so Fauré looked for other means of unifying the song cycle. In *La chanson d'Eve*, a sequel to *La bonne chanson*, he reduced the number of recurrent themes from six to two, concentrated the vocal style and gave a new polyphonic richness to the piano accompaniment. The last three cycles, *Le jardin clos* op.106, *Mirages* op.113 and *L'horizon chimérique* op.118, no longer have common themes; the unity is in the subject, the atmosphere and mainly in the writing, which renounces luxuriance and moves in the direction of total simplicity.

Fauré's stylistic evolution can also be observed in the works for piano. The elegant and captivating first pieces, which made the composer famous, show the influence of Chopin, Saint-Saëns and Liszt. The lyricism and complexity of Fauré's style in the 1890s are evident in the Nocturnes nos.6 and 7, the Fifth Barcarolle and the *Thème et variations*. Finally, the stripped-down style of the final period informs the last nocturnes (nos.10–13), the series of great barcarolles (nos.8–11) and the astonishing Fifth Impromptu. The piano writing, based on the flexible undulations of the arpeggio, achieves a free counterpoint that is always expressive, as in the opening of the 13th Nocturne, the summit of Fauré's piano writing, where the dissonances result from a kind of time-lag between the hands.

Unlike Saint-Saëns, Fauré was not interested in piano writing as such and cannot be recognized from particular formulae. Characteristic is the way in which arpeggios break the music into pieces like a mosaic, the accompaniment, in syncopation, working itself into the interstices of the melody. Even more original and characteristic is the equal importance of the hands which, in many passages, alternate and complement each other for the presentation of a theme or the execution of a run. This trait (which reflects the fact that Fauré was ambidextrous), together with the finger substitutions familiar to organists, have discouraged many performers from attempting these otherwise admirable pieces. Nevertheless, the piano is central to his work. It is used

4. *Gabriel Fauré (seated) with (from left to right) Pablo Casals,
Jacques Thibaud and Alfred Cortot*

in all his songs and in his two concertante works, the Ballade and the *Fantaisie*.

In Fauré's chamber music the piano is also prominent; he freed himself from it only in his last work, the String Quartet op.121. With the songs, the chamber music constitutes Fauré's most important contribution to music; he enriched all the genres he attempted – the violin sonata, cello sonata, quintet, quartet and trio. In chamber music he established his style most rapidly; the First Violin Sonata (1875–6, 11 years before Franck's), and the First Piano Quartet (1876–9) display astonishing novelty of conception.

Fauré's apparent lack of interest in the orchestra is sometimes criticized as a weakness. He had a horror of vivid colours and effects and showed little interest in combinations of tone-colours, which he thought were too commonly a form of self-indulgence and a disguise for the absence of ideas. Nevertheless, his orchestral writing has substance, and certain piano pieces and his greatest chamber music, even *La bonne chanson*, have convincing power and an almost symphonic breadth.

For long Fauré did not attempt musical stage works; he felt no contempt for them (as has been suggested), but had difficulty in finding a subject that suited him. There are about ten abandoned projects. His early incidental music led to the highly successful *Prométhée* (1900), a lyric tragedy with spoken interludes, which is easily adapted to concert performance with a narrated text (the usual solution, for the original text is now dated). In *Pénélope*, begun seven years later, Fauré found a subject that enchanted him, and this lyric drama contains his personal solution to the problem of post-Wagnerian opera; *Pénélope* can be described as a 'song opera' since

26

it uses neither the classical aria with recitative nor Wagner's continuous melody, but a sequence of short lyrical flights, without repetition, linked by passages of arioso and, less often, plain recitative, sometimes without accompaniment. *Pénélope* thus meets the challenge of maintaining a balance between the voices and the orchestra, whose role is important because it provides a commentary on the action by means of several leitmotifs in the manner of Debussy's *Pelléas et Mélisande*, which in other respects it does not resemble at all. Like *Pelléas* and *Wozzeck* this proposed an original solution, but like them it had no true successors. Yet Fauré felt too much distaste for theatrical effects to be able to create a popular work. *Pénélope* is a powerful masterpiece, but a masterpiece of pure music.

WORKS

(printed works published in Paris unless otherwise stated; most MSS in F-Pn)

Numbers in the right-hand column denote references in the text.

STAGE

op.	Title	Description	Libretto	First performance	Published	Remarks	
							26–7
—	Barnabé	opéra comique, 1	J. Moineaux	unperf.		inc.; 6vv, pf in MS, 1879	
52	Caligula	incidental music	A. Dumas *père*	Paris, Odéon, 8 Nov 1888	1888	orch, female chorus	6
57	Shylock	incidental music	E. de Haraucourt, after Shakespeare	Paris, Odéon, 17 Dec 1889	1890	see also 'Orchestral'	6–7
—	La Passion	incidental music	Haraucourt	Paris, Société Nationale, 21 April 1890		preview, Paris, Cirque d'hiver, 4 April 1890	
—	Le bourgeois gentilhomme	incidental music	Molière			see also 'Songs', 'Orchestral' and 'Chamber'	
80	Pelléas et Mélisande	incidental music	M. Maeterlinck, Eng. trans., J. W. Mackail	London, Prince of Wales, 21 June 1898		1st version orchd C. Koechlin; 2nd version orchd Koechlin, Fauré, see also 'Orchestral'	9
82	Prométhée	tragédie lyrique, 3	J. Lorrain, A. F. Hérold	Béziers, Arènes, 27 Aug 1900	1900	1st version, 3 wind bands, str, harps, C. Eustace, Fauré, 1900; 2nd version, orch, Fauré, Roger-Ducasse, 1917	9, 11, 14, 16, 26
88	Le voile du bonheur	incidental music	G. Clemenceau	Paris, Théâtre de la Renaissance, 4 Nov 1901			
—	Pénélope	drame lyrique, 3	R. Fauchois	Monte Carlo, 4 March 1913	1913	dedicated to Saint-Saëns	12, 14, 26–7
112	Masques et bergamasques	comédie musicale	Fauchois	Monte Carlo, 10 April 1919	1919	see also 'Songs', 'Secular choral' and 'Orchestral'	

SONGS

(many published in collections: i (1879), ii (1897), iii (1908); numbering follows revised order of 1908)

op.	Title, key	Text	Composed	Collection	Published	
1/1	Le papillon et la fleur, C	V. Hugo	1861	i/1	1869	
1/2	Mai, F	Hugo	?1862	i/2	1871	
5/2	Rêve d'amour (S'il est un charmant gazon), E♭	Hugo	?1862	i/10	1875	
—	L'aube naît	Hugo	?1862		lost	
—	Puisque j'ai mis ma lèvre, C	Hugo	8 Dec 1862			
—	Tristesse d'Olympio, e	Hugo	c1865			
2/1	Dans les ruines d'une abbaye, A	Hugo	c1866	i/3	1869	
2/2	Les matelots, E♭	T. Gautier	c1870	i/4	1876	
4/2	Lydia, F	Leconte de Lisle	?1870	i/8	1871	
7/2	Hymne, G	C. Baudelaire	?1870	i/16	1871	
3/1	Seule!, e	Gautier	1871	i/5	1871	
5/3	L'absent (Seniers où l'herbe se balance), a	Hugo	3 April 1871	i/11	1879	15, 21
—	L'aurore, A♭	Hugo	?1871		ed., Mw, xvi (1958)	
8/2	La rançon, c	Baudelaire	?1871	i/18	1879	
5/1	Chant d'automne, a	Baudelaire	c1871	i/9	1879	
4/1	La chanson du pêcheur (Lamento), f	Gautier	?1872	i/7	1877; orchd (n.d.)	15, 21
6/1	Aubade, F	L. Pomey	c1873	i/12	1879	
6/2	Tristesse, c	Gautier	c1873	i/13	1876	
7/3	Barcarolle, g	M. Monnier	1873	ii/20	1877	
8/3	Ici-bas!, f♯	Sully-Prudhomme	?1874	i/19	1877	21
8/1	Au bord de l'eau, c♯	Sully-Prudhomme	Aug 1875	i/17	1877	
3/2	Sérénade toscane (O tu che dormie riposata stai), b♭	anon., trans. R. Bussine	?1878	i/6	1879	15, 21
7/1	Après un rêve (Levati sol que la luna è levata), c	anon., trans. Bussine	?1878	i/15	1878	21
6/3	Sylvie, F	P. de Choudens	1878	i/14	1879	
18/1	Nell, G♭	Leconte de Lisle	1878	ii/1	1880	15, 21
18/2	Le voyageur, a	A. Silvestre	?1878	ii/2	1880	15
18/3	Automne, b	Silvestre	1878	ii/3	1880	
21	Poème d'un jour 1 Rencontre, D♭; 2 Toujours!, f♯; 3 Adieu, G♭	C. Grandmougin	1878	ii/4–6	1880	
23/1	Les berceaux, b♭	Sully-Prudhomme	1879	ii/7	1881	21, 23
23/2	Notre amour, E	Silvestre	c1879	ii/8	1882	
23/3	Le secret, D♭	Silvestre	1880–81	ii/9	1881	

op.	Title, Key	Text	Composed	Collection	Published	
27/1	Chanson d'amour, F	Silvestre	1882	ii/10	1882	
27/2	Le fée aux chansons, F	Silvestre	1882	ii/11	1883	
39/1	Aurore, G	Silvestre	20 May 1884	ii/12	1885	
39/2	Fleur jetée, f	Silvestre	25 May 1884	ii/13	1885	
39/3	Le pays des rêves, Ab	Silvestre	30 May 1884	ii/14	1885; orchd (1897)	18–19
39/4	Les roses d'Ispahan, D	Leconte de Lisle	1884	ii/15	1885; orchd (1888)	15, 21, 179
43/1	Noël	V. Wilder	1886	i/20	1886	
43/2	Nocturne, Eb	Villiers de l'Isle Adam	1886	ii/17	1886	
46/1	Les présents, F	Villiers de l'Isle Adam	1887	ii/18	1888	
46/2	Clair de lune, bb	P. Verlaine	1887	ii/19	1888; orchd (1888)	21
51/1	Larmes, c	J. Richepin	1888	iii/1	1888	
51/2	Au cimetière, e	Richepin	1888	iii/2	1888	
51/3	Spleen, d	Verlaine	1888	iii/3	1888	
51/4	La rose, F	Leconte de Lisle	Aug 1890	iii/4	1890	
57	Chanson, Bb, Madrigal, F [from Shylock]	Haraucourt	1889	iii/5–6	1889	
—	En prière, Eb	S. Bordèse	1889	ii/16	1890; orchd (1890)	
58	Cinq mélodies 'de Venise' 1 Mandoline, G; 2 En sourdine, Eb; 3 Green, Gb; 4 A Clymène, e; 5 C'est l'extase, Db	Verlaine	1891	iii/7 11	1891	7, 23
posth.	Sérénade du Bourgeois gentilhomme, f	Molière	1893		1957	7, 8, 16, 23, 26, 45, 209
61	La bonne chanson 1 Une sainte en son auréole, Ab; 2 Puisque l'aube grandit, G; 3 La lune blanche luit dans les bois, F#; 4 J'allais par des chemins perfides, f#; 5 J'ai presque peur, en vérité, e; 6 Avant que tu ne t'en ailles, Db; 7 Donc, ce sera par un clair jour d'été, Bb; 8 N'est-ce pas?, G; 9 L'hiver a cessé, Bb; arr. pf, str qt but repudiated (by Fauré)	Verlaine	1892–4		1894	
83/1	Prison, eb	Verlaine	4 Dec 1894	iii/14	1896	
83/2	Soir, Db	A. Samain	17 Dec 1894	iii/15	London and Paris, 1896	21
76/1	Le parfum impérissable, E	Leconte de Lisle	22 Aug 1897	iii/12	London and Paris, 1897	21

posth.			20 Sept 1897	iii/13	London and Paris, 1897	
	Mélisande's song, d [for op.80]	Maeterlinck, trans. Mackail	31 May 1898		1937	
85/1	Dans la forêt de septembre, G♭	C. Mendès	29 Sept 1902	iii/18	1902	
85/2	La fleur qui va sur l'eau, b	Mendès	13 Sept 1902	iii/19	1902	
85/3	Accompagnement, G♭	Samain	28 March 1902	iii/20	1903	
87/1	Le plus doux chemin (Madrigal), f	Silvestre	1904	iii/16	1907	
87/2	Le ramier (Madrigal), e	Silvestre	1904	iii/17	Milan, 1904	
92	Le don silencieux, E	J. Dominique [M. Closset]	20 Aug 1906		1906	21
94	Chanson, e	H. de Regnier	1906		1907	
—	Vocalise-étude, e		1907		1907	
95	La chanson d'Eve 1 Paradis, e; 2 Prima verba, G♭; 3 Roses ardentes, E; 4 Comme Dieu rayonne, c; 5 L'aube blanche, D♭; 6 Eau vivante, C; 7 Veilles-tu ma senteur de soleil?, D; 8 Dans un parfum de roses blanches, G; 9 Crépuscule, d; 10 O mort poussière d'étoiles, D♭	C. Van Lerberghe	1906-10		no.9 (1906), nos.1, 2 (1907), nos.3, 5 (1908), nos.6, 8 (1909), no.10 (1910)	12, 23
106	Le jardin clos 1 Exaucement, C; 2 Quand tu plonges tes yeux dans mes yeux, F; 3 La messagère, G; 4 Je me poserai sur ton coeur, E♭; 5 Dans la nymphée, D♭; 6 Dans la pénombre, E; 7 Il m'est cher, Amour, le bandeau, F; 8 Inscription sur le sable, e	Van Lerberghe	July-Nov 1914		1915	13, 22, 23-4
113	Mirages 1 Cygne sur l'eau, F; 2 Reflets dans l'eau, B♭; 3 Jardin nocturne, E♭; 4 Danseuse, d	Baronne A. de Brimont	1919		1919	23-4
114	C'est la paix, A	G. Debladis	8 Dec 1919		1920	
118	L'horizon chimérique 1 La mer est infinie, D; 2 Je me suis embarqué, D♭; 3 Diane Séléné, E♭; Vaisseaux nous vous aurons aimés, D	J. de la Ville de Mirmont	1921		1922	13, 24

Sight-reading exercises for the Conservatoire, 1906-16, MSS. Archives nationales, Paris

ORCHESTRA AND SOLO INSTRUMENT (continued)

112	Masques et bergamasques, suite 1919 (1920): 1 Ouverture, 2 Menuet, 3 Gavotte, 4 Pastorale; movts 1 and 3 reworked from earlier works	
—	Chant funéraire, 1921, transcr. as 2nd movt Vc Sonata no.2, arr. wind band, G. Balay (1932) (for centenary of Napoleon's death)	

ORCHESTRA AND SOLO INSTRUMENT

14	Vn Conc., 1878–9, 2nd movt destroyed, ? rev. as Andante op.75	6
16	Berceuse, vn, 1880 (1898) [2nd version]	
19	Ballade, pf, April 1881 (1901) [2nd version]	26
24	Elégie, vc, 1895 (1901) [2nd version]	
28	Romance, vn, 1882 (1920) [2nd version]	13, 26
111	Fantaisie, pf, 1918 (1919)	20, 26

CHAMBER

PC – Paris Conservatoire

SN – Paris, Société nationale de musique

13	Vn Sonata no.1, A, 1875–6, SN, 27 Jan 1877 (Leipzig, 1877)	5, 20, 26
15	Pf Qt no.1, c, 1876–9, SN, 14 Feb 1880, finale rev. 1883 (1884)	5, 26
28	Romance, vn, pf, Bb, 1877, SN, 3 Feb 1883 (1883), also orchd, P. Gaubert (1920)	
16	Berceuse, vn, pf, 1879, SN, 14 Feb 1880 (1880), also orchd (1898)	
24	Elégie, vc, pf, 1880, SN, 15 Dec 1883 (1883), also orchd (1901)	15
77	Papillon, vc, pf, before 1885 (1898)	
45	Pf Qt no.2, g, ?1885–6, SN, 22 Jan 1887 (1887)	6
49	Petite pièce, vc, ?c1888	
78	Sicilienne, vc/vn, pf, 16 April 1898 (London and Paris, 1898) [orig. for Le bourgeois gentilhomme, 1893; orch version for Pelléas et Mélisande also pubd]	9
69	Romance, vc, pf, 1894, Geneva, 14 Nov 1894 (1895)	
75	Andante, vn, pf, July 1897, SN, 22 Jan 1898 (London and Paris, 1897),? rev. of 2nd movt, Vn Conc., op.14	
—	Morceau de lecture, vc, acc. 2nd vc, 1897	
—	Morceau de lecture, fl, pf, 1898	
79	Fantaisie, fl, pf, 1898, PC, 28 July 1898 (1898), orchd L. Aubert, 1957 (1958)	
—	Morceau de lecture, vn, pf, 1903, Monde musical (30 Aug 1903)	
89	Pf Qnt no.1, d, 1887–95, 1903–5, Brussels, Cercle Artistique, 23 March 1906 (New York, 1907)	13, 16, 24
98	Sérénade, vc, pf, 1908 (1908)	13
108	Vn Sonata no.2, e, 1916–17, SN, 10 Nov 1917 (1917)	13
109	Vc Sonata no.1, d, 1917, SN, 19 Jan 1918 (1918)	13, 16
115	Pf Qnt no.2, c, 1919–21, SN, 21 May 1921 (1921)	13
117	Vc Sonata no.2, g, 1921, SN, 13 May 1922 (1922)	14
120	Pf Trio, d, 1922–3, SN, 12 May 1923 (1923)	14, 26
121	Str Qt, e, 1923–4, PC, 12 June 1925 (1925)	3, 16, 24

PIANO

(all for piano solo unless otherwise stated)

17	3 romances sans paroles, ?1863 (1880)	3, 9
—	Intermède symphonique, 4 hands, 30 March 1869; incl. as Ouverture in Masques et bergamasques, op.112	
—	Gavotte, c#, 16 May 1869; incl. in Sym., op.20, and Masques et bergamasques, op.112	
—	Prélude et fugue, e, 1869, only fugue pubd (1903) (=op.84 no.6)	
33/1	Nocturne no.1, eb, c1875 (1883)	
19	Ballade, F#, 1877–9 (1880), rev. acc. orch, 1881	5, 15, 20
32	Mazurka, Bb, c1878 (1883)	
33/2	Nocturne no.2, B, c1880 (1883)	9
26	Barcarolle no.1, a, c1880 (1881)	
25	Impromptu no.1, Eb, 1881 (1881)	
30	Valse-caprice no.1, A, 1882 (1883)	
33/3	Nocturne no.3, Ab, ?1882 (1883)	9
31	Impromptu no.2, f, May 1883 (1883)	9
34	Impromptu no.3, Ab, ?1883 (1883)	
36	Nocturne no.4, Eb, ?1884 (1885)	
37	Nocturne no.5, Bb, ?1884 (1885)	
38	Valse-caprice no.2, Db, July 1884 (1884)	
41	Barcarolle no.2, G, Aug 1885 (1886)	
42	Barcarolle no.3, Gb, 1885 (1886)	
44	Barcarolle no.4, Ab, 1886 (1887)	
59	Valse-caprice no.3, Gb, 1887–93 (1893)	9
posth.	Souvenirs de Bayreuth: Fantaisie en forme de quadrille sur les thèmes favoris de l'Anneau de Nibelung, 4 hands, ?1888, (1930): collab. Messager	

62	Valse-caprice no.4, A♭, 1893–4 (1894)	9
56	Dolly, 4 hands, 1894–7, no.1 (1894), nos.2–5 (1896), no.6 (1897): 1 Berceuse, 2 Mi-a-ou, 3 Le jardin de Dolly, 4 Kitty-Valse [orig. Ketty], 5 Tendresse, 6 Le pas espagnol; orchd H. Rabaud, 1906 (1906)	8
63	Nocturne no.6, D♭, 3 Aug 1894 (1894)	24
66	Barcarolle no.5, f♯, 18 Sept 1894 (1894)	24
68	Allegro symphonique, 4 hands, c1865, arr. L. Boëllmann from Suite op.20 (1895)	
73	Thème et variations, c♯, 1895 (London and Paris, 1897)	9, 24
70	Barcarolle no.6, E♭, 1896 (London and Paris, 1896)	
74	Nocturne no.7, c♯, 1898 (1899)	24
84	8 pièces brèves [names supplied by publisher against Fauré's wishes], 1869–1902 (1903): 1 Capriccio, E♭, 2 Fantaisie, A♭, 3 Fugue, a, 4 Adagietto, e, 5 Improvisation, c♯, 6 Fugue, e, 7 Allegresse, C, 8 Nocturne no.8, D♭	
90	Barcarolle no.7, d, 1905 (1905)	12
91	Impromptu no.4, D♭, 1905–6 (1906)	
96	Barcarolle no.8, D♭, 1906 (1908)	12, 24
97	Nocturne no.9, b, 1908 (1908)	12
99	Nocturne no.10, e, 1908 (1909)	12, 24
101	Barcarolle no.9, a, 1909 (1909)	12, 20, 24
102	Impromptu no.5, f♯, 1909 (1909)	16, 17, 24
103	9 préludes, D♭, c♯, g, F, d, c♭, A, c, c, 1909–10 (1910–11)	9
104/1	Nocturne no.11, f♯, 1913 (1913)	12, 16, 17, 24
104/2	Barcarolle no.10, a, Oct 1913 (1913)	12, 24
105	Barcarolle no.11, g, 1913 (1914)	12, 24
106bis	Barcarolle no.12, E♭, Sept 1915 (1916)	
107	Nocturne no.12, e, 1915 (1916)	24
116	Barcarolle no.13, C, 1921 (1921)	24
119	Nocturne no.13, b, 1921 (1922)	13, 24
Several	transcrs. of works by Saint-Saëns, for pf 4 hands, 2 pf, 2 pf 8 hands	
posth.	Cadenza for Beethoven's Pf Conc. no.3, 27 April 1869 (1927)	
—	Cadenza for Mozart's Pf Conc. K37, c1878	
posth.	Cadenza for Mozart's Pf Conc. K491, 15 April 1902 (1927)	

OTHER INSTRUMENTAL WORKS

—	Improvisation, org, c1900	9
86	Impromptu, harp, 1904 (1904)	8
—	Morceau de lecture, harp, 1904, MS, Archives nationales, Paris	
110	Une châtelaine en sa tour, harp, 1918 (1918)	

WRITINGS

ARTICLES

'Lettres à propos de la réforme religieuse', Monde musical, xvi/3 (1904), 35

'Joachim', Musica (1906), April

'Edouard Lalo', Courrier musical, ii (15 April 1908), 245

'André Messager', Musica (1908), Sept

'La musique étrangère et les compositeurs français', Le Gaulois (10 Jan 1911)

'Sous la musique que faut-il mettre', Musica (1911), Feb, 38

Preface to G. Jean-Aubry: La musique française d'aujourd'hui (Paris, 1916)

'Camille Saint-Saëns', ReM, iii/4 (1922), 97

'Souvenirs', ReM, iii/11 (1922), 3

Hommage à Eugène Gigout (Paris, 1923)

Opinions musicales (Paris, 1930) [selection of articles originally in Le Figaro, 1903–21]

LETTERS

'Lettres à une fiancée', ed. C. Bellaigue, Revue des deux mondes, xlvi [année xcviii] (1928), 911–43

Lettres intimes, ed. P. Fauré-Fremiet (Paris, 1951) [Fauré's letters to his wife]

'Correspondance Saint-Saëns Fauré', ed. J.-M. Nectoux, RdM, lviii (1972), 65, 190–252; lix (1973), 60–98

Saint-Saëns, Fauré, correspondance, soixante ans d'amitié, ed. J.-M. Nectoux (Paris, 1973)

Correspondance, ed. J.-M. Nectoux (Paris, 1980; Eng. trans. as Gabriel Fauré: his Life through his Letters, 1984)

BIBLIOGRAPHY

MONOGRAPHS

L. Vuillemin: *Gabriel Fauré et son oeuvre* (Paris, 1914)
L. Aguettant: *Le génie de Gabriel Fauré* (Lyons, 1924)
A. Bruneau: *La vie et les oeuvres de Gabriel Fauré* (Paris, 1925)
C. Koechlin: *Gabriel Fauré* (Paris, 1927, 2/1949; Eng. trans., 1945)
P. Fauré-Fremiet: *Gabriel Fauré* (Paris, 1929, enlarged 2/1957) [incl. extensive bibliography]
G. Servières: *Gabriel Fauré* (Paris, 1930)
V. Jankélévitch: *Gabriel Fauré et ses mélodies* (Paris, 1938, enlarged, 2/1951, enlarged, 3/1974 as *Gabriel Fauré et l'inexprimable*)
G. Faure: *Gabriel Fauré* (Paris, 1945)
C. Rostand: *L'oeuvre de Gabriel Fauré* (Paris, 1945; Ger. trans., 1950)
N. Suckling: *Fauré* (London, 1946)
G. Fauré: publications techniques et artistiques (Paris, 1946)
M. Favre: *Gabriel Faurés Kammermusik* (Zurich, 1949)
E. Vuillermoz: *Gabriel Fauré* (Paris, 1960; Eng. trans., 1969 with extensive discography by S. Smolian)
M. Long: *Au piano avec Gabriel Fauré* (Paris, 1963; Eng. trans., 1981)
J. L. Kurtz: *Problems of Tonal Structure in Songs of Gabriel Fauré* (diss., Brandeis U., 1970)
J.-M. Nectoux: *Fauré* (Paris, 1972, 2/1986) [with discography and iconography]
M.-Cl. Beltrando-Patier: *Les mélodies de G. Fauré* (diss., U. of Strasbourg, 1978)
J.-M. Nectoux: *Phonographies I: Gabriel Fauré, 1900–1977* (Paris, 1979)
R. Orledge: *Gabriel Fauré* (London, 1979)
J.-M. Nectoux: *Gabriel Fauré et le théâtre* (diss., U. of Paris, 1980)
E. K. Scott jr: *The Requiem by Gabriel Fauré* (diss., Indiana U., 1980)
G. Hilson Woldu: *Gabriel Fauré as Director of the Conservatoire National de Musique et de Déclamation 1905–1920* (diss., Yale U., 1983)
R. C. Tait: *The Musical Language of Gabriel Fauré* (diss., U. of St Andrews, 1984)

ARTICLES, ESSAYS ETC

C. Saint-Saëns: 'Une sonate', *Journal de musique* (7 April 1877), 3
H. Imbert: *Profils de musiciens* (Paris, 1888)
P. Dukas: 'Prométhée de G. Fauré', *Revue hebdomadaire* (6 Oct 1900) [repr. in P. Dukas: *Les écrits sur la musique* (Paris, 1948)]

35

P. Ladmirault: 'La bonne chanson', *Courrier musical*, iii/13 (1900), 1

L. Aguettant: 'Les mélodies de Gabriel Fauré', *Courrier musical*, vi/3 (1903), 34

Musica (1909), no.77 [special Fauré issue]

C. Malherbe: 'Gabriel Fauré', *BSIM*, vi (1910), p.xvii [within section 'Französisches Musikfest in München: Festschrift']

O. Séré [J. Poueigh]: *Musiciens français d'aujourd'hui* (Paris, 1911, 2/1921) [incl. bibliography]

J. de Marliave: *Etudes musicales* (Paris, 1917)

ReM, iii/11 (1922) [special issue, incl. articles by M. Ravel, J. Roger-Ducasse, A. Cortot, C. Koechlin, F. Schmitt, N. Boulanger]

A. Copland: 'Gabriel Fauré, a Neglected Master', *MQ*, x (1924), 573

L. Rohozinski, ed.: *Cinquante ans de musique française* (Paris, 1925–6)

F. Schmitt: 'Fauré, Gabriel Urbain', *Cobbett's Cyclopedic Survey of Chamber Music* (Oxford, 1929, 2/1963)

A. Cortot: *La musique française de piano*, i (Paris, 1930; Eng. trans., 1932)

R. Dumesnil: *Portraits de musiciens français* (Paris, 1938)

ReM (May 1945) [special issue, incl. articles by P. Fauré-Fremiet, R. Dumesnil, G. Jean-Aubry]

M. Cooper: 'Some Aspects of Fauré's Technique', *MMR*, lxxv (1945), 75

V. Jankélévitch: 'Pelléas et Pénélope', *Revue du Languedoc*, vi (1945), 123

E. Lockspeiser: 'Fauré and the Song', *MMR*, lxxv (1945), 79

L. Orrey: 'Gabriel Fauré: 1845–1924', *MO*, lxviii (1945), 197, 229

——: 'Gabriel Fauré, 1845–1924', *MT*, lxxxvi (1945), 137

——: 'The Songs of Gabriel Fauré', *MR*, vi (1945), 72

N. Suckling: 'The Unknown Fauré', *MMR*, lxxv (1945), 84

W. Mellers: *Studies in Contemporary Music* (London, 1947)

V. Jankélévitch: *Le nocturne: Fauré, Chopin et la nuit, Satie et le matin* (Paris, 1957)

F. Gervais: 'Etude comparée des langages harmoniques de Fauré et de Debussy', *ReM* (1971), nos.272–3

Bulletin de l'Association des amis de Gabriel Fauré (1972–9), pubd as *Etudes fauréennes* (1980–84)

'Gabriel Fauré (1845–1924)', *A Dictionary of 20th-century Composers, 1911–71*, ed. K. Thompson (London, 1973) [incl. work-list and extensive bibliography]

J.-M. Nectoux: 'Les orchestrations de Gabriel Fauré: légende et vérité', *SMz*, cxv (1975), 243

——: 'Ravel, Fauré et les débuts de la Société musicale indépendante', *RdM*, lxi (1975), 295 [incl. letters]

R. Orledge: 'Fauré's "Pelléas et Mélisande"', *ML*, lvi (1975), 170

Bibliography

J.-M. Nectoux: 'Flaubert/Gallet/Fauré ou le démon du théâtre', *Bulletin du bibliophile*, i (1976), 33 [incl. letters]

——: 'Works Renounced, Themes Rediscovered: *Eléments pour une thématique fauréenne*', *19th Century Music*, ii (1978–9), 231

J.-M. Nectoux: 'Debussy et Fauré', *Cahiers Debussy*, new ser., no.3 (1979), 13

R. Orledge: 'The Two Endings of Fauré's "Soir" ', *ML*, lx (1979), 316

J.-M. Nectoux: 'Gabriel Fauré et l'esthétique de son oeuvre théâtrale', *Revue musicale de Suisse Romande*, xxxiii (1980), 50

——: 'Le "Pelléas" de Fauré', *RdM*, lxvii (1981), 169

Interviews with Fauré, *Excelsior* (12 June 1922), 2; *Comoedia* (31 Jan 1910), 1; (20 April 1910), 1; (10 Nov 1924), 4; *Candide* (9 Dec 1937), 19; *Paris-Comoedia* (3 March 1954), 106

CLAUDE DEBUSSY

Roger Nichols

CHAPTER ONE

Life

Achille-Claude Debussy was born at St Germain-en-Laye on 22 August 1862. At that time Debussy's parents were running a china shop; his father subsequently became a travelling salesman, a printer's assistant and later a clerk, while his mother worked for a time as a seamstress. Surprise at the emergence of a composer from such a background, unwittingly supported by the remarks of one of his biographers, has led some writers to doubt Debussy's legitimacy: this notion may finally be scotched by juxtaposing a sketch of him on his deathbed with a photograph of his paternal grandfather.

The unsettled life of the young Debussy reached a climax with the Commune of 1871, when his father was imprisoned for revolutionary activities. However, during this period Debussy was receiving piano lessons from Mme Mauté, the mother-in-law of Verlaine, who, even if she was never a pupil of Chopin as has been claimed, at least recognized the quality of the material in her hands. In October 1872 Debussy was accepted into the piano class of Marmontel and the theory class of Lavignac at the Paris Conservatoire, where his other teachers were to include Durand, Bazille, Guiraud and, for a brief unofficial spell, Franck. Already in 1874 he was playing Chopin's F minor Concerto and a career as a virtuoso was clearly in view, but in both 1878 and 1879 his efforts in the piano examinations went unrewarded and these dreams had to be abandoned. At the end of 1880 he joined the composition class of Guiraud and under his guidance won the second Prix de Rome in 1883 and the first Prix de Rome the following year with his cantata *L'enfant prodigue*.

Debussy had already travelled to Italy, Vienna and Russia in the company of Tchaikovsky's patron, Mme von Meck, but his enforced stay at the Villa Medici in Rome gave him no joy; he was separated from the woman he loved (Mme Vasnier, an amateur singer) and he was irked by the Villa's architecture, the pretensions of his fellow students and the necessity to produce a series of 'envois' for the Académie des Beaux Arts. He remained in Rome for the minimum permitted period of two years and returned to his parents' home in Paris in February 1887. In 1888 and 1889 he visited Bayreuth and in the latter year was enthralled by the Javanese gamelan at the World Exhibition in Paris. From about this time dates Debussy's liaison with Gabrielle Dupont with whom he lived in penury for the next nine years. He further marked his independence in 1890 by refusing to write the customary overture for the official performance of two of his 'envois', the *Fantaisie* for piano and orchestra and *La damoiselle élue*, as a result of which the whole concert was abandoned.

In 1892 Debussy became a close friend of Chausson, having completed *Fêtes galantes* (1891) on poems by Verlaine, and began the *Prélude à l'après-midi d'un faune* and a first version of the *Nocturnes*, but it was not until the performance of *La damoiselle élue* at the Société Nationale in April 1893 that his music came to the notice of the public. The next month he attended a performance of Maeterlinck's play *Pelléas et Mélisande*,

5. *Madame von Meck's trio, 1880; (left to right) Danil'chenko,
Rakhul'sky and Debussy*

and probably began to sketch his opera at once. In December the Ysaÿe Quartet gave the first performance of his String Quartet in G minor. Early in 1894 he became engaged to the singer Thérèse Roger, but the engagement was broken off in unpleasant circumstances which led to a permanent severance of Debussy's friendship with Chausson. The crowning achievement of these 'Bohemian years' was undoubtedly the performance of *Prélude à l'après-midi d'un faune* in December 1894. By the spring of 1895 he had finished the first version of *Pelléas et Mélisande*, but no completed work appeared until the *Trois chansons de Bilitis* in the summer of 1897, a year in which Dupont (still his mistress) attempted suicide and which ushered in a period of despair in his own life.

On 19 October 1899 Debussy married Rosalie (Lily) Texier, a mannequin and a friend of Dupont, and in December he completed the *Nocturnes* for orchestra. In 1901 he became music critic of *La revue blanche* and in May of that year *Pelléas et Mélisande* was formally accepted for performance at the Opéra-Comique. It is a cruel irony that during rehearsals of this masterpiece in April 1902 Debussy should have been prosecuted for non-payment of debts; in spite of a stormy dress rehearsal, the first performance on 30 April was soon hailed as a landmark in French music. The opera received its 100th performance in Paris only 11 years later.

The years 1904 and 1905 were especially prolific: new works written at this time included the second set of *Fêtes galantes*, the first set of *Images* for piano, *L'isle joyeuse* and *La mer*. The newly confident tone that critics have remarked in these works, especially in the last two, may partly be ascribed to the change in

Debussy's domestic situation. In the autumn of 1903 he met Emma Bardac, the wife of a banker and an amateur singer, to whom Fauré 11 years previously had dedicated his song cycle *La bonne chanson*. In June 1904 Debussy left his wife and in the autumn moved with Bardac into an apartment (rented with her money) in the Avenue du Bois de Boulogne, where he lived for the rest of his life. In October his wife attempted to commit suicide and in the resulting scandal a number of Debussy's friends broke off relations with him. A year later, on 30 October 1905, a fortnight after the first performance of *La mer*, a daughter was born to Debussy and Bardac and named Claude-Emma (Chou-Chou). The parents were married on 20 January 1908.

1906 was marked only by the first performance of the first set of *Images* for piano and the publication of one tiny piano piece; the next first performance of a major work did not take place until February 1908, when Viñes played the second set of *Images*. By this time Debussy had seen his hopes of material prosperity dashed; in 1907 Bardac's uncle, the financier Osiris, disinherited her, and over the next seven years Debussy was forced to undertake ten journeys to England, Belgium, Holland, Austria, Hungary, Italy and Russia, playing the piano and conducting his own works.

At the end of 1908 Debussy finished *Ibéria*, the second of three orchestral *Images*, and in 1909 he enjoyed a year of particular musical success: he was appointed a member of the advisory board of the Paris Conservatoire, he was in London for the triumphant British première of *Pelléas et Mélisande* (even if he had strong reservations about the production), the first French biography of him by Laloy was published and he

6. Claude
Debussy with his
second wife,
Emma Bardac

46

began five of the first book of *Préludes* for piano. Early in the year, however, he began to be troubled by the rectal cancer that was to kill him, and had to take drugs to alleviate the pain. The following year *Ibéria* and *Rondes de printemps* were given their first performances and he received two commissions, both of which he seems to have accepted largely for financial reasons. The second of these, *Le martyre de St Sébastien*, on a text by D'Annunzio, achieved some notoriety, but little success. On both commissions, *Khamma* and *Le martyre*, Debussy engaged the help of other musicians, Koechlin and Caplet respectively, and there is evidence that he was not clear about the way his style could develop. In 1913 he finished orchestrating *Jeux* – given in the spring of that year by Dyagilev's company, a fortnight before the première of *The Rite of Spring*, which largely overshadowed it.

In 1914 Debussy made his last visit abroad, to London, although he continued to make plans for tours of the USA, England and Switzerland. Early in 1915 his publisher Jacques Durand commissioned him to produce an edition of the works of Chopin and from this labour of love sprang the 12 *Etudes* for piano. These were only part of his output during the months July to October which he spent at Pourville; in this final creative burst he also finished *En blanc et noir* and composed the first two of a projected set of six sonatas for various combinations of instruments. On his return to Paris he began to suffer acute pain and in December he had a colostomy. He wrote nothing the following year except the final version of the libretto of *La chute de la maison Usher*, based on a story by Poe, a project cherished probably for some 25 years but never completed. His last work, the Violin Sonata, received its first performance in May 1917 with the composer at the piano; it was the last music that he played in public, at St Jean-de-Luz in September. From the early days of 1918 he was confined to his room and he died on 25 March.

Dramatic, orchestral and choral works

Of Debussy's dramatic works before *Pelléas* nothing survives complete. Two fragments from *Hymnis*, a setting of Banville's *comédie-lyrique*, show a conventional sweetness of harmony and melody, with a little vocalise in honour of Mme Vasnier to whom it was dedicated. Far more interesting are the 29 surviving pages of *Diane au bois* (see fig.7). In tackling Banville's comedy Debussy recognized eventually that he had overreached himself; but the dream world of forests, lakes, of distant horns and seductive flutes had made its impression, and in a general sense the work may be regarded as a preparation for *L'après-midi*. The third unfinished work is the opera *Rodrigue et Chimène*, which Debussy undertook unwillingly in response to parental pressure and in the hope that association with its librettist, Mendès, would open doors for him at the Paris Opéra. After two years of work Debussy finally decided he could no longer stomach the work's epic nature and claimed that the manuscript had been destroyed in an accidental fire. But the opinion voiced by several distinguished musicians, some of whom have seen the almost complete piano score, that it is undiluted Wagner cannot be supported. In addition to occasional 'Tristan' chords there is considerable Russian influence (perhaps from Rimsky-Korsakov's music performed at the 1889 Exhibition) and not a little

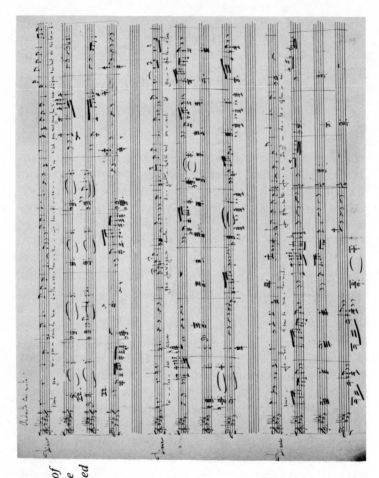

7. The fifth
surviving
autograph page of
Debussy's 'Diane
au bois', composed
c1884–6

50

Vocal dramatic works

from French opera, especially Chabrier's *Gwendoline*, also on a libretto by Mendès. There are also a number of features (spreading diatonic chords, throbbing offbeat accompaniments) which regularly appear in his mature work; and Act 2 begins prophetically 'dans une salle sombre et vaste dans le château de Bivar'.

The genesis of *Pelléas et Mélisande*, produced at the Opéra-Comique in 1902, was as early as 1889. Some of Debussy's conversations with his teacher Guiraud are on record: 'Music in opera is far too predominant', 'My idea is of a short libretto with mobile scenes', 'No discussion or argument between the characters, whom I see at the mercy of life or destiny'. Whether or not Debussy read Maeterlinck's play before seeing it on the stage, it is clear enough why he was attracted to it as a libretto (he had already applied unsuccessfully in 1889 to Maeterlinck for permission to set *La princesse Maleine*). In finding music too predominant in opera Debussy was obviously thinking of Wagner. He adored *Tristan* above all Wagner's operas, but in setting a similar story of love, jealousy and revenge he realized that he had to find a new means of expression, and *Pelléas*'s stormy reception was due in part to its negative characteristics: it is in a superficial sense anti-Wagner, anti-Massenet and wholly anti-Leoncavallo. The fact that Debussy seriously considered a Pelléas *en travesti* demonstrates his view of this operatic hero as no Des Grieux, let alone a Siegfried. On the other hand the opera is not lacking in positive features: the primacy of text over music (he made only a few cuts and changes in Maeterlinck's original), a total respect for the inflections of the French language, and a revolutionary use of discreet orchestral colour and of silence. During the years 1893–5, when *Pelléas* was taking shape, Debussy got to know the vocal score of *Boris Godunov* and it is reasonable to suppose that it made its mark, in principle rather than in detail.

One of Debussy's main achievements in *Pelléas* was to prolong by his music the equivocal yet palpable atmosphere of the play. The story, set in the allegorical kingdom of Allemonde, is almost embarrassingly simple and Debussy turned this simplicity to advantage. The very lack of action allowed him time to capture the often unexpressed feelings of the characters so that without, for the most part, any histrionics they come across the footlights as far more than cardboard figures. At the same time they lack the definition that a Verdi would have given them. Everything lies in the mode of suggestion to which the orchestra is dedicated and in the sparing (and often misunderstood) use of recurring themes. Debussy does not use these as material for any symphonic argument essential to the opera, still less as agents of what he called the 'visiting card' technique of the *Ring*. These themes refer not so much to individual characters as to states of mind. True, Golaud is often tormented in spirit, but it is simplistic to speak of 'Golaud's theme'. The uncertain progress of this motif, characterized by a dotted rhythm (ex.1), symbolizes not

Ex.1

so much Golaud himself as his struggle against fate, and this is a struggle in which Pelléas and Mélisande are also involved. We may compare this phrase with what has been called 'Arkel's motif' (ex.2) but which, in its rounded contours, more nearly symbolizes the old man's acceptance of fate as the dominating factor of life.

Ex.2

The vocal score was probably finished by April 1895, and in 1901 Debussy was promised a production the following year by the director of the Opéra-Comique. Before that date the composer had firmly to refuse the giving of fragments of the work or the making of a symphonic suite; indeed, so precious to him was the image of the opera that the cold actuality of a full-scale production filled him with misgivings. In May 1901 he began the orchestration, then in November began again. From the start of 1902 difficulties mounted: countless mistakes in the orchestral parts, Maeterlinck's hostility caused partly by the rejection of his mistress for the part of Mélisande, and the discovery that interludes were needed to allow time for scene changes. After a noisy public dress rehearsal the première on 30 April 1902 was quieter, but hostility and incomprehension were if anything more widespread. The critics were divided. Among the opposition Théodore Dubois, the director of the Conservatoire, forbade his students to go to it, while even some supporters were puzzled: the critic Gustave Bret wrote: 'This music overwhelms you, drives deep into your heart with a power of inspiration that I admire but cannot fully understand'. Accusations were largely of formlessness (no arias), melodic and rhythmic mon-

8. Stage design by Jusseaume for the scene of the death of Pelléas in Debussy's 'Pelléas et Mélisande', first performed in Paris, 30 April 1902

otony (no dances), lack of noise (sparing use of trombones) and unintelligible harmonic progressions (few perfect cadences). Possibly these criticisms might have been tempered by a perusal of the vocal score but this did not appear in print until ten days after the première and by that time positions were entrenched. The opera's supporters were mostly young and they made a vociferous defence of this work which for them opened a door to the 'new music': 'what will survive in *Pelléas* . . . is the human soul which there finds its expression; the work's humanity' (Fernand Gregh, quoted in Vallas, 1932). The symbolist movement, which reached its peak in Paris about 1890, had belatedly engendered an operatic masterpiece.

Debussy's career was littered with abandoned dramatic projects (see work-list), but the two to which he probably devoted most time were *Le diable dans le beffroi* and *La chute de la maison Usher*, both on tales of Poe. Only fragments survive of the music for this varied double bill. In *Le diable* Debussy was intent on finding a new style of choral writing to express the mingled sentiments of a crowd; neither the antiphonal groups of *Boris Godunov* nor the organized army of *Die Meistersinger*. The part of the Devil himself was not to be sung but whistled. In contrast with this ironic fantasy *La chute* was a study of pathological melancholia. The grey stones of Usher's house, like the dungeons of Golaud's castle, shadow the existence of the characters and it cannot be doubted that Debussy to some extent saw himself mirrored in the over-sensitive person of Roderick Usher. He absorbed himself in this opera as he had not done in anything since the composition of *Pelléas*; in 1908 he wrote to his editor: '. . . there are times when I lose contact with my surroundings and if Roderick Usher's sister were suddenly to appear I should not be all that surprised'.

Debussy's last vocal work for the stage was the incidental music to *Le martyre de St Sébastien* (1911), a synthesis of orchestral and vocal music, speech, mime and dancing on a text by D'Annunzio. In spite of the haste in which Debussy was forced to complete the music, he was not displeased with the result. The mixture of paganism and Christianity in the text may have evoked memories of the occultism in which he had dabbled in the 1890s, but it did not please the Archbishop of Paris, who forbade Catholics to attend. On the day of the ban Debussy declared to a journalist: 'I assure you, I have written the music as though it were commissioned for a church', and certainly it seems to have been widely admired. Less acceptable to the Church were the glorification of cruelty in D'Annunzio's text and the beautiful legs of Ida Rubinstein, who played the part of the saint. For all the money spent on it, *Le martyre* was a flop and has never again been staged in its original five-hour form. Debussy received considerable help with the scoring from his friend Caplet and the final chorus has been widely assumed to be wholly Caplet's work; it does have an unusually academic flavour but recent research supports the view that it is indeed by Debussy. Of the five 'mansions' into which the work is divided the fourth, 'Le laurier blessé', is of the highest inspiration throughout, while elsewhere individual passages, such as the saint's dance on the red-hot coals and the prelude to the second mansion, 'La chambre magique', show Debussy moving towards an orchestral texture that is at the same time evocative and hard as iron.

A study of Debussy's orchestral works before his successful Prix de Rome cantata *L'enfant prodigue* (1884) is
profitable only in showing that Debussy was no infant
Mozart and that he was only comfortable when writing
pastiche of the conventional French idiom of the period.
Some undigested Russian influence may be noted in a
work such as the B minor Symphony (1880) and
some imaginative but ill-judged attempts at sinister
trombone writing in *Le gladiateur* (1883), but only in
L'enfant prodigue does the music flow with any
conviction. Through the ten years 1884–94 he directed
his efforts towards achieving a similar sense of
conviction while using a more advanced musical
language and pursuing ideas both radical and elusive.

Of the four 'envois' which Debussy was obliged to
submit to the Académie only two were composed in
Rome: *Zuleima* (now lost) and the symphonic suite
Printemps, finished, apart from the orchestration, a
month before his return to Paris in March 1887. This is
the earliest of his orchestral works to find a place in the
modern repertory and in its two movements Debussy
tried 'to express somehow the slow, agonizing birth of
beings and of objects in nature, then the gradual
blossoming, and finally an outburst of joy at being
reborn to a new life'. It was to be a work 'of an individual
colour' and 'without a programme'. The jury of the
Académie censured its 'vague impressionism' (the first
recorded use of this dangerous term to describe
Debussy's music) while admitting that, whatever
Debussy's faults, banality was not one. Unfortunately the
original full score is lost, and the version made from a
piano score in 1912 by Büsser, excluding as it does the
female chorus, can give only a rough idea of it. Debussy

himself wanted the piano duet included but it seems that his interest in this work of his youth was by that time financial rather than aesthetic. The most interesting features of the score are the pentatonic opening of unaccompanied melody and the amalgamation of the two main tunes to form the climax (see *Petite suite*). The first movement begins and ends in F♯ major in spite of (or perhaps because of) Saint-Saëns' objection to this key for the orchestra in *Zuleima*; there are Wagnerian echoes at the beginning of the second movement; and the 'outburst of joy' is rather brashly Lisztian.

A female chorus also plays an important part in the third 'envoi', *La damoiselle élue* (1887–8). In setting a French translation of *The Blessed Damozel* by Rossetti Debussy avoided the pitfalls of sentimentality, and the chastely syllabic chanting of the chorus is strangely impressive; more so than the solo vocal writing which is somewhat wooden, though the Damozel herself has some beautiful turns of phrase. Debussy clearly had *Parsifal* in mind when he wrote it, and he used a medium-sized orchestra with restraint. As in so many later works, flute, oboe and english horn have prominent parts, and strings and harp are frequently used for colouristic effects, such as the surprisingly syncopated passage portraying the angels playing their guitars and lutes, where the two main themes are again played simultaneously. The strings frequently divide; for the final C major chord into 18 parts. The material too is in many ways individual. Inside the basic C major, out of mind for much of the work, E minor–major becomes almost a subsidiary tonic, in accord with the often modally inspired harmony, and the blatant consecutive 5ths of the opening phrase indicate that Debussy was not one to let academic formulae restrain his 'plaisir'.

The final 'envoi' was the *Fantaisie* for piano and orchestra. This was never performed in Debussy's lifetime, but it is clear from his correspondence of the early 1890s that he was not at the time dissatisfied with the work. In fact he withdrew it before the intended first performance only because d'Indy wanted to perform the first movement alone; as it is a cyclic work and the three movements are played continuously, Debussy's attitude is understandable. It contains several imaginative passages, including some extended use of the whole-tone scale to build tension, but in general the orchestral writing looks to Liszt, the piano writing to Saint-Saëns and the result is not wholly satisfactory. In August 1909 Debussy wrote to Edgard Varèse 'For some time I've been intending to rewrite it almost entirely ... I've changed my mind about how to treat the piano with an orchestra. The orchestral scoring has to be different too, otherwise you end up with a slightly ridiculous battle between the two participants'. Certainly the *Fantaisie* gives little warning of the stature of Debussy's next major orchestral work.

In the words of Boulez, 'just as modern poetry surely took root in certain of Baudelaire's poems, so one is justified in saying that modern music was awakened by *L'après-midi d'un faune*'. While few might disagree with this judgment, few would agree about what makes *L'après-midi* such a revolutionary work. Like Mallarmé's poem the music works by suggestion, and in a sense any careful analysis is likely to be right, as far as it goes. At any rate it is not a straightforward piece of programme music; as the composer said, 'if the music were to follow more closely it would run out of breath,

9. Vaclav
Nizhinsky (right,
also the choreo-
grapher) and the
nymphs in
Debussy's
'L'après-midi
d'un faune'

60

Choral and orchestral works

like a dray horse competing for the Grand Prix with a thoroughbred'. The unique sound of the work comes partly from the richness of the woodwind section (including three flutes, english horn and four horns) and the prominent roles which they play in the absence of trumpets, trombones and timpani. The only percussion instruments, unless one counts the two harps as such, are the two antique cymbals, to which Debussy entrusted a mere five notes apiece, a highly 'unprofessional' use of a commodity, justified beyond question by its effect. Texture apart, the trance-like quality of the score also stems from the nature of the opening theme, whose languorously syncopated outline and emphasis on the tritone (C♯–G) weaken the claims of the E major tonality. It is possible to analyse the whole work as a series of perpetual variations on this theme. Debussy used the sound of the flute as a symbol of the faun's dreaming, and, as in dreams, the same ideas recur but in different configurations, while the reedy timbres of oboe and clarinet act as modulators from one state to another. The friction between theme and distorted echo is taken up on another level by that between the contrary suggestions of melody and harmony, some chords producing rich 'frissons' simply by their context. Similarly, the total silence of the sixth bar is bursting with music. Even the central D♮ section, regretted by some critics, can be seen as a mirage of activity, an unattainable state as the returning flute theme soon shows; here too there is friction, between the 'real' and the 'ideal' (which is which?), here too a development from the chromatic–tonal conflict of the opening bars.

For all its revolutionary character, *L'après-midi* was an instant success. Mallarmé wrote to Debussy that the music 'set up no dissonance with my text, except indeed to explore further the nostalgia and the atmosphere of light, delicately, disturbingly, deeply'. Not unexpectedly, Saint-Saëns saw this truth with other eyes: '[It] is pretty sound, but it contains not the slightest musical idea in the real sense of the word. It's as much a piece of music as the palette a painter has worked from is a painting'. Dyagilev produced it as a ballet in 1912 for which Nizhinsky danced the name part and provided the choreography. Although this production had its defenders, Debussy was not one of them. Contemporary accounts make it clear that the fluid construction of the music was belied by the architectural poses of the dancers and that the subtle suggestions of sexuality were made all too explicit.

It seems likely that the *Nocturnes* began life as *Trois scènes au crépuscule* in 1892 and went through other metamorphoses before reaching their final form (see work-list). The strings in *Nuages* are unusually predominant for Debussy, and are something more than a mere background to the chromatic line of the english horn, suggested to Debussy by the hooter of a 'bateau-mouche' on the Seine. Their textures are extraordinarily varied; the spare two-part counterpoint doubled at the octave, widespread divisions, and a blending of arco and pizzicato in which they throb like an enormous heart. In the central section the pentatonic tune and its scoring are obviously suggested by the lie of the hands on the keyboard, whereas the masterly dissolution of the final bars is purely orchestral in inspiration, described by Debussy as a 'grey agony, gently tinged with white'. *Fêtes* is one of the most truly descriptive of all his works. The brass band of the Garde Républicaine moves

through the festivities and its tune is just vulgar enough
to set it apart from the surrounding music which has
passed through the prism of Debussy's own insight; it
also has the advantage of working with it to form a
contrapuntal climax. Less clumsy than *Printemps*, less
solid than the last movement of *La mer*, less raucous
than *Ibéria*, this movement is unique in Debussy's music
for the grace of its high spirits. In its unconstrained use
of triads and major 9ths and in the entirely natural
vacillation between triple, quadruple and quintuple
metre, the rustic dream of the faun has been civilized
and given substance in contemporary surroundings. The
coda distils that sense of pleasurable exhaustion
Debussy had already tapped in his song *Chevaux de bois*
15 years earlier. *Sirènes*, including a vocalising female
chorus, is a study in 'sea-texture' before *La mer* but
without that work's subtleties of construction. It is a
rare chorus that surmounts the difficulties of intonation.
Laloy, reviewing the first performance, claimed somewhat ironically to have found intellectual pleasure in the
historically correct quarter-tones of these Greek
mythological figures. On a more serious level, the controlled monotony and regular phrase lengths may be
taken as a symbol of the sirens' power, dependent as it
was on an appearance of unsophisticated charm.

Those enthusiasts who expected to find in *La mer* a
repetition of *Sirènes* or of the grotto scene in *Pelléas*
were disappointed, and admittedly the complex structure and the anti-melodic conception of certain passages
were calculated to disturb the casual listener. At the
opening of the first movement (up to fig.[3]) there is a
bewildering succession of textures, ranging from themes
to noises via arabesques and accompanimental figures.

Themes, such as that played by the horns at fig.[3], and including the sharp 4th and flat 7th characteristic of this period, have to be fought for and are subject to interruptions from the surrounding materials; or rather, reinterpretations, because nearly all the material derives from the four superimposed 5ths, announced in a reordered form at the opening and subsequently presented both horizontally and vertically. For sheer complexity the passage at fig.[18] is a prime example. Seven different rhythms are sounding simultaneously and three different patterns of dynamics.

The second movement, 'Jeux de vagues', is a masterpiece of suggestion in which Debussy blurred the outlines by trills and heterophonic scoring. It is instructive to compare the end of this movement with the coda of *L'après-midi*, also in E major and making use of flute, harp and muted brass. The later passage is less compact, perhaps less 'perfect', but Debussy continues to imbue it with a strong sense of expectancy; it is not surprising that he was not satisfied with his earliest version. The answer to this expectancy is the simple but menacing noise of the tumultuous sea. If the second movement was a study of light, the third movement is a study of colour and space, and of the elemental power at which the first movement had only hinted. Some critics have found the Franckian main tune rather blatant, even weak, but if this is true the final grafting on to it of the chorale takes advantage of the weakness to good effect. At the theme's second appearance the high A♭ harmonic on the first violins creates an amazing impression of space, an orchestral use of the 'technique of illusion' which Lockspeiser has mentioned in connection with the piano works; the listener tends not to hear the harmonic itself, only the effect it has on the texture as a whole, a procedure which we may legitimately term 'impressionist'. But in general the logic of this movement is traditional enough and leads to the first wholly extrovert ending since the piano *Fantaisie*. This masculine element in *La mer* was no doubt what Lockspeiser had in mind when he wrote that 'a latent force that for years had been lying dormant is brought to a head'. More recently Howat has marshalled detailed and convincing arguments to show that this force and more especially the work's structural solidity are the result of Debussy's use of Golden Section proportioning.

La mer occupied Debussy for nearly two years from the summer of 1903. In the meantime he wrote the two *Danses* for cross-strung chromatic harp and string orchestra, commissioned by the firm of Pleyel in liaison with the Brussels Conservatory as a test piece for a class that was being initiated there in this new instrument. Compared with *La mer*, the *Danses* are chaste and formal. The first, based on a piano piece by the Portuguese composer Francisco de Lacerda, belongs to the stately genre of *Danseuses de Delphes*; the second sparkles rather more – certainly it is hard to find in either a musical explanation for Fauré's review, in which he referred to the 'usual collection of harmonic peculiarities'. Much the same directness and simplicity governs the *Trois chansons de Charles d'Orléans* for unaccompanied chorus. Debussy had finished the two outer songs in 1898. The first is largely based on the Aeolian mode, addressed with decently restrained adoration to the beloved. The last illustrates the cruel sterility of winter not only by fairly obvious chromaticism but also (a typical *jeu d'esprit*) by a passage of fugal imitation. In the central song, composed ten years later, the word 'tabourin' is enough to turn Debussy towards Spain, especially since he was at the time already involved in his largest 'Spanish' work.

The three movements collectively entitled *Ibéria* themselves form the central movement of his orchestral *Images*. Here Debussy, with the resources of a large orchestra, faced the temptations of direct sound-painting, whereas on the piano any imitation had to pass through the filter of his own 'plaisir'. Perhaps the most impressive thing about *Ibéria* is Debussy's skill (as in *Fêtes*) in flirting with vulgarity without ever losing his aristocratic poise. Guitars and castanets are plentiful, even trombone glissandos, but involvement is tempered with objectivity. The clarinets for example, which gain a new melodic importance in these *Images*, are directed on their first entry to be 'elegant and fairly rhythmical' as opposed to sloppily sentimental. In the central 'Parfums de la nuit' sultry passion is suggested by the orchestration but there is no romantic dénouement; instead the darkness dissolves into the morning light of a festival, a transitional passage of which Debussy was particularly proud. This last movement consists of what Debussy called 'realities', thrown at the audience in an apparently incoherent assembly of ideas and bathed in a hard, garish luminosity. Even if the procedure is not subtle in the sense of contrived, it is certainly a crucial step in the abandonment of linear motivic thinking in much 20th-century music. Equally certainly it is not 'impressionist'.

Gigues and *Rondes de printemps* together balance this largely extrovert central movement. *Gigues* is not so much sad as tragic. Throughout there is a feeling that happiness is within reach, and the music of the *Keel Row* brings with it a certain desperate jollity, like that of the fool in *King Lear*. But as the flute rules *L'après-midi*, so the baleful timbre of the oboe d'amore is stronger than any mere tune. There are no 'realities' in *Gigues*, nor in *Rondes*, in which Debussy for the fourth time used the nursery tune 'Nous n'irons plus au bois'. The mood of the piece is a kind of refined nostalgia. But unlike nostalgia proper, it never becomes self-indulgent or repetitive. Indeed a contemporary critic found that, while it was based with an almost academic strictness on the nursery tune, it lacked emotional coherence. Part of the secret lay no doubt in the complexity of the orchestration; the primal function of timbre, entrusted in *Gigues* to the oboe d'amore, is here disseminated among the whole orchestra. The interplay of rhythms, too, is complex and contained within an overall fluidity of tempo.

Debussy's last three orchestral works were all ballets, two of which were orchestrated with the assistance of others. Of these, *La boîte à joujoux* is undoubtedly a success on its own modest terms as 'a work to amuse children, nothing more' (or was this description of Debussy's merely disingenuous?), but *Khamma*, an Egyptian ballet written for the Canadian dancer Maud Allan has generally and unfairly been written off as a failure. Debussy referred to its 'trumpet calls which suggest revolt and fire and which send a shiver down your back', indicating that if he wrote it in the first place for money he had nevertheless responded in some degree to the 'childishly simple' scenario.

Debussy harboured similar feelings about the plot of

67

Jeux, which he wrote for Dyagilev in the late summer of 1912, but in this case a simple structure encouraged a particularly rich response. As in 'Jeux de vagues' from *La mer*, the title 'games' seems to have suggested to Debussy a framework of rules which was but the starting-point for the substance of the game itself, consisting of an infinite variety of strokes and gestures. In *Jeux* the substance is the endless variation of the basic, undulating phrase, the orchestral colours and the proliferating arabesques; even if these 'accessories' do not help to get the ball over the net, they are what makes the game worth watching. Stravinsky considered *Jeux* an orchestral masterpiece, but found some of the music (that is, the ideas) too easy on the ear ('trop lalique'). It is at least questionable whether this distinction is valid. The logic of the work is hard to see on the page. The fragments coalesce towards the end into a promising theme, but this is cut short at the climax and leads to a poetic disintegration, which, like that in 'Jeux de vagues', Debussy was content to rework, this time at Dyagilev's instigation. Certain ideas, such as the dark stillness of the park at the opening or the flight and force of the tennis ball, find traditional expression, but there is at no time a jarring between such external ideas and the inner development of the music. *Jeux* was first greeted with incomprehension, then forgotten. 50 years later, at the other extreme, it became a cult object of the avant garde who, in their admiration for its technical wonders, perhaps lost sight of its emotional power. As in Ravel's *La valse*, and yet how differently, the waltz is isolated as a cultural phenomenon and placed in a new and disturbing context; we see that the opium of the dancing classes is no longer potent. To borrow Debussy's own phrase about *The Rite of Spring*, *Jeux* is 'a beautiful nightmare'.

CHAPTER THREE

Chamber music and songs

Apart from an early Piano Trio in G (*c*1879) and a
Nocturne et scherzo for cello and piano, both written
for the composer himself and his partners in von
Meck's musical establishment, Debussy's earliest essay
in this genre is his String Quartet (1893), although
'essay' is hardly appropriate for such a radical reinter-
pretation of the medium. The opening theme provides
material for three of the four movements but, characteristically, Debussy allowed himself freedom from cyclic
tyranny in the slow movement where a certain Russian
melancholy comes to the fore. One of the chief novelties
of the first movement is that the rhythm and overall
shape of the main theme assume priority over its
original harmonic structure and over the exactness of
melodic details. It is meaningful to distinguish between
the endless variation which Debussy applies here and
the intervallic kind of development which appeals more
to the German mentality. Of the four movements the
scherzo is undoubtedly the most startling. In the combination of arco and pizzicato and in the pervading
cross-rhythms the listener loses track of any thematic
thread and instead is forced to appreciate the texture as
texture. The result is almost orchestral in its variety and
stands as the earliest model for those quartet writers of
the 20th century (Webern, Bartók) for whom timbre has
assumed a dominant role. It is no surprise to find the

composer 15 years later complaining of the difficulty of making a piano arrangement of the work. The immediate critical reaction was mostly of puzzlement. Dukas recognized its stature but Chausson, to whom Debussy had confided details of the work in progress, was profoundly disappointed and said so. A second quartet was destined by Debussy to soothe this disappointment, but the break in their friendship no doubt explains why this work never became more than a project.

In 1910, for the annual practical examinations at the Conservatoire, Debussy completed two pieces for clarinet and piano: the *Première rapsodie* as the test piece proper and a sight-reading exercise later published as the *Petite pièce*. The latter is unpretentiously charming (rather like *The Little Shepherd* in *Children's Corner*) but the *Rapsodie* is, in the words of Debussy's friend Robert Godet, 'the most dreamlike of his rhapsodies'; he exploited both the cantabile and *con agilità* aspects of the clarinet's character in a truly Mozartian fashion, without plumbing Mozartian depths. The work gains greatly from the composer's own orchestral arrangement.

Debussy's final chamber works were the three sonatas, of a projected set of six, which he wrote between the summer of 1915 and the spring of 1917. In the Cello Sonata (1915) the traditionally sustained legato of the instrument is almost ignored. Instead Debussy seems to have been bent on turning it into a bass guitar – he himself dubbed the work 'Pierrot angry with the moon'. Where there are passages of legato they eventually dissolve into nervous ornaments. Logical continuity is stretched beyond one's immediate understanding by persistent variation of speed and by a free modulation which often becomes a surrealistic juxtaposition of different ideas. The second movement in particular is an extension of the essentially non-thematic structure in the scherzo of the String Quartet. When, in the third and final movement, something in the nature of a theme does appear, it has the effect of a sarcastically disingenuous remark dropped into an otherwise wholly allusive conversation. If the tone of the Sonata for flute, viola and harp is less challenging, it too is built on understatements. The harmonic language is surprisingly simple and the occasional turn of phrase harks back to Debussy's melodic style of the 1890s, but the message thus conveyed is undeniably of the 20th century. Partly this is a question of the scoring: Debussy had originally planned to use an oboe instead of the viola, but the string instrument is undoubtedly more effective not only for pitch but also in mediating between plucked strings and woodwind, between the evanescent and the controlled sound. Partly it is the free assembly, even more pronounced than in the Cello Sonata, of thematic elements: the six ideas of the first movement return, with or without extensive variation, in the order 2–5–6–3–4–1–5–3. Partly it is such innovations in the sonata tradition as the narcissistic echoes which bring the work to a halt in the second bar of the first movement. The composer said of it: 'I don't know whether it should move us to laughter or tears. Perhaps both?'

The Violin Sonata (1917) was the last work Debussy finished. He had particular difficulty with the final movement, settling in the end for a version of his original idea; and even if the end may seem a rather too facile solution, it is surely wrong to dismiss the work as worthless. The middle movement is an exercise in the fantastic, including some surprisingly wholehearted tunes, and the first is remarkable for its fluid extensions of the rhythms one expects. The writing for the violin betrays Debussy's admiration for the true 'gypsy' style, and at the recapitulation he was patently torn between the claims of form and those of fantasy. The result is two parallel streams of invention in which it is possible to see foreshadowed many of the concepts of dualism to be found in later 20th-century music.

Debussy's early songs present chronological problems: dates of composition and extent of revision are often untraceable. But one can begin to describe the general character of much of this early work. Two influences are apparent above all others: that of French opera (whether Gounod or Massenet, the atmosphere at least is very similar) and that of the amateur singer Mme Vasnier. The smooth, unsurprising lines of the 19th-century French tradition are everywhere in evidence in the songs Debussy wrote before leaving for Rome in 1885. A song such as *Rondeau* (1882) is almost a pre-echo of Manon's apostrophe to her 'petite table'; the melody is suspended in a glutinous diatonic substance, compounded chiefly of added 6th or dominant 7th, gently stirred from time to time, but which binds the melody to a complaisant servitude. The influence of Vasnier works in a different direction. She possessed a high, agile voice, and for her Debussy wrote the great majority of his songs before 1885. The unpublished *Rondel chinois* is a diverting vocalise and little more, but the first version of *Fantoches* and two other settings, *Pantomime* and *Pierrot*, manage to extract some expressive content from the style.

In view of Debussy's deficient education, it is perhaps surprising that even in his early 20s he was responding to the quality of the poets he set. Generally the sentimental effusions of Banville and Bourget get what they deserve, the former's *Zéphyr* becoming almost a parody of itself. But where a second-rate poet surpasses himself (Bourget in *Beau soir*), or when the poet is of the order of Verlaine or Mallarmé, Debussy's setting reflects this. The style may still be that of French opera, and there may still be passages of vocalise, but the germ of sincerity is transmitted. In *Beau soir* (to which the chronological provisos apply) the antithesis of E major and G minor at the end of the piano introduction is a warning of the ambivalent mood of the poem, leaving the details of such ambivalence to be filled in by the singer. The penultimate chord, as in several songs of this period, is an augmented 5th, but here Debussy integrated the cliché by aligning it chillingly with the second syllable of 'tombeau'. The only published song to show a foretaste of genius is *Apparition* on a poem by Mallarmé. Perhaps it is noteworthy that with *Beau soir* this is one of the few not dedicated to Vasnier. Certainly there is nothing wanton or irrelevant in the vocal line, from which Debussy was to extract one complete phrase for use in *Pelléas et Mélisande*. Some of the word-setting is still a little heavy and stilted, but the lines themselves are magnificently wide, resting on harmonies and textures that are always changing. Both the opening phrase, on one note, marked 'rêveusement', and the ending, lulled by juxtaposed major triads, take the listener into the dream world of Mallarmé's poem.

With the *Ariettes oubliées* Debussy moved decisively towards the style of his maturity. In *Green* the piano part provides a framework of two-bar phrases on which the varied melodic line is built; it concerns itself with melody and atmosphere, the voice with rhythm and words, a division that enabled Debussy to mould the vocal line after the natural inflections of the French language. At the same time he was alive to the overall shape of the poem: as the poet's mood passes from ardour, through fear, to hope, so the initial A♭ minor only at the end finds some repose in the tonic G♭ major. The confinement of the vocal line within narrower limits also gave Debussy the opportunity to make an expressive point with occasional wide leaps or melismata. In *C'est l'extase*, Debussy marked in this way the 'muted rolling of the pebbles under the water' and 'the soft cry of the ruffled grass', the climactic points in the poet's imagery, and he caught the plainer language of the final verse in a return to syllabic word-setting and a high proportion of repeated notes. To convey the tragic monotony of *Il pleure dans mon coeur*, the vocal line coincides throughout with the 40 two-bar phrases of the piano part, and the opening Dorian modality is consciously exploited as an atmospheric device. A refined symbolism is at work in *Chevaux de bois*, dating in essentials from 1885, where the circular movement of the horses on the merry-go-round is mirrored by 'circular' melody and harmony that return predictably to their starting-point; and in *L'ombre des arbres*, where the recurring octave E♯ discreetly but powerfully suggests the unidentified fate by which the traveller's hopes are shattered. Even though this E♯ octave is heard at three pitches, it is hardly an exaggeration to see it as an early example of an 'objet sonore', a single sound conceived in terms of one particular instrument or combination of instruments, and one which plays a structural role.

Simultaneously with the *Ariettes* Debussy worked on the *Cinq poèmes de Baudelaire*. Laloy, in his biography of 1909, noted that 'finding a vocal line and a consistent mood to fit these works, which resemble the pictures of Manet and sometimes those of Cézanne in their dense complexity, was something of a tour de force'. The effect of the piano part is indeed that of reduction from a well-filled orchestral score, and in general Debussy continued along the path he had abandoned after *Apparition*. The influence of Wagner is prevalent, especially in *Recueillement* with its images of love, night and death. Debussy coped with the formal problems of setting the long poem *Le balcon* by development through insertion as against development through repetition, and in *Harmonie du soir* he even reflected in the music the stringent 'pantoum' form of the poem, in which the second and fourth lines of one quatrain become the first and third lines of the next. Unique in the set is *Le jet d'eau*, completed in March 1889. The image of water obviously moved Debussy to abandon the almost experimental style of the other songs; the texture is more open and nearly devoid of chromatic inner parts. Debussy later orchestrated this song alone of the five but Vuillermoz's criticism, 'listening to this unblended and colourless orchestration one misses the piano', points, if in a backhanded way, at the essentially pianistic style of the accompaniment, depending for its effect on the sympathetic resonance between the vibrating strings.

These preoccupations with sonority and with the idiomatic setting of the French language continued in the songs of the next decade. *Les angélus*, *Les cloches*

and *De soir*, show three imaginative attempts at captur-
ing the sound of bells while in *L'échelonnement des
haies* Debussy even managed to evoke the synthetic
sound of 'cloches comme des flûtes'. The variety of style
between songs is very wide; compare for instance the
conversational tone of *Dans le jardin* with the heroic
sweep and bold colours of *La mer est plus belle*. All
these tendencies came together for the first time in the
masterly first set of *Fêtes galantes*. Debussy had made
two versions of an earlier setting of *En sourdine*, in
which the piano pulsates on expressively dissonant
chords; in this published setting he exploited the same
kind of texture but the subtleties of interplay between
voice and piano were made finer and the whole song
became a logical development, in terms not of notes but
of mood, from the insistent melancholy of the nightingale's refrain. *Fantoches* is essentially a song of 1882,
but the revision mixed triple rhythms with the original
duple ones and integrated the ending into the rest of the
song, both the sort of improvements that one might have
expected. It is an extraordinary little Harlequinade that
seems at first insubstantial, but the economy of the
writing masks passages of heavy irony – one rarely
hears the Spanish imitation in the middle section given
its full weight – and it is a perfect partner for the other
two songs, lightening but not dispelling their nostalgic
lyricism. In the final *Clair de lune* Debussy combined a
sensitivity to every inflection of the text with a grasp of
the structure of the whole and consciously manipulated
his by now extensive harmonic vocabulary to serve both
these ends, as in the evocative but also structurally valid
use of successive triads, and the perfect cadence at the
words 'et sangloter d'extase les jets d'eau'.

It is typical of Debussy, with his motto 'toujours plus

10. *Claude Debussy (right) with Raymond Bonheur on the bank of the River Marne at Luzancy, 1893*

loin', that he should have followed this achievement with
an experiment. Throughout the 1890s he toyed with the
idea of becoming a writer, and the *Proses lyriques* are
settings of four of his own poems. In general the
imagery is dense, and occasionally unfortunate; the aims
of Debussy the poet were hardly compatible with those
of Debussy the composer, and he was forced thereby to
compose in a rather convoluted musical style. The last
two are generally considered better than the others, a
view that Debussy possibly held himself, since he chose
these two to form part of the first ever all-Debussy
programme, given in Brussels on 1 March 1894. *De
fleurs* begins simply and includes several well-
characterized passages, but clumsy tremolos invade the
texture towards the end. *De soir* is probably the best.
Once more the bells ring and in the transformation of
the holiday scene as evening falls Debussy caught some
of the magic of the similar passage in *Chevaux de bois*.
The final apostrophe to the Virgin is spare and unaf-
fected, an understated summary more in accordance
with the composer's true nature.

By the summer of 1895 Debussy had finished the first
and basic version of *Pelléas et Mélisande* and his involvement with Maeterlinck's dream world is reflected in
the settings he made between 1897 and 1898 of three of
the *Chansons de Bilitis* by his friend Louÿs. The poet's
technique is the same as in his novel *Aphrodite*, to lend
blatantly erotic situations a certain dignity by placing
them in an antique never-never land. Like Mélisande,
Bilitis is so innocent that one is almost persuaded to
believe in her enduring chastity. Debussy's music
catches the ambiguity of these prose poems by a mixture
of modality (largely Dorian) and chromaticism, and by

a style of word-setting that is melodically simple with many repeated notes, but rhythmically fluid. Particularly in the third song, *Le tombeau des naïades*, the tension between the flexible vocal line and the unrelenting semiquavers of the accompaniment perhaps suggests Bilitis's unwillingness to come to terms with realities. Only in the middle song, *La chevelure*, is passion released and the narrow range of the vocal line expands (see ex.3). The major 9th harmony is activated by the gradually accelerating rhythm of the voice and the climax is balanced not only by the contrary motion of voice and piano but by their coincidence on B and E.

The two settings of Charles d'Orléans in the *Trois*

Ex.3

par la mê-me che-ve-lu-re la bouche sur la bou -
- - - che

chansons de France (1904) mark the beginning of what has been called a 'classical' style. Certainly they are not as sensual as the Bilitis songs and the piano writing is unusually non-atmospheric. Also of 1904 is the second set of *Fêtes galantes*. If the first set was a celebration of his ardent affair with Gaby, this one marks Debussy's final break with his first wife and the beginning of his liaison with Emma Bardac. It is not surprising that his view of love is less than wholeheartedly enthusiastic. The disenchantment, hinted at by Verlaine but not brought out by Debussy in the first set, is here plainly evident. The nostalgia of *Les ingénus* is more painful than sweet, as Debussy suggested by frequent use of the whole-tone chord, and the figure of the statue in *Le faune* warns the lovers of 'an unhappy end to these moments of content'; this song contains one of Debussy's most extended and imaginative passages of ostinato, a dry, distant drumming on two notes that from the fourth bar carries through to the end. Call it 'fate' or whatever, the effect is powerfully sinister. No more hopeful message is to be found in the final *Colloque sentimental*, arguably the most moving song Debussy ever wrote. Two ghosts recall their old love. For one the passion is still real, for the other love too is dead: ' "Does your heart beat faster at the mention of my name? Or in your dreams do you still find me?" "No" '. It is a mark of Debussy's genius that this monosyllable, bald and even risible on the page, provokes tears rather than laughter. He also integrated into the song different styles to project the three characters: a plain chordal style for the disenchanted lover; a richer, more operatic one for the other; and a spare, linear recitative for the narrator who frames the lovers' conversation. Perhaps the touch most revealing of what Debussy had learnt in the 13 years since the first set of *Fêtes galantes* is the reappearance of the nightingale's song from *En sourdine* as the first ghost begins to reminisce. The warm 9ths and triads of the original accompaniment become acidly dissonant diminished 7ths over the A♭ which pulses through the uncommunicative dialogue.

The move towards melodic and harmonic simplicity continued in the cycle *Le promenoir des deux amants* of which the first song, *La grotte*, had originally formed part of the *Trois chansons de France*. Although in this later set *La grotte* is followed by two other songs also on texts by the 17th-century poet Tristan Lhermite, it is possible to feel that its post-*Pelléas* evocative style assorts ill with their clearcut elegance; added to which there was something about stagnant water that struck deep into Debussy's imagination. In combining passion with precision he was more successful in the *Trois ballades de Villon* (1910). The singer is commanded to deliver the *Ballade de Villon a s'amye* 'with an expression as much of anguish as of regret' and the lover's shifting emotions are beautifully underlined by the subtle modulations, hesitant rhythms and imaginative timbres of the piano writing, while the vocal line returns from time to time to the superficially ungrateful chromaticism of the *Chansons de Bilitis*. The central prayer runs the risk of seeming like a pastiche of itself with its bare 5ths, parallel triads and modal contours but Debussy's control is absolute, as it is over the delicate touches of chromaticism that paint the damned in Hell and over a tonal scheme that suggests the contentment of a deep, orthodox faith through the movement from A minor to C major. The final *Ballade des femmes de Paris* bears the palm for the wittiest, most zestful song of his output. Through the incessant chatter of semiquavers comes an affection for the failings and peculiarities of Parisian woman, of whose charms Debussy, like Villon, was not wholly without experience.

Apart from the musically insignificant *Noël des enfants* (1915) Debussy's last songs were the *Trois poèmes de Mallarmé* (1913). In returning from Renaissance to contemporary poetry Debussy was possibly motivated by the move his own style had made in the last few years towards abstraction and non-traditional syntax, particularly in *Jeux*, which he had completed the previous autumn. Certainly these settings match the texts in their elliptical harmonic progressions and mere suggestions of melody. *Placet futile* is an avowal of love to a shepherdess painted on a Sèvres teacup. The playful artificiality of Mallarmé's poem finds an echo in the distorted memories of an 18th-century minuet and in a profusion of ornaments that are just as important to the texture as any of the more solid materials beneath. In *Eventail* such ornaments assume the principal role; just as the fan itself is a substitute for the crude spoken language, so Debussy enriched the atmosphere of the poem with discreet agitations of the fingers.

CHAPTER FOUR

Piano works

The fact that Debussy developed slowly as a writer for
the piano may be something of a mystery but it is not a
total one. His teacher Marmontel is quoted as saying
'Debussy isn't very fond of the piano, but he loves
music'. From this one may gather that even at the
Conservatoire Debussy was aware of the limitations of
the instrument. There are descriptions of him launching
himself at the piano, overdoing every effect, as though
moved by a deep hatred. On the other hand Fargue
remembered his playing in the 1890s: 'he cradled it [the
piano], talked softly to it, like a rider to his horse, a
shepherd to his flock or a thresher to his oxen'. It is
significant that on this occasion he was performing the
uncompleted score of *Pelléas*. Among the varied
accounts of his playing, agreement is reached on only
two points: that it was like nobody else's, and that it had
about it an orchestral quality. At all events, the two
approaches outlined above, at the extremes of boldness
and refinement, both display an unwillingness to treat
the piano as it had been treated in the past, and a
determination to subdue it to his will.

In his earlier years Debussy shied away from the
challenge which the piano held ready for him. Quite
possibly he identified it also with the 'castles in the air'
built by the father of the budding virtuoso, and with their
ultimate collapse. The *Deux arabesques* are the earliest

84

of his pieces that have held even a small place in the modern repertory, and are charming, unpretentious salon pieces. Five other works published in 1890–92, although heard even less often, are in many ways more interesting and in places prophetic of Debussy's mature style, even if he still lacked the technique or the vision to expand such passages beyond a few bars. Among the palpable weaknesses are the lumpy bridge-passages leading into the middle sections and the endings, either awkward or predictable, but the *Nocturne* is an accomplished piece of lyrical writing, like Fauré without the harmonic surprises. The opening theme of the *Danse* begins in pentatonic fashion and Debussy remembered it in the song *L'échelonnement des haies*, composed during 1891; for 36 bars, in the central section, he avoided a cadence and built textures that look ahead to *Masques* 15 years later. Ravel liked the *Danse* well enough to produce an orchestral version in 1922.

The exact placing of the *Suite bergamasque* in Debussy's output is problematical since there are no means of knowing what alterations he made to it between its composition in 1890 and its publication in 1905. Individual bars of the *Prélude* are fluid and sensuous in effect but the resolutions are too often through scales and other traditional devices for the magic to last, although the final passage treats the major and minor 7th degrees of the scale as equal alternatives in the manner of *L'après-midi*. The *Menuet* is the most revealing of the transition taking place in Debussy's musical language; within the delicate framework of an 18th-century pastiche are encompassed a lyrical tune à la Massenet, solid blocks of four-part writing à la Chausson and an ending that evaporates through a

Debussian glissando. Reliance on traditional arpeggio patterns in the left hand robs *Clair de lune* of the prophetic air it might otherwise have breathed but, as in the *Nocturne* and *Danse*, there are moments at least when the texture lures attention away from the syntax. Unfortunately the final *Passepied* is bedevilled by a trite second theme, and all Debussy's modal ingenuity is deployed in an attempt to save it, so that out of this uninspiring fragment he produces two magical passages. These are achieved by the use first of inversion and second of a successive combination of triple and duple rhythms. Once more, the ending breaks away from conventional practice in its widespread texture and its modal opposition of B major and F♯ minor.

The year before the first performance of *Pelléas* Debussy published the three pieces entitled *Pour le piano*. The *Prélude* shows, quite apart from the forcefulness of its ideas, a tightness of construction that Debussy had not so far achieved. The interweaving of two complementary themes and the subtlety with which chords of the augmented 5th prepare the way for the extended whole-tone passage, both show a craftsman's hand, as do many points of detail. Ravel claimed that *Pour le piano* 'said nothing really new' but there is no precedent for the individual sound of ex.4. The novelty resides not just in the whole-tone harmony, but in the texture created by the trill and (surely) the pedal, in the melodically otiose but beautiful minim A♭s, in the teasing antithesis of triplets against semiquavers and in the syncopated placing of the triplets' repeat. The final *Toccata* similarly mixes brilliant fingerwork with evocative textures, and Aeolian modality with the whole-tone scale, and it is crowned with an ending that

is, for Debussy, unusually emphatic. Seven successive, loud chords of the tonic major will not be found again in his output. It is to be noted, however, that the marking 'le double plus lent', found in many editions, is not Debussy's. The best of the set is undoubtedly the *Sarabande*. Again the mode is basically Aeolian but the control of chromaticism within it is masterly. For the first time in Debussy's piano works there are times when tonality is momentarily submerged and it is a measure of his extension of the key system that D major can follow G♯ minor with complete inevitability. An earlier version of the *Sarabande* exists as the second of three *Images* written in 1894 and all dedicated, like the final *Sarabande*, to Yvonne Lerolle, Chausson's niece. The 80 or so changes that Debussy made to the first version were largely in suppressing excessive chromatic alterations and allowing the modal harmony to stand uncluttered. The first *Image*, marked 'mélancolique et doux', is rather in the nostalgic style of Chausson, while the third, usually referred to as an early version of

Jardins sous la pluie because it contains the tune 'Nous n'irons plus au bois', is in fact a totally different and very exciting piece. The discreet, almost private nature of these *Images* is reflected in Debussy's own words at the head of the score: 'These pieces would shrink in terror from the brilliantly illuminated salons regularly frequented by those who do not like music. They are rather "conversations" between the piano and oneself'.

But, for all the beauties that these earlier pieces contain, it was not until 1903 that Debussy really faced the challenge of the instrument. His new approach proclaims itself in the title of the set, *Estampes*, as well as in those of the individual pieces. In calling them 'prints' he possibly intended to convey a refinement, an abjuration of the grand manner, yet they are not self-evident pastiches such as the *Passepied* from *Pour le piano*. *Pagodes* reflects his interest in Eastern music, and it is revealing that in the first of his pieces to break away from traditional piano textures Debussy should have chosen to look beyond Western civilization altogether. It is difficult to write about the piece without mentioning 'impressionism', a word which Debussy found meaningless or at best ill-used, but a short example (ex.5) shows what the term denotes in this context. The low B dictates that the sustaining pedal be held throughout and the effect on the rest of the three-fold texture bears obvious resemblances to the way that impressionist painters tended to use light: beyond that assertion lie the areas of controversy. One can see also that the movement in the three parts is graded according to their pitch, so that in performance all emerge at a similar volume and are heard as one, composite sound. With the second piece Debussy provoked another of the many

'affaires' with which his life was studded. After the first performance in 1898 of Ravel's *Habanera* for two pianos, Debussy had borrowed the score. Five years later he produced *La soirée dans Grenade*, marked 'mouvement de Habanera' and centred, like Ravel's piece, round languorously repeated C♯s. Some 70 years later it is possible to judge what different conclusions the two men drew from similar propositions. Whereas Ravel developed his ideas with perceptible logic, Debussy threw together a series of impressions and out of their friction grows an understandable excitement. *Jardins sous la pluie* is, in a sense, a reworking of the *Prélude* from *Pour le piano* in terms of Debussy's latest discoveries; the final 11 bars in particular are a miraculous synthesis of prestidigitation and expressive effect.

The two piano works of 1904, *Masques* and *L'isle joyeuse*, were both inspired by 18th-century subjects. In *Masques* Debussy returned for inspiration to the world of 'fêtes galantes' (he had finished his second set of songs of this title a few months earlier) and in particular to a texture of alternating hands that is first found in the song *Mandoline*. Many of Debussy's special effects – curling chromatic tunes in the middle of the keyboard, passages of whole-tone and pentatonic harmony, juxtaposed chromatic triads in root position – here go to make up a vigorous yet strangely touching work, and one that is all too rarely played. The more popular *L'isle joyeuse*, suggested by Watteau's *L'embarquement pour Cythère*, is one of Debussy's happiest inspirations. It manages to be extrovert without ever tending towards the plebeian; even the traditional left-hand arpeggios have 'a touch of class', arranged in groups of five against the three quavers in the right. Certainly Debussy plays no jokes with the listener's expectations; 'happiness is no laughing matter'.

One can relate the last two of the first series of *Images* (1905) to earlier works of the composer; considering the *Hommage à Rameau* as a development in both size and harmonic subtlety of the earlier *Sarabande*, and *Mouvement* as a more whimsical and elusive version of *Jardins sous la pluie*. But the opening piece, *Reflets dans l'eau*, has no clear ancestry. The rhythms of water, symmetrical to the casual eye, but in fact full of life-giving asymmetries, the sound of water, monotonous and hypnotic, even (in a good performance) the feel of water, come across with a fidelity that Liszt and Ravel had not achieved. Debussy used a wide area of keyboard, often at a low dynamic level, and built his material from short phrases. These he treated rather like the pebble dropped into the water, which initiates a series of movements only indistinctly related to its own shape but defined by its size, force and density. The final bars, marked 'lent, dans une sonorité harmonieuse et lointaine', afford a glimpse of Debussy's preoccupation, already audible in *Fêtes*, with the movement of sounds in space.

With the second series of *Images* (1907) Debussy reached the country towards which his steps had been leading for some 15 years, the country where sensation is king. The sounds of bells through leaves, the sight of a goldfish lit by sunlight shining through water, both are complex sensations, and the first a mixture of sound and sight in the manner of *Reflets dans l'eau*. But all three pieces of this set go beyond the earlier work in their harmonic richness, in their mercurial changes of mood, and in their demands on independence of finger; all are written on three staves. *Cloches à travers les feuilles* is notable for passages of mixed dynamics which suggest an orchestral sound, although no orchestra could match the rich texture of Debussy's piano writing. The name of the second, *Et la lune descend sur le temple qui fut*, was suggested to Debussy, after he had written the piece, by the dedicatee, Laloy, who was deeply interested in the Orient: the balance of this title admirably reflects the poise and precision of Debussy's music, in which traditionally 'oriental' features such as open 4ths and 5ths acquire a new dignity from being combined. The dangers of adapting a literally visual approach to this music are illustrated by the third piece, *Poissons d'or*, where the sight of the goldfish is merely the spark that kindles the composer's imagination. The quick movements of the fish suggest trills, trills suggest arpeggios and arpeggios suggest chords, while tunes and accompaniments exchange roles with bewildering speed. The final cadenza in its alternation of black-note and

91

white-note groups perhaps recalls Ravel's *Jeux d'eau*, but the whole is guided by a powerful fantasy which leaves ornamental fountains, and goldfish, far behind.

In writing *Children's Corner* that same year for his daughter, Debussy was pleased to aim two lighthearted blows at targets which especially attracted him: finger exercises and Wagner, in *Doctor Gradus* and the *Golliwogg's Cake-walk*. These mark the entry of humour into his piano writing, but at least two of the other four pieces merit a deeper response. In *The Little Shepherd* the free, natural, unaccompanied tune of the shepherd's pipe is three times caught by a web of harmonies and dragged down to a cadence; finally it abandons its dreams of freedom and conforms. *The Snow is Dancing* portrays the not entirely disagreeable ennui that grows from looking out at a snowy landscape.

The two sets of *Préludes*, published in 1910 and 1913, contain Debussy's last important offerings to the amateur pianist and also his last homage to the genre of descriptive writing that began with Schumann. In placing his evocative titles at the ends of the pieces he seems to have recognized that they are often less of a help than an impediment to understanding. As with *Poissons d'or*, a title like *Ce qu'a vu le vent d'ouest* may have planted the seed but the piece should certainly not be viewed literally as a west–east itinerary; the title is merely symbolic of the violence and mystery in which the music abounds. Perhaps the most remarkable feat, in the first book at least, is Debussy's success in incorporating elements of popular music: Neapolitan song in *Les collines d'Anacapri*, music-hall song in *Minstrels*, guitar-strumming in *La sérénade interrompue* and an unidentifiable but definitely non-serious style in *La*

11. Claude Debussy with his daughter Chou-Chou at Moulleau, 1916

danse de Puck. At the other extreme lie the hieratic *Danseuses de Delphes*, perhaps suggested to Debussy by his project in collaboration with Segalen on the myth of Orpheus, and the well-known *La cathédrale engloutie*, his most thorough exploration of the points of contact between the piano and bells. It is a piece that needs a virtuoso command of the sustaining pedal, for which, characteristically, Debussy wrote indications addressed not to the player's feet but to his ears – 'in a gentle, harmonious haze', 'gentle and fluid', 'emerging from the haze gradually'. In every piece he established a unique identity at the start through melody (*La fille aux cheveux de lin*), texture (*Danseuses de Delphes*), harmony (*Voiles*), ornaments (*Minstrels*) or rhythm (the iambic opening of *Des pas sur la neige* which 'should sound like a melancholy, snowbound landscape') and then allowed his fancy to play upon it.

The second book does not maintain this high level of inspiration and craftsmanship throughout. Some of the pieces (*Bruyères, Canope, Hommage à S. Pickwick Esq.*) sound rather as though they were rescued from a bottom drawer and *Les tierces alternées* hardly belongs with its companions – unless Debussy inserted it as a joke, tempting us to invent an evocative title. *General Lavine – excentric* is the only successful comic number, a sketch of a music-hall juggler, but three of the scenic pieces are of the highest quality: *Brouillards*, where he depicted the disembodying fog in bitonal harmonies; *La terrasse des audiences du clair de lune*, in which the twin inspirations of moonlight and the Orient led him to write in a style of powerful delicacy, almost a compendium of his favourite piano techniques and textures; and *Feuilles mortes*, in which the subtle colours of dead leaves are matched by the subtle and precisely graded harmonies (ex.6). The different weighting of what is effectively the same chord is a detail with which many a lesser composer might not have concerned himself, and one that shows clearly the value to Debussy of the sonority of a chord quite apart from its harmonic function.

Ex.6

Debussy's last important works for the instrument were the two books of *Etudes*, which he wrote at Pourville during August and September 1915. Earlier in the year he had edited the piano works of Chopin for his publisher, Jacques Durand; and, while he realized that in dedicating his own studies 'to the memory of Chopin' he was certainly meeting the challenge that he had earlier chosen to ignore, he had a confidence in these pieces which one rarely finds in him during his last years. In the first book he explored the traditional areas of study-writing – 3rds, 6ths, octaves and the dexterity of the fingers – with the exception of *Pour les quartes*. Here the manipulation of 4ths led him to write music of a percussive clarity, full of wayward chromaticism and

95

strong bell-like sonorities in which rhythm, melodic outline and harmonic tension interact. One could call it Classical, in the sense that it is a work of understatement in which every nuance produces an effect, or Romantic in that it is informed with a certain wistful, almost sly humour. Debussy kept the cascading 4ths in the middle of the piece just this side of tea-house chinoiserie.

In the second book he was concerned not with the letters but with the vocabulary of music. The studies *Pour les degrés chromatiques* and *Pour les notes répétées*, quite apart from their technical difficulties, are by their nature fitted to stretching tonality beyond the limits of what was generally considered comfortable in 1915. If *Pour les notes répétées* relies for its coherence almost entirely on consistent textures and rhythms, *Pour les agréments* lives by the delicious uncertainty as to what is or is not an *agrément*. The 'divine arabesque' which Debussy recognized in Bach's music permeates the whole structure so that traditional distinctions between melody and accompaniment can no longer be made. Movement between keys is effortless and often elliptical. In the ten bars, for example, that lead to the return of the opening idea, Debussy threw several amusing asides into the conversation but the main point is never for a moment lost. In *Pour les sonorités opposées* he explored further the possibilities of the layered textures in which bells and distant trumpet calls combine to repudiate their source in a box of hammers. One may also note the juxtapositions of disparate materials, a technique introduced in *La soirée dans Grenade*, flaunted in *La sérénade interrompue*, and here used with a fine discretion. The central section of *Pour les arpèges composés* brings the only hint of levity into this second

12. *Autograph of part of the second movement of Debussy's 'En blanc et noir', composed 1915*

book which ends with the massive *Pour les accords*. In a
letter to Durand Debussy wrote: 'these *Etudes* will be
useful in teaching pianists that to embark on a musical
career they must first have a formidable technique'. The
fierce outer sections of this final piece constitute
Debussy's nearest approach to the 19th-century 'war-
horse'. Having faced the piano's challenge and won, he
now threw out a challenge of his own. If pianists were to
succeed where he himself had failed, they must have 'les
mains redoutables'.

Debussy's works for piano duet begin with the four
movements of the *Petite suite*, probably better known in
Büsser's orchestral version. With four hands at his
disposal Debussy was able to experiment more easily
with unusual textures; for example the *Menuet* contains
two beautiful passages where melodies are doubled at
the 10th below. Only the long-drawn tune of *En bateau*
gains undeniably from transcription. The most surprising movement is the final *Ballet*, of a festive bluntness
uncharacteristic of Debussy at any period, for which he
seems to have taken Chabrier as his model. All the
movements are in simple ternary form, but he seems to
have been aiming at further integration, because in every
case the repeat of the opening section is accompanied by
elements from the central one. Apart from the lively
Marche écossaise, a fantasy written for a Scottish general on an air which purported to be a family tune of the
Earls of Ross, the only other pieces Debussy wrote for
this medium were the *Six épigraphes antiques* (1914),
based on music he had composed 14 years earlier to
accompany a recitation of some of Louÿs's *Chansons de
Bilitis*. The world of the *Préludes* is re-created in images
of exotic lands (Greece and Egypt) and of nature (rain

and night). The writing is spare and Debussy cultivated a carefully defined monotony, either of harmony or rhythm or both. Five of the six pieces end *pianissimo* or less, and in the final one the optimistic return of the theme from the first is tactfully but irrecoverably stifled.

Of the works for two pianos, *Lindaraja* is a feeble essay in the Spanish style, and only *En blanc et noir* merits description here (see fig.12). The composer wrote of these pieces that they 'derive their colour and feeling merely from the sonority of the piano'. In spite of this adjuration not to read any programme into the work, it is hard not to see it as Debussy's considered statement on war. The central movement, which he thought the best, is dedicated to a young friend killed in action that year and resorts to trumpet calls and relentless intonations of *Ein' feste Burg*. The first movement is a display of the strength and confidence that made such a holocaust possible; the last, dedicated to Stravinsky, a presentiment of the shattered morale and exhausted resources that were to be its aftermath, illumined only by the light of hope. Among the many miracles in this masterpiece are the textures, some of a rich clarity, others hard-edged (as at the end of the second movement), and the freedom of harmonic movement already remarked on in the *Etudes*, in spite of which the D major ending to the D minor last movement conveys consolation in a wholly traditional manner.

CHAPTER FIVE

Ideals, contemporaries, influence

Although Debussy was no infant prodigy from a technical point of view, he seems to have realized early that for him the ideal music was radically different from that which surrounded him. One of his teachers at the Conservatoire, Emile Durand, saw his individuality in another light: one of his reports for 1878 reads 'With his feeling for music and abilities as an accompanist and sight-reader, Debussy would be an excellent pupil if he were less sketchy and less cavalier'; and for the following year: 'A pupil with a considerable gift for harmony, but desperately careless'. If Durand had been more perceptive he might have gone further than to find Debussy's harmonizations 'certainly ingenious', but then Debussy himself had no clear idea of where he was going. With the Prix de Rome behind him and several years' security ahead, he attacked the problem, realizing that the conventional minds of the Institut might well be shocked by the results. Working on *Diane au bois* he wrote to M. Vasnier from Rome in 1886: 'It may be in fact that I have taken on a task that is too much for me; there is no precedent so I am obliged to invent new forms. I could turn to Wagner but I don't need to explain to you the folly of such an attempt'. This objective view of Wagner, at this time the god to whom the French musical world was busy making obeisance, seems to have been somewhat disturbed by his visit to Bayreuth in 1888. On his return the next year the magic was no longer so powerful even though, as Holloway has shown, Wagnerism remained as a lingering but periodically eruptive infection in Debussy's bloodstream at least up to and including *Jeux*. In conversations with his composition teacher Ernest Guiraud, already referred to, Debussy showed that his aims had now clarified, even if his technique was still not sufficient to realize them: of musical drama 'The ideal would be two associated dreams'; 'A prolonged development does not, cannot fit the words'; In general, 'rhythms cannot be contained within bars'; 'Themes suggest their orchestral colouring'; 'There is no theory. You have merely to listen. Fantasy [plaisir] is the law'. At the same time he was not advocating musical anarchy: 'I feel free because I have been through the mill, and I don't write in the fugal style because I know it'.

The first fruit of this search for a music that was precisely imagined yet fluid and untramelled by rules was *L'après-midi*; significantly, a work based on a symbolist poem. Debussy recognized in the writings of Baudelaire, Verlaine and especially Mallarmé not only a fantasy and freedom that were missing from contemporary music, but also a concentration of feeling. The opening flute solo is just such a concentration of diverse emotions, dreamy idleness, good humour and speculative lust, and one may judge its potency by comparing it with the innocuous solo line at the beginning of *Printemps*. Certainly the chromatic outline of the faun's phrase is no mere imitation or 'impression' of a panpipe; it is the primary symbol of the work and one should appreciate the silence that surrounds it.

If one has to accord Debussy an '-ism', then 'symbolism' would probably be the most truthful. In a letter to Chausson in 1893 he wrote of his newly begun work on *Pelléas* 'I have found, and what is more quite spontaneously, a technique which strikes me as fairly new, that is silence (don't laugh) as a means of expression and perhaps the only way to give the emotion of a phrase its full power'. This desire for simplicity and space never left him. As a child he used to prefer small pictures with large margins, and in 1913 he wrote of the Annamite theatre he had seen nearly 25 years earlier: 'A small, shrieking clarinet is the guide of the emotion; a tam-tam the organizer of terror . . . and that is all'. *Pelléas* itself is the most complete summary of Debussy's ideals up to his 40th year. Critics have written of its reticence without noticing that this reticence is a concentration of feeling not a lack of it; obviously for those writing at the time, nurtured on Verdi, Wagner and Strauss, it was hard to appreciate that passion need not be measured in decibels. Indeed Strauss himself, in a box at the Opéra-Comique with Ravel and Romain Rolland, greeted the end of Act 1 with the words, 'Is it like this all the time?'; on being assured that it was, he could find no kinder comment than a disdainful 'It's very refined'.

From 1901 Debussy wrote articles for a number of magazines in which one can follow the development, without radical change, of the views he expressed to Guiraud. In April 1902 he wrote of his reasons for choosing *Pelléas*: 'I wanted from music a freedom which it possesses perhaps to a greater degree than any other art, not being tied to a more or less exact reproduction of Nature but to the mysterious correspondences between Nature and Imagination'. To reinforce this freedom, there must be others. The public must be free to state their opinion: 'In art there can be no obligatory

Ideals

respect; that is the sort of nonsense that has been off-loaded on to a number of people who have become respectable only through having lived a long time ago'. The response itself should be free, unfettered by a formal musical education – 'Love of art does not depend on explanations' – or by experience as in the case of those who say of a new work ' "I need to hear that several times". Utter rubbish! When we really listen to music, we hear immediately what we need to hear'. But the hardest-won freedom of all is that of the artist, who must please only himself. 'Truly, that day far in the future – I hope as far as possible – when I shall no longer stir up controversy, I shall reproach myself bitterly'; but (in a letter of 1911) 'how much one has first to find and then suppress, to reach the naked flesh of emotion'.

One theme that runs through Debussy's later thoughts is the need for French music to be true to itself. Gluck and the imitators of Wagner came under heavy fire and he held up Rameau as the great neglected figure of French musical history. Rather than Wagner, the model should be Musorgsky; not for imitation, but as an example of directness and truth of utterance within a native tradition. This is not a call for provincial narrow-mindedness, and indeed Debussy could hardly be convicted of this; his taste in the visual arts was catholic, embracing Turner, Moreau and Hokusai, and in music itself the styles of the Near and Far East as well as Spain. But all influences had to be held in balance and the neck of eloquence well and truly wrung. Music, for Debussy, lay neither in the scholastic nor the bombastic, but in the playing of the gypsy violinist Radics: 'In a cheap, ordinary café, he gives the impression of playing in the depths of a dark forest, and calls up from the

103

bottom of your soul a kind of melancholy that we rarely bring to the surface. He could drag secrets from an iron safe'. Here was the 'naked flesh of emotion'.

Such ideals, intransigently held and eloquently expressed, did not help make Debussy an establishment figure. Until *Pelléas* was produced he remained remote from the mainstream of French musical life, happier in the 'Chat Noir' than at the meetings of the Société Nationale. He entertained a secret love for the music of Massenet but had little time for the Franckian school headed by d'Indy and did his best to persuade Chausson not to overdo the counterpoint but to let his imagination run (he himself felt that the end of the *Poème* for violin and orchestra marked Chausson's finest inspiration). Among composers his most faithful friend was Satie, his most implacable enemy Saint-Saëns who as late as 1915 wrote to Fauré: 'I advise you to look at the pieces for two pianos, *Noir et blanc* [sic], which M. Debussy has just published. It's incredible, and the door of the Institut must at all costs be barred against a man capable of such atrocities'. Saint-Saëns had his way.

Pelléas suddenly made Debussy an 'important' composer. For his parents' sake he accepted the Légion d'honneur in 1903 and every major work from then on was eagerly scrutinized by the critics. He was content to leave his piano works chiefly in the hands of Viñes until his debts forced him on to the platform in 1910. His career as a conductor was similarly motivated, although he was certainly unhappy about early performances of *La mer* under Chevillard, and his own performance in 1908 came as a revelation to many. He also found Pierné's conducting in the rehearsals of *Ibéria* 'rather left-bank' (i.e. intellectual), and in both conductors he missed the improvisational fluidity that he sought, even if his own unavailing struggles with *Ibéria* in Turin convinced him that the task was no easy one.

Apart from money, Debussy's chief problems in the first decade of the century were the estrangement from a majority of his friends over his second marriage, and the rise of 'debussysme'. As one may easily imagine, the last thing he wanted was to be the head of a school of composers, but many critics and journalists seemed determined to force the role on him, and the affair reached a climax with the publication of *Le cas Debussy* in 1909, and in particular 'M. Claude Debussy et le snobisme contemporain', an article in it by Raphaël Cor. The article, full of bigotry and spite, asks such questions as: 'Has anyone noticed that among the many beautiful passages in *Ariane et Barbe-Bleue* by Dukas, produced in 1907, the least successful act is certainly the second, in which Debussy's influence is predominant?' Debussy was just as annoyed by those who wanted him to turn out endless replicas of *Pelléas*, and he had to find his own way between the opposing camps of hostility and blind devotion. Worst of all was his realization that so few of his contemporaries could see beyond the trills and the whole-tone chords to the spirit of his music. *Le martyre* brought him a short-lived notoriety and *Jeux* not even that, after which World War I put a stop to any but small-scale music-making. The effect of the war was thus to reinforce Debussy's desire, in his illness, to turn in upon himself and to work in his own way for the preservation of French culture. The destructive intrusion of *Ein' feste Burg* into the second movement of *En blanc et noir* is his most poignant comment on the world as he saw it; the last three sonatas, signed 'Claude

Debussy, musicien français', the pledge of his hope for the future.

(*i*) *Debussy and Ravel.* There is no record of any Debussy–Ravel correspondence but it seems likely that they first met early in 1898 at the first performance of Ravel's *Sites auriculaires.* Two years later Ravel was present at a private play-through that Debussy gave of *Pelléas* and their relations were certainly friendly until the time of its production. The break in their friendship occurred for various complementary reasons: the supposed similarity between Ravel's *Habanera,* from *Sites auriculaires,* and Debussy's later *La soirée dans Grenade*; Debussy's disappointment that Ravel should squander his undoubted gifts in the 'factitious Americanism' of the *Histoires naturelles*; no doubt a good measure of jealousy on Debussy's part; and possibly a remark that Ravel made on the morality of Debussy's second marriage – a mutual friend, Misia Sert, later claimed that Ravel contributed to a small weekly allowance for Debussy's first wife after Debussy abandoned her. Already in 1904 such an intelligent layman as Rolland could write: 'I have met a variety of musicians. Among them, one who is more Debussyste than Debussy: Ravel'. Such remarks annoyed Debussy extravagantly. As Lockspeiser pointed out, in Debussy's letters Ravel's name is never mentioned 'without a note of sarcasm, irony or concern' and he expressed considerable annoyance in 1913 when he found that Ravel had set two of the same Mallarmé poems as himself – largely, one imagines, because he was afraid that this would be the signal for another orgy of comparison. On the other hand, apart from an understandable feeling of propriety for the new textural and harmonic ideas in

Jeux d'eau, Ravel all his life revered Debussy as a master. Besides making a number of arrangements of Debussy's music, he gave the first performance of *D'un cahier d'esquisses*, and to the 'Tombeau de Debussy' printed in the *Revue musicale* of 1920 he contributed no brief *pièce d'occasion* but the first movement of his Sonata for violin and cello. Towards the end of his life he said to a friend, of *L'après-midi*: 'It was hearing this work, so many years ago, that I first understood what real music was'.

(*ii*) *Debussy and Stravinsky*. Debussy and Stravinsky first met backstage after the first performance of *The Firebird* on 25 June 1910. Debussy's immediate reactions were commendatory, although Stravinsky related that Debussy later qualified his praise with: 'After all, you had to begin somewhere'. In Russia Stravinsky had been impressed by Ziloti's performances of *L'après-midi* and the *Nocturnes* but there is little of Debussy's manner to be found in *The Firebird*, rather more of Rimsky-Korsakov's. *Petrushka* was the one work of Stravinsky over which Debussy never expressed a reservation, referring to an 'orchestral infallibility that I have found only in *Parsifal*' and to the 'sonorous magic' in the 'Tour de passe-passe' (figs.[58–64] in the miniature score). There followed a period of close friendship, during which Debussy asked Stravinsky's advice about the scoring of *Jeux*, and together they performed the piano-duet version of *The Rite of Spring*, Debussy playing the bass at sight without apparent difficulty. However, after the première of *The Rite* Debussy's appreciation of Stravinsky became tinged almost with fear. In a letter of 1916 he described Stravinsky as 'a spoilt child who, from time to time, makes rude gestures at music

... He professes to be friends with me because I have helped him climb to a rung on the ladder from which he lobs grenades that don't all explode'. If Debussy felt that Ravel was squandering his gifts, then perhaps Stravinsky was being all too successful. Acknowledging the present of a score of *The Rite* Debussy wrote to him: 'for me, who descend the other slope of the hill but keep, however, an intense passion for music, for me it is a special satisfaction to tell you how much you have enlarged the boundaries of the permissible in the empire of sound', a task which Debussy had begun but which he knew he was now too ill to pursue very far. On the other hand, Stravinsky, like Ravel, never doubted his debt to the older man. He may have found *Pelléas* 'a great bore on the whole, in spite of many wonderful pages' but he also confirmed that 'the musicians of my generation and I myself owe the most to Debussy'.

(*iii*) *Debussy's musical style and its posthumous influence*. The details of Debussy's technique are easy to catalogue but, as with catalogues, they give little idea of the quality of the product. His desire to free himself from tonality led him to use the church modes and melodic lines inspired by plainsong, the whole-tone scale and chords, synthetic modes such as the major scale with sharp 4th and flat 7th and parallel 9ths and triads in which each chord is no more than a colouring of the melodic line. Rhythmically he was for a long time bound by the four-bar phrase (often a two-bar one repeated, with or without variation in the fourth bar) but the combination and succession of duplets and triplets frequently rounds off the squareness of the structure. From *La mer* onwards he achieved a new fluidity of rhythm, particularly in orchestral works where he tended to present several planes of timbre and material simultaneously. The influence of the Orient, especially of the Javanese gamelan, operated not only on his scoring as such but on his conception of what was 'permissible in the empire of sound' – what in the 19th century had been noise was now music. Above all, as has been well said, Debussy brought music out of the salon and the concert hall and into the open air, even to an immaterial existence independent of place or space.

If one omits Schoenberg, who quite failed to recognize his rival's stature, a list of 20th-century composers influenced by Debussy is practically a list of 20th-century composers *tout court*. Bartók acknowledged the 'insights' that Debussy's music gave him into harmony and orchestration, as *Bluebeard's Castle* and *The Miraculous Mandarin* testify; *Wozzeck* owes much to *Pelléas*, and Webern's interest in timbre stems in part from Debussy; for Varèse the beginning of *L'après-midi* provided the model for those numerous opening paragraphs where a single note sets up a gravitational field; and even Les Six, after Cocteau's initial diatribes, came round individually to a more sober appreciation.

Among the leading musical minds of the 1950s and 1960s, Cage obviously looks back to Debussy's example of 'letting sounds be themselves', on the need to re-educate ourselves in what we expect of music, and on the value of silence; for Messiaen at ten years old *Pelléas* was 'a veritable bombshell', and works of Boulez like *Pli selon pli* and *Eclat/multiples* can be seen as further extensions of the fragmentary coherence in *Jeux*; while the whole *raison d'être* of electronic music is the same extension of those boundaries on which *L'après-midi* first exerted an insidious pressure. Can it be

entirely fortuitous that the major 9th, Debussy's best
beloved among chords, sounds throughout the 70
minutes of Stockhausen's *Stimmung*, coupled with the
recitation of magic names? Let Debussy have the last
word: 'We must agree that the beauty of a work of art
will always remain a mystery, in other words we can
never be absolutely sure "how it's made". We must at all
costs preserve this magic which is peculiar to music and
to which, by its nature, music is of all arts the most
receptive'.

WORKS

Numbers in the right-hand column denote references in the text.

OPERAS

Title	Acts; libretto	Composed	First performance	Publication	Remarks	
Axël	1 scene; l'Isle-Adam	c1888		unpubd	lost	
Rodrigue et Chimène	3; C. Mendès, after G. de Castro and Corneille	vocal score of Acts 1 (in part), 2 and 3, 1890–92		short score, ed. R. Langham Smith (in preparation)		49, 51
Pelléas et Mélisande	5; Maeterlinck, abridged Debussy	1893–5, 1898, 1900–02	Paris, Opéra-Comique, 30 April 1902	vocal score (1902, rev. 1907), full score (1904)	sketches facs. (Geneva, 1977)	15, 27, 44, 45, 49, 51–5, 63, 74, 79, 82, 84, 86, 102, 104, 105, 106, 108, 109, 221
Le diable dans le beffroi	2 tableaux; Debussy after Poe	1902–?12			inc.; sketches for scenario and music in Lockspeiser: *Debussy et Edgar Poe* (1962)	55
La chute de la maison Usher	2 scenes; Debussy after Poe	1908–17	New Haven, 25 Feb 1977	vocal score, full score, ed. J. Allende-Blin (1979)	inc., orig. planned as 3 scenes; complete text and vocal score of scene i and part of scene ii (Usher's monologue) in Lockspeiser: *Debussy and Edgar Poe* (1962)	47, 55–6
Fêtes galantes	opéra-ballet, 3 tableaux; L. Laloy after Verlaine	1913–15			libretto and sketches for scene i in Orledge: *Debussy and the Theatre* (1982)	

111

BALLETS

Title	Description; scenario	Composed	First performance	Publication	Remarks	
Khamma	légende dansée; W. L. Courtney, M. Allan, ?Debussy	1911–12	Paris, Opéra-Comique, 26 March 1947	pf score (1916)	beginning orchd Debussy, rest Koechlin under Debussy's supervision	47, 67
Jeux	poème dansé; Nizhinsky, ?Dyagilev	1912–13	Paris, Champs-Elysées, 15 May 1913	pf score (1912), full score (1914)		47, 68–9, 83, 101, 105, 107, 109
La boîte à joujoux	ballet pour enfants; A. Hellé	1913	Paris, Lyrique, 10 Dec 1919	pf score (1913), full score (1920)	beginning orchd Debussy, rest Caplet from Debussy sketches	67
No-ja-li (Le palais du silence)	ballet; G. de Feure	1913–14			sketches for prelude and scene i in Orledge: Debussy and the Theatre (1982)	

INCIDENTAL MUSIC

Berceuse for La tragédie de la mort (R. Peter), 1v, 1899; unpubd
Le roi Lear (Shakespeare), 1904, inc.; 7 sections sketched, 2 completed and orchd Roger-Ducasse (1926); Fanfare d'ouverture, Le sommeil de Lear
Le martyre de St Sébastien (mystère, 5, D'Annunzio), 1911, orchd Debussy and Caplet; Châtelet, 22 May 1911; vocal score (1911), full score (1911)   47, 56, 105
Pièce for Psyché (Flûte de Pan) (G. Mourey), fl, 1913; pubd as Syrinx (1927)

OTHER DRAMATIC WORKS

(early choral works from dramatic sources)
Diane au bois (Banville), overture (pf duet), vocal score of end of Act 2 scene iii and scene iv, 1881–6; unpubd   49, 50, 100
Hymnis (Banville), scenes i, ii (in part) and vii, c1882; 'Il dort encore (scene i) (1984)   49

(music to accompany readings of poems)
Chansons de Bilitis (Louÿs), 2 fl, 2 harps, cel, 1900–01, lost cel part reconstructed Boulez (1954) and Hoérée (1971); recomposed as Six épigraphes antiques, pf 4 hands, 1914 (1915)   98

(projects)
Florise (dramatic choral, Banville), c1882
As You Like It (incidental music, M. Vaucaire, after Shakespeare), 1886
Salammbô (opera, ?Debussy, after Flaubert), 1886
L'embarquement pour ailleurs (sym. commentary, Mourey), 1890–91
La princesse Maleine (opera, Maeterlinck), 1891
Les noces de Sathan (incidental music, J. Bois), 1892
Prélude, interludes et paraphrase finale pour L'après-midi d'un faune (incidental music, Mallarmé), 1892
Amphion (ballet, Valéry), c1895
La grande bretèche (opera, Debussy, after Balzac), 1895
Cendrelune (opera, Louÿs), 1895–8; text extant
Daphnis et Khloé (ballet, Louÿs, after Longus), 1895–8
Les uns et les autres (opera, Verlaine), 1896
Aphrodite (ballet, Louÿs), 1896–8
Le chevalier d'or (pantomime, Mme J.-L. Forain), 1897
La tentation de St Antoine (incidental music, G. de Voisins, after Flaubert), 1897
La fille de Pasiphaé (incidental music, V. de Balbiani, after Racine), 1898

Orphée (opera, Valéry), c1900
Le voyage de Pausole (sym. suite, Louÿs), 1901
Comme il vous plaira (opera, P. J. Toulet), 1902–4
Le pèlerin d'amour (incidental music, V.-E. Michelet), 1902–3
Don Juan (?opera, after Byron or Molière), 1903
Joyzelle (opera, Maeterlinck), 1903
Dionysos (lyric tragedy, J. Gasquet), 1904–5
Siddartha (opera, Segalen), 1907
L'histoire de Tristan (opera, Mourey, after J. Bédier), 1907–9
Orphée-roi (opera, Segalen and Debussy), 1907–9
Huon de Bordeaux (Mourey), 1909
Le chat botté (Mourey, after La Fontaine), 1909
Le marchand de rêves (Mourey), 1909
L'Orestie (opera, Laloy, after Aeschylus), 1909
Masques et bergamasques (ballet, Debussy), 1909–10, scenario (1910); also known as L'Amour masqué and L'éternelle aventure
Pygmalion (ballet, Rameau 1748), reorch planned 1911
La dame à la faulx (incidental music, Saint-Pol-Roux), 1911
Ballet persan (ballet, Toulet), 1912
Crimen amoris (Morice after Verlaine), 1912–13, later Fêtes galantes [see 'Operas']
Drame indien (D'Annunzio), 1914
Tania, (?opera, ? after Pushkin), 1914–16
As You Like It (incidental music, Toulet, after F. Gémier), 1917

ORCHESTRAL   57
Symphony, b. 1880; Allegro arr. pf 4 hands (1933)
Intermezzo (after Heine), vc, orch, 1882 (1944); also arr. pf 4 hands: unpubd
Le triomphe de Bacchus (after Banville), suite, c1882, lost; Allegro arr. pf 4 hands (1928), orchd Gaillard (1928)
Première suite, c1883: Fête, Ballet, Rêve, Bacchanale; also arr. pf; unpubd
Printemps, sym. suite, female chorus, orch, 1887, orig. score lost; arr. pf 4 hands (1904); reorchd from pf version by Büsser under Debussy's supervision, 1912 (1913)   57–8, 63, 101
Fantaisie, pf, orch, 1889–90; full score (1920)   42, 59, 65
Prélude à l'après-midi d'un faune (after Mallarmé), 1892–4; arr. 2 pf (1895), full score (1895)   42, 44, 49, 59–62, 64, 67, 85, 101, 107, 109

Nocturnes, 1897–9: Nuages, Fêtes, Sirènes [? after Trois scènes au crépuscule, 1892–3]; full score (1900)   42, 44, 62–3, 66, 107
La mer, 3 sym. sketches, 1903–5: De l'aube à midi sur la mer, Jeux de vagues, Dialogue du vent et de la mer; arr. pf 4 hands (1905), full score (1905)   44, 45, 63–5, 68, 104, 108
Danse sacrée et danse profane, chromatic harp, str, 1904: full score (1904), arr. 2 pf (1904)   65
Images, 1905–12: Gigues, 1909–12, full score (1913); Ibéria, 1905–8, full score (1910): Rondes de printemps, 1905–9, full score (1910)   45, 47, 63, 66–7, 104–5

(orchestrations)
March écossaise sur un thème populaire [after pf work], ?1891–6, completed 1908 (1911)
Deux gymnopédies [nos.1 and 3 of Satie: Trois gymnopédies], 1896 (1898)
Première rapsodie [after chamber work], cl, orch, 1911; full score (1911)
La plus que lente [after pf work]; full score (1912)
Berceuse héroïque [after pf work], 1914; full score (1915)
Rapsodie [after chamber work], a sax, orch, 1901–8: orchestration sketched, completed by Roger-Ducasse (1919)

(projects)
Symphony, after Poe, 1890; lost
Trois scènes au crépuscule, after Régnier, 1892–3   62
Poème (Concerto), vn, orch, c1894
Trois nocturnes, vn, orch, c1894: no.1 with str; no.2 with 2 fl, 4 hn, 3 tpt, 2 harps; no.3 with both groups

VOCAL ORCHESTRAL
Daniel (E. Cécile), cantata, 3 solo vv, orch, 1882; c1881: unpubd
Le printemps (Comte de Ségur), female chorus, orch, 1882; pubd as Salut printemps, chorus, pf arr. Gaillard (1928); full score 1956)
Invocation (Lamartine), male chorus, orch, 1883; vocal score with pf 4 hands (1928), full score (1957)
Le gladiateur (E. Moreau), cantata, 3 solo vv, orch, 1883; unpubd
Le printemps (J. Barbier), chorus, orch, 1884; unpubd   57
L'enfant prodigue (E. Guinand), scène lyrique, 1884: vocal score (1884); rev. 1906–8, full score (1908): Prélude, Cortège et air de danse arr. pf duet (1884)   42, 57

Barcarolle (Guinand), c1885; lost

Ariettes, paysages belges et aquarelles (Verlaine) (1888), repubd as Ariettes oubliées (1903): C'est l'extase, 1887; Il pleure dans mon coeur, 1887; L'ombre des arbres, 1885; Chevaux de bois, 1885; Green, 1886; Spleen, between 1885 and 1887 — 63, 74–6, 79

Cinq poëms de Baudelaire (1890): Le balcon, 1888; Harmonie du soir, 1889; Le jet d'eau, 1889; Recueillement, 1889; La mort des amants, 1887 — 76

La belle au bois dormant (E.-V. Hyspa), 1890 (1902)

Deux romances (Bourget), 1891 (1891): L'âme évaporée, Les cloches — 76

Les angélus (G. Le Roy), 1891 (1891) — 76

Trois mélodies (Verlaine), 1891 (1901): La mer est plus belle, Le son du cor, L'échelonnement des haies — 77, 85

Fêtes galantes (Verlaine), set 1, 1891 (1903): En sourdine, Fantoches [rev. of 1882 setting], Clair de lune — 42, 77, 81, 82

Proses lyriques (Debussy) (1895): De rêve, 1892; De grève, 1892; De fleurs, 1893; De soir, 1893 — 77, 79

Chansons de Bilitis (Louÿs), 1897–8 (1899): La flûte de Pan, La chevelure [pubd separately], 1897], Le tombeau des naïades — 44, 79–80, 81, 82

Dans le jardin (P. Gravollet), 1903 (1905) — 77

Trois chansons de France, 1904 (1904): Rondel I, Le temps a laissié son manteau (d'Orléans); La grotte (Lhermite); Rondel II, Pour ce que Plaisance est morte (d'Orléans) — 80–81, 82

Fêtes galantes (Verlaine), set 2, 1904 (1904): Les ingénus, La faune, Colloque sentimental — 44, 81–2, 89–90, 91

Le promenoir des deux amants (Lhermite), 1904–10 (1910): La grotte, 1904 [no.2 of Trois chansons de France]; Crois mon conseil, chère Climène, 1910; Je tremble en voyant ton visage, 1910 — 82

Trois ballades de Villon, 1910 (1910): Ballade de Villon à s'amye, Ballade que Villon feit à la requeste de sa mère, Ballade des femmes de Paris — 82–3

Trois poèmes de Mallarmé, 1913 (1913): Soupir, Placet futile, Eventail — 83

Noël des enfants qui n'ont plus de maison (Debussy), 1915 (1916), arr. children's chorus 2vv, pf (1916) — 83

(projects)

Nuits blanches (Debussy), cycle, 1899–1902

Rapsodie in the style of Liszt; lost

Danse bohémienne, 1880 (1932)

Deux arabesques, 1888–91 (1891)

Ballade slave, 1890 (1891), repubd as Ballade (1903) — 84–5

Rêverie, 1890 (1891)

Suite bergamasque, 1890, rev. 1905 (1905): Prélude, Menuet, Clair de lune, Passepied — 85–6, 179

Tarantelle styrienne, 1890 (1891), repubd as Danse (1903) — 85, 86

Valse romantique, 1890 (1890)

Mazurka, ?1890 (1904) — 85, 86

Nocturne, 1892 (1892)

Images, 3 pieces, 1894 (1978) [no.2 (1896) differs only in detail from Sarabande of Pour le piano] — 87–8, 89

Suite: Pour le piano, 1894–1901 (1901): Prélude, Sarabande, Toccata — 86–7, 88, 89, 90, 107, 130

D'un cahier d'esquisses (Esquisse), 1903 (1904) — 88–9, 90, 96,

Estampes, 1903 (1903): Pagodes, La soirée dans Grenade, Jardins sous la pluie — 106, 156, 179

Pièce pour piano, 1903–4 (1905) [based on sketch from Le diable dans le beffroi] — 44, 89, 90

L'isle joyeuse, 1904 (1904) — 89–90

Masques, 1904 (1904) — 44, 45, 90–91

Images, set 1, 1905 (1905): Reflets dans l'eau, Hommage à Rameau, Mouvement — 45, 71

Sérénade à la poupée, 1906 (1906), incorporated in Children's Corner — 92

Children's Corner, 1906–8 (1908): Doctor Gradus ad Parnassum, Jimbo's Lullaby, Serenade for the Doll, The Snow is Dancing, The Little Shepherd, Golliwogg's Cake-walk

Images, set 2, 1907 (1908): Cloches à travers les feuilles, Et la lune descend sur le temple qui fut, Poissons d'or — 45, 91–2

Hommage à Haydn, 1909 (1910)

The Little Nigar, 1909 (1909)

Préludes, bk 1 (1910): Danseuses de Delphes, 1909; Voiles, 1909; Le vent dans la plaine, 1909: 'Les sons et les parfums tournent dans l'air du soir', 1910; Les collines d'Anacapri, 1909; Des pas sur la neige, 1909; Ce qu'a vu le vent d'ouest; La fille aux cheveux de lin, 1910; La sérénade interrompue; La cathédrale engloutie; La danse de Puck, 1910; Minstrels, 1910 — 47, 65, 92, 94, 96, 98

La plus que lente, 1910 (1910)

Préludes, bk 2, 1911–13 (1913); Brouillards, Feuilles mortes, La Puerta del Vino, 'Les fées sont d'exquises danseuses', Bruyères, General Lavine – excentric, La terrasse des audiences du clair de lune, Ondine, Hommage à S. Pickwick Esq. P.P.M.P.C., Canope, Les tierces alternées, Feux d'artifice

Berceuse héroïque, 1914 (1915)

Six épigraphes antiques [arr. pf 4 hands], 1914 (1915)

Élégie, 1915 (1916)

Études, 1915 (1916): Pour les cinq doigts, Pour les tierces, Pour les quartes, Pour les sixtes, Pour les octaves, Pour les huit doigts, Pour les degrés chromatiques, Pour les agréments, Pour les notes répétées, Pour les sonorités opposées, Pour les arpèges composés, Pour les accords [2 bks] [1st version of Pour les arpèges composés (realized R. Howat, 1980)]

Pièce pour le Vêtement du blessé, 1915; pubd as Page d'album (1933)

(four hands)

Andante, c1880; unpubd

Petite suite, 1886–9 (1889): En bateau, Cortège, Menuet, Ballet

Marche écossaise sur un thème populaire, 1891 (1903)

Six épigraphes antiques [in part from Chansons de Bilitis, 1900–01], 1914 (1915): Pour invoquer Pan, Pour un tombeau sans nom, Pour que la nuit soit propice, Pour la danseuse aux crotales, Pour l'égyptienne, Pour remercier la pluie au matin

(two pianos)

Lindaraja, 1901 (1926)

En blanc et noir, 3 pièces, 1915 (1915)

(arrangements)

P. Tchaikovsky: Three dances from Swan Lake, pf 4 hands, 1880 (1965)

92, 94–5, 98

47, 95–6, 98, 99

58, 98
98
98–9

99, 179
47, 97, 99, 104, 105

C. Saint-Saëns: Caprice on airs from the ballet in Gluck's Alceste, pf 4 hands, 1889 (1891); Introduction et Rondo capriccioso, 2 pf, 1889 (1889); Airs de ballet d'Étienne Marcel, 2 pf, 1890: Symphony no.2, 2 pf, 1890

R. Wagner: Overture: The Flying Dutchman, 2 pf, 1890 (1890)

R. Schumann: Six studies in canon form, 2 pf, 1891: Am Springbrunnen (A la fontaine), 2 pf, 1903 (1904)

J. Raff: Humoresque en forme de valse, 1893 (1903)

For arrs. of own works see other sections of list

92, 94–5, 98

Principal publishers: Choudens, Durand, Fromont, Hamelle, Jobert, Schott/Eschig

MSS in *F-ASO, Pn; GB-Lbm; US-AUS, Bc, NYpm, R, STu, Wc* and numerous private collections

EDITION

J.-P. Rameau: *Les fêtes de Polymnie*, Oeuvres complètes, xiii (Paris, 1908)

WRITINGS

Preface to Durand edn. of piano works by Chopin (Paris, 1915)

Monsieur Croche antidilettante (Paris, 1921, 2/1926; Eng. trans., 2/1962)

ed. F. Lesure: *Monsieur Croche et autres écrits* (Paris, 1971; Eng. trans., 1977)

Unpubd plays written with R. Peter: *Les mille et une nuits de n'importe où et d'ailleurs*, c1897; *Les 'Frères en art'* [F. E. A.], 1897–8, rev. Debussy, c1903; *Le roman de Rosette*, c1898–1901; *L'utile aventure*, c1898; *L'herbe tendre*, c1899; *Esther et la maison de fous*, c1899

102

BIBLIOGRAPHY

CATALOGUES AND BIBLIOGRAPHY

G. Andrieux: Catalogue of sale of all Debussy's possessions, Paris, 30 Nov–8 Dec (Paris, 1933)

A. Martin: *Catalogue de l'exposition Debussy* (Paris, 1942)

Catalogue de la collection Walter Straram: manuscrits de Claude Debussy (Rambouillet, 1961)

F. Lesure: *Catalogue de la collection André Meyer* (Abbeville, 1961)

——: *Catalogue de l'exposition Claude Debussy* (Paris, 1962)

C. Abravanel: *Claude Debussy: a Bibliography* (Detroit, 1974)

M. G. Cobb: *Discographie de l'oeuvre de Claude Debussy* (Geneva, 1975)

F. Lesure: *Catalogue de l'oeuvre de Claude Debussy* (Geneva, 1977)

SOURCE MATERIAL

'Correspondance inédite de Claude Debussy et Ernest Chausson', *ReM*, vi (1925), 116

J. Durand, ed.: *Lettres de Claude Debussy à son éditeur* (Paris, 1927)

Correspondance de Claude Debussy et P.-J. Toulet (Paris, 1929)

M. Denis: *H. Lerolle et ses amis* (Paris, 1932) [incl. 3 letters]

G. Doret: 'Lettres et billets inédits de C. A. Debussy', *Lettres romandes* (Geneva, 23 Nov 1934)

C. Oulmont: 'Deux amis: Claude Debussy et Ernest Chausson: documents inédits', *Mercure de France* (1 Dec 1934)

J. André-Messager, ed.: *La jeunesse de Pelléas: lettres de Claude Debussy à André Messager* (Paris, 1938)

'3 lettres à B. Molinari de 1914–1915', *Suisse romande*, ii (1939)

Claude Debussy: lettres à deux amis: 78 lettres inédites à Robert Godet et G. Jean-Aubry (Paris, 1942)

H. Borgeaud, ed.: *Correspondance de Claude Debussy et Pierre Louÿs* (Paris, 1945)

A. Ysaÿe: *Eugene Ysaÿe: sa vie, son oeuvre, son influence* (Brussels, 1947) [incl. letters]

G. Tosi, ed.: *Debussy et d'Annunzio* (Paris, 1948)

A. Gauthier: *Debussy: documents iconographiques* (Geneva, 1952)

E. Lockspeiser, ed.: *Lettres inédites de Claude Debussy à André Caplet* (Monaco, 1957)

P. Vallery-Radot, ed.: *Lettres de Claude Debussy à sa femme Emma* (Paris, 1957)

I. Stravinsky and others: *Avec Stravinsky* (Monaco, 1958) [incl. 7 letters]

P. Vallery-Radot: *Tel était Claude Debussy* (Paris, 1958) [incl. 17 letters]

117

Catalogue Nicolas Rauch no.20, 24: *Letters to Gabriel Mourey* (Geneva, 1958)
A. Joly and A. Schaeffner: *Ségalen et Debussy* (Monaco, 1962) [incl. 21 letters]
F. Lesure, ed.: 'Claude Debussy: textes et documents inédits', *RdM*, xlviii (1962)
F. Lesure: 'Lettres inédites de Claude Debussy', *Candide* (21 June 1962)
——: ' "L'affaire" Debussy–Ravel: lettres inédites', *Festschrift Friedrich Blume* (Kassel, 1963)
——: 'Claude Debussy, Ernest Chausson et Henri Lerolle', *Mélanges d'art et de littérature offerts à Julien Cain* (Paris, 1968)
——: 'Lettres inédites de Claude Debussy à Pierre Louÿs', *RdM*, lvii (1971), 29
Mme G. de Tinan: 'Memories of Debussy and his Circle', *Recorded Sound*, nos.50–51 (1973), 158
F. Lesure: *Icongraphie musicale: Debussy* (Geneva, 1975)
——, ed.: *Claude Debussy: lettres 1884–1918* (Paris, 1980)

MONOGRAPHS

W.-H. Daly: *Debussy: a Study in Modern Music* (Edinburgh, 1908)
L. Liebich: *Claude-Achille Debussy* (London, 1908)
L. Laloy: *Claude Debussy* (Paris, 1909, enlarged 2/1944)
C. F. Caillard and J. de Bérys: *Le cas Debussy* (Paris, 1910)
D. Chennevière: *Claude Debussy et son oeuvre* (Paris, 1913)
E. Vuillermoz: *Claude Debussy* (Paris, 1920)
'Numéro spécial consacré à Debussy', *ReM*, i (1920), 98–216
R. Jardillier: *Claude Debussy* (Dijon, 1922)
L. Sabaneyev: *Claude Debussy* (Moscow, 1922); Eng. trans. in *ML*, x (1929), 1–34
A. Suarès: *Debussy* (Paris, 1922, enlarged 2/1936)
R. Paoli: *Debussy* (Florence, 1924, 2/1947)
F. Gysi: *Claude Debussy* (Zurich, 1926)
R. van Santen: *Debussy* (The Hague, 1926, 2/1947)
'La jeunesse de Claude Debussy', *ReM*, vii (1926), 99–236
C. Koechlin: *Debussy* (Paris, 1927)
L. Vallas: *Debussy* (Paris, 1927)
——: *Les idées de Claude Debussy* (Paris, 1927; Eng. trans. 2/1967)
M. Boucher: *Claude Debussy* (Paris, 1930)
R. Peter: *Claude Debussy* (Paris, 1931, enlarged 2/1944)
M. Dumesnil: *How to Play and Teach Debussy* (New York, 1932)
L. Vallas: *Claude Debussy et son temps* (Paris, 1932, 2/1958; Eng. trans., 2/1973)
E. Decsey: *Claude Debussy* (Graz, 1936)

Bibliography

E. Lockspeiser: *Debussy* (London, 1936, rev. 4/1963)

H. Kölsch: *Der Impressionismus bei Debussy* (Düsseldorf, 1937)

A. Liess: *Claude Debussy und das deutsche Musikschaffen* (Würzburg, 1939)

H. Strobel: *Claude Debussy* (Zurich, 1940, rev. 3/1948)

O. Thompson: *Debussy, Man and Artist* (New York, 1940)

L. Vallas: *Achille-Claude Debussy* (Paris, 1944)

A. Gauthier: *Sous l'influence de Neptune: dialogues avec Debussy* (Paris, 1945)

L. Oleggini: *Au coeur de Claude Debussy* (Paris, 1947)

R. Paoli: *Debussy* (Florence, 1947, 2/1951)

R. Malipiero: *Debussy* (Brescia, 1948)

J. van Ackere: *Claude Debussy* (Antwerp, 1949)

E. Decsey: *Debussys Werke* (Graz, 1949)

V. Jankélévitch: *Debussy et le mystère* (Neuchâtel, 1949)

R. Myers: *Debussy* (New York, 1949)

J. d'Almendra: *Les modes grégoriens dans l'oeuvre de Claude Debussy* (Paris, 1950)

W. Danckert: *Claude Debussy* (Berlin, 1950)

G. and D.-E. Inghelbrecht: *Claude Debussy* (Paris, 1953)

E. Vuillermoz: *Claude Debussy* (Geneva, 1957)

J. Barraqué: *Debussy* (Paris, 1962; Eng. trans., 1972)

Debussy et l'évolution de la musique au XXe siècle: CNRS Paris 1962

M. Dietschy: *La passion de Claude Debussy* (Neuchâtel, 1962)

E. Lockspeiser: *Debussy, his Life and Mind* (London, 1962–5)

Y. Tiénot and O. d'Estrade-Guerra: *Debussy, l'homme, son oeuvre, son milieu* (Paris, 1962)

'Souvenir et présence de Debussy', *RBM*, xvi (1962), 43–149

'Claude Debussy 1862–1962: livre d'or', *ReM* (1964), no.258

I. Kremlev: *Claude Debussy* (Moscow, 1965)

S. Jarocinski: *Debussy, a impresionizm i synmbolizm* (Kraków, 1966; Fr. trans., 1971; Eng. trans., 1975)

R. Park: *The Later Style of Claude Debussy* (diss., U. of Michigan, 1967)

V. Jankélévitch: *La vie et la mort dans la musique de Debussy* (Neuchâtel, 1968)

G. Gourdet: *Debussy* (Paris, 1970)

M. Schneider and others: *Debussy*, Génies et réalités (Paris, 1972)

S. Jarocinski: *Debussy, kronika zycia, dziela, epoki* (Kraków, 1972)

R. Nichols: *Debussy* (London, 1973)

C. M. Zenck: *Versuch über die wahre Art Debussy zu analysieren* (Munich, 1974)

V. Jankélévitch: *Debussy et le mystère de l'instant* (Paris, 1976)

A. B. Wenk: *Debussy and the Poets* (Berkeley and Los Angeles, 1976)

119

T. Hirsbrunner: *Debussy und seine Zeit* (Berne, 1981)

M. G. Cobb: *The Poetic Debussy: a Collection of his Song Texts and Selected Letters* (Boston, 1982)

R. Orledge: *Debussy and the Theatre* (Cambridge, 1982)

R. Howat: *Debussy in Proportion: a Musical Analysis* (Cambridge, 1983)

A. B. Wenk: *Claude Debussy and Twentieth-century Music* (Boston, 1983)

OTHER GENERAL LITERATURE

F. Liebich: 'An Impressionist Composer, Claude Debussy, and his Music of Legend and Dream', *Musical Standard* (20 Feb 1904)

M.-D. Calvocoressi: 'Les "Histoires naturelles" de M. Ravel et l'imitation debussyste', *Grande revue* (10 May 1907), 508

P. Lalo: 'M. Ravel et le debussysme', *Le temps* (19 March 1907)

F. Santoliquido: *Il dopo Wagner: Claude Debussy e Richard Strauss* (Rome, 1909)

L. Laloy: 'Claude Debussy et le debussysme', *BSIM*, vi (1910), Aug

G. Jean-Aubry: 'Claude Debussy', *MQ*, iv (1918), 542

G. Mourey: 'Memories of Claude Debussy', *Musical News and Herald* (11 June 1921), 747

J. Durand: *Quelques souvenirs d'un éditeur de musique* (Paris, 1924–5)

R. Godet: 'Weber and Debussy', *The Chesterian*, vii (1926), 220

L. Laloy: *La musique retrouvée* (Paris, 1928)

V. d'Indy: *R. Wagner et son influence sur l'art musical français* (Paris, 1930)

L. Laloy: 'Debussy', *Revue des deux mondes* (15 July 1932)

L. Vallas: 'Debussy, poète', *Les nouvelles littéraires* (15 April 1933)

H. Prunières: 'Autour de Debussy', *ReM* (1934), no.146, p.349; no.147, p.21; no.149, p.189

O. Wartisch: *Studien zur Harmonik des musikalischen Impressionismus* (Erlangen, 1934)

C. Koechlin: 'Sur l'évolution de la musique française avant et après Debussy', *ReM*, xvi (1935), no.155, 264

P. Vallery-Radot: 'Souvenirs de Claude Debussy', *Revue des deux mondes* (15 May 1938)

W. Mellers: 'The Final Works of Debussy or Pierrot fâché avec la lune', *ML*, xx (1939), 168

R. Godet: 'Claude Debussy: souvenirs (à propos des dernières oeuvres)', *Information musicale* (26 March 1943)

C. Saint-Saëns: 'Correspondance entre Saint-Saëns et Maurice Emmanuel à propos de Debussy', *ReM* (1947), no.206, p.30

G. Samazeuilh: *Musiciens de mon temps* (Paris, 1947)

Bibliography

L. Vallas: 'Claude Debussy aurait 85 ans', *Figaro littéraire* (23 Aug 1947)

P. Landormy: *La musique française de Franck à Debussy* (Paris, 1948)

A. Poniatowski: *D'un siècle à l'autre* (Paris, 1948)

S. Bonmariage: *Catherine et ses amis: Claude Debussy, Pierre Louÿs etc* (Gap, 1949)

O. Thompson: 'Claude Debussy', *International Cyclopedia of Music* (New York, 1949), 413

M. de Falla: *Escritos sobre música y músicos, Debussy, Wagner, el 'cante jondo'* (Buenos Aires, 1950)

M. Cooper: *French Music from the Death of Berlioz to the Death of Fauré* (London, 1951)

M. Garden and L. Biancolli: *Mary Garden's Story* (New York, 1951)

F. Gervais: *Etude comparée des langages harmoniques de Fauré et de Debussy* (Paris, 1951)

A. Schaeffner: 'Debussy et ses rapports avec la musique russe', *Musique russe*, i (1953), 95–138

H. Mondor: 'Mallarmé et Debussy', *Cahiers de marottes et violons d'Ingres* (1954), Sept–Oct

P. Boulez: 'La corruption dans les encensoirs', *Melos*, xxiii (1956), 276

C. Brăiloiu: 'Pentatonismes chez Debussy', *Studia memoriae Belae Bartók sacra* (Budapest, 1956, 3/1959; Eng. trans., 1959), 385–426

A. Jakobik: *Zur Einheit der neuen Musik* (Würzburg, 1957)

F. Gervais: 'La notion d'arabesque chez Debussy', *ReM* (1958), no.241, p.3

E. Lockspeiser: 'New Literature on Debussy', *ML*, xl (1959), 140

M. Dietschy: 'The Family and Childhood of Debussy', *MQ*, xlvi (1960), 301

E. Souffrin-Le Breton: 'Debussy lecteur de Banville', *RdM*, xlvi (1960), 200

E. Ansermet: 'Le langage de Debussy', *Feuilles musicales*, xv (1962), 63

F. Lesure: 'Debussy et le XVIe siècle', *Hans Albrecht in memoriam* (Kassel, 1962), 242

M. Dietschy: 'Claude Debussy et André Suarès', *Revue musicale de Suisse romande*, xvi/3 (1963)

F. Lesure: 'Claude Debussy after his Centenary', *MQ*, xlix (1963), 277

E. Lockspeiser: 'Debussy's Concept of the Dream', *PRMA*, lxxxix (1962–3), 49

H. Schmidt-Garré: 'Parallelen zwischen Dichtung und Musik', *NZM*, cxxv (1964), 290

R. Myers: 'Debussy and French Music', *MT*, cviii (1967), 899

J. Noble: 'Debussy and Stravinsky', *MT*, cviii (1967), 22

G. W. Hopkins: 'Debussy and Boulez', *MT*, cix (1968), 710

E. Lockspeiser: 'Debussy in Perspective', *MT*, cix (1968), 904

E. Brody: 'La famille Mendès: a Literary Link between Wagner and Debussy', *MR*, xxxiii (1972), 177

E. Lockspeiser: *Music and Painting* (London, 1973)

R. L. Smith: 'Debussy and the Art of the Cinema', *ML*, liv (1973), 61

R. Orledge: 'Debussy's Musical Gifts to Emma Bardac', *MQ*, lx (1974), 544

Mme G. de Tinan: 'Souvenirs de Claude Debussy', *SMz*, cxv (1975), 293

A. Whittall: 'Tonality and the Whole-tone Scale in the Music of Debussy', *MR*, xxxvi (1975), 261

Musik-Konzepte, nos.1–2 (1977) [Debussy issue]

R. Holloway: *Debussy and Wagner* (London, 1979)

J.-M. Nectoux: 'Debussy et Fauré', *Cahiers Debussy*, new ser., no.3 (1979), 13

W. Spencer: 'The Relationship between André Caplet and Claude Debussy', *MQ*, lxvi (1980), 112

R. L. Smith: 'Debussy and the Pre-Raphaelites', *19th Century Music*, v (1981–2), 95

STUDIES OF PARTICULAR WORKS
(*dramatic works*)

V. d'Indy: 'A propos de Pelléas et Mélisande: essai de psychologie du critique d'art', *L'occident* (Brussels, 1902), June

E. Evans: 'Pelléas et Mélisande', *Musical Standard* (29 May 1909)

D.-E. Inghelbrecht: *Comment on ne doit pas interpréter Carmen, Faust, Pelléas* (Paris, 1933)

R. Peter: 'Ce que fut la "générale" de Pelléas et Mélisande', *Inédits sur Claude Debussy*, Collection Comoedia Charpentier (Paris, 1942), 3

J. van Ackere: *Pelléas et Mélisande* (Brussels, 1952)

A. Goléa: *Pelléas et Mélisande* (Paris, 1952)

J. Kerman: 'Music and Play: *Pelléas et Mélisande*', *Opera News*, xviii/8 (1953), 13

F. Merkling: 'The Ultimate Dim Thule', *Opera News*, xviii/8 (1953), 5

M. Abraham: 'Sous le signe de Pelléas', *Annales du Centre universitaire Méditerranéen*, vii (1953–4), 99

H. Büsser: *De Pelléas aux Indes galantes* (Paris, 1955)

J. Kerman: *Opera as Drama* (New York, 1956)

O. d'Estrade-Guerra: 'Les manuscrits de Pelléas et Mélisande', *ReM* (1957), no.235, p.5

Bibliography

R. Leibowitz: '*Pelléas et Mélisande* ou le "No-Man's Land" de l'art lyrique', *Critique*, xiii (1957), 22

'Le martyre de Saint-Sébastien', *ReM* (1957), no.234

H. Eimert: 'Debussys Jeux', *Die Reihe* (1959), no.5, p.3; Eng. trans., *Die Reihe* (1961), no.5, p.3

W. Paap: '*La boîte à joujoux* van Debussy', *Mens en melodie*, xvii (1962), 347

E. Lockspeiser: *Debussy et Edgar Poe* (Monaco, 1962)

C. Van Lerberghe: '*Pelléas et Mélisande': notes critiques* (Liège, 1962)

A. Schaeffner: 'Claude Debussy et ses projets Shakespeariens', *Revue de la société d'histoire du théâtre*, xvi (1964), 446

F. Lesure: 'Retour à *Khamma*', *RBM*, xx (1966), 124

E. Lockspeiser: 'The Martyrdom of St Sebastian', *The Listener* (5 May 1966)

——: 'Debussy's Dream House', *Opera News*, xxxiv/21 (1969–70), 8

——: '*Frères en Art:* pièce de théâtre inédite de Debussy', *RdM*, lvi (1970), 165

J.-J. Nattiez and L. Hirbour-Paquette: 'Analyse musicale et sémiologie: à propos du Prélude de Pelléas', *Musique en jeu* (1973), no.9, p.42

R. L. Smith: 'The Parentage of *Pelléas*', *Music and Musicians*, xxii (1973), 38

F. Lesure: 'Une interview "inédite" de Debussy', *Cahiers Debussy*, no.1 (1974), 7

R. Orledge: 'Debussy's Orchestral Collaborations', *MT*, cxv (1974), 1030; cxvi (1975), 30

M. Dietschy: 'À propos d'une interview inédite de Debussy', *Cahiers Debussy*, no.2 (1975), 1

B. Williams: 'L'envers des destinées: Remarks on Debussy's *Pelléas et Mélisande*', *Cambridge University Quarterly* (1975), 389

R. Orledge: 'Another Look inside Debussy's "Toybox" ', *MT*, cxvii (1976), 987

——: 'Debussy's *House of Usher* Revisited', *MQ*, lxii (1976), 536

——: 'Debussy's Second English ballet: *Le palais du silence* or *No-ja-li*', *CMc*, xxii (1976), 73

C. M. Zenck: 'Form- und Farbenspiele: Debussys "Jeux" ', *AMw*, xxxiii (1976), 28

Esquisses de Pelléas et Mélisande (1893–1895) (Paris, 1977) [facs. with introduction by F. Lesure]

L'avant-scène, no.9 (1977) [*Pelléas et Mélisande* issue]

J. McKay: 'The Bréval Manuscript: New Interpretations', *Cahiers Debussy*, new ser., no.1 (1977), 5

H.-K. Metzger and R. Riehn, eds.: *Musik-Konzepte*, nos.1–2 (1977), 10–41 [on *La chute de la maison Usher*]

A. Porter: 'Fragments of the *House of Usher*', *New Yorker* (14 March 1977), 130

J. Allende-Blin: 'À la découverte de Debussy (à propos de la *Chute de la maison Usher*)', *Musique en jeu* (1978), no.31, p.7

M. Chimènes: 'Les vicissitudes de *Khamma*', *Cahiers Debussy*, new ser., no.2 (1978), 11

L. McDearmon: 'Maud Allan: the Public Record', *Dance Chronicle*, ii/2 (1978), 85

R. Myers: 'The Opera that never was: Debussy's Collaboration with Victor Segalen in the Preparation of *Orphée*', *MQ*, lxiv (1978), 495

T. Hirsbrunner: 'Debussys Ballett: *Khamma*', *AMw*, xxxvi (1979), 105

M. Rinaldi: '*Le martyre de Saint Sébastien* de Debussy su testo d'Annunzio', *Nuova antologia*, no.2131 (1979), 378

L. Berman: '*Prelude to the Afternoon of a Faun* and *Jeux*: Debussy's Summer Rites', *19th Century Music*, iii (1979–80), 225

C. Abbate: '*Tristan* in the Composition of *Pelléas*', *19th Century Music*, v (1981–2), 117

(*orchestral and choral works*)

M. Ravel: 'L'art et les hommes: à propos des Images de Claude Debussy', *Cahiers d'aujourd'hui*, iii (1913), 135

L. Laloy: 'La dernière oeuvre de Claude Debussy: l'Ode à la France', *Musique* (15 March 1928), 245

W. Austin, ed.: *Debussy: Prelude to 'The Afternoon of a Faun*' (New York, 1970)

D. Cox: *Debussy Orchestral Music* (London, 1974)

C. K. Baron: 'Varèse's Explication of Debussy's *Syrinx* in *Density 21.5* and an Analysis of Varèse's Composition: a Secret Model Revealed', *MR*, xliii (1982), 121

E. Kasaba: ' "Le martyre de Saint Sébastien": étude sur sa genèse', *Cahiers Debussy*, new ser., nos.4–5 (1980–81), 19

J. Pasler: 'Debussy, *Jeux*: Playing with Time and Form', *19th Century Music*, vi (1982–3), 60

R. L. Smith: 'La genèse de "La Damoiselle élue" ', *Cahiers Debussy*, new ser., nos.4–5 (1980–81), 3

R. Howat: 'Dramatic shape in *Jeux de vagues*, and its relationship to *Pelléas*, *Jeux* and other scores', *Cahiers Debussy*, new ser., no.7 (1983), 7

(*chamber music*)

R. Moevs: 'Intervallic Procedures in Debussy: Serenade from the Sonata for Cello and Piano, 1915', *PNM*, viii/1 (1969), 82

124

Bibliography

(*songs*)

E. Lockspeiser: 'Debussy's Unpublished Songs', *Radio Times* (23 Sept 1938)

G. Samazeuilh: 'La 1ère version inédite de "En sourdine" avec facsimile', *Inédits sur Claude Debussy*, Collection Comoedia Charpentier (Paris, 1942), 34

J. Bathori: *Sur l'interprétation des mélodies de Claude Debussy* (Paris, 1953)

P. Ruschenburg: *Stilkritische Untersuchungen zu den Liedern Claude Debussys* (diss., U. of Hamburg, 1966)

E. Hardeck: *Untersuchungen zu den Klavierliedern Claude Debussys* (Regensburg, 1967)

P. Bernac: *The Interpretation of French Song* (London, 1970)

(*piano works*)

A. Cortot: 'La musique de piano de Debussy', *ReM*, i (1920), 127; Eng. trans. (1922) as *The Piano Music of Debussy*

A. Jakobik: *Die assoziative Harmonik in den Klavier-Werken Claude Debussys* (Würzburg, 1940)

R. Schmitz: *The Piano Works of Claude Debussy* (New York, 1950, 2/1966)

R. Réti: 'Claude Debussy: La cathédrale engloutie', *The Thematic Process in Music* (New York, 1951, 2/1961), 194

M. Long: *Au piano avec Claude Debussy* (Paris, 1960; Eng. trans., 1972)

F. Dawes: *Debussy Piano Music* (London, 1969)

R. Howat: 'A Thirteenth Etude of 1915: the Original Version *pour les arpèges composés*', *Cahiers Debussy*, new ser., no.1 (1977), 16

R. di Benedetto: 'Congetture su *Voiles*', *RIM*, (1978), 312–44

R. Orledge: 'Debussy's Piano Music: Some Second Thoughts and Sources of Inspiration', *MT*, cxxii (1981), 21

ERIK SATIE

Patrick Gowers

Nigel Wilkins

CHAPTER ONE

Life

Eric (he later adopted the spelling 'Erik') Alfred Leslie
Satie was born in Honfleur on 17 May 1866, son of
Alfred Satie, a French ship broker, and his Scottish wife.
After the Franco-Prussian war (1870–71) the family
moved to Paris, but two years later his mother died and he
was sent back to live with his grandparents. In 1878 his
grandmother died and he was returned once more to Paris
where his father organized an informal education for
him. If this gave him any joy it was short-lived, for in
1878 Alfred Satie married Eugénie Barnetsche, a pianist
and mediocre Romantic composer whom the child
disliked.

In 1879 Satie entered the Paris Conservatoire.
Records show him as gifted, exceptionally lazy and
often absent; in 1882 he was dismissed for failing to
reach the required standard, but he spent a year attending Taudou's harmony class, and in 1885 was just
accepted into the piano class of Mathias, who assessed
him thus: 'Nothing. Three months to learn a piece.
Incapable of sight-reading'. His greatest friend of the
time, Contamine de Latour, stated that he persisted with
his wearisome studies to qualify for the one-year *volon-
tariat* in place of five years' military service. In
November 1886 he duly joined the 33rd Infantry, but
by April of the next year he had contracted bronchitis
and he spent several months convalescing.

Alfred Satie was now trying to establish a music publishing business and brought out five songs by Satie and de Latour. Meanwhile Chabrier's *Le roi malgré lui* had had its first performance and shortly afterwards Satie wrote his three Sarabandes (1887), which owe a debt to Chabrier, and in their turn probably influenced the Sarabande of Debussy's *Pour le piano*. In the following year he produced his *Gymnopédies*, and in 1890, in the wake of the Paris World Exhibition of 1889, his orientally tinged *Gnossiennes*.

Satie, always a keen reader, had by now developed an absorbing interest in mystical religion, Gregorian chant, Gothic art and the lives of the saints. He had also begun, with de Latour, to frequent Montmartre where, when the *Gymnopédies* were still little known, Vital-Hocquet introduced him to Rudolph Salis's café Chat Noir as 'Erik Satie, gymnopédiste!' His narrow, bourgeois upbringing had left him shy, discreet, reserved, elegant and well mannered. The Chat Noir was a revelation; under the influence of its camaraderie, escapades and endless revolutionary artistic debates, his character began to evolve. Relations with his family grew strained and he moved to Montmartre with 1600 francs in his pocket, going to smaller and smaller lodgings as his money ran out. His religious interests led him, in the early 1890s, to join the flamboyant Joséphin Péladan, 'Sâr Merodack' of the 'Rose + Croix' artistic movement for which Satie became the official composer. Péladan was an avid Wagnerian. Satie, however, wrote him scores that were hieratic and aloof, notably *Le fils des étoiles* (1891), justly called a 'static sound décor'. During the composition of it he first met the man who for some 25 years was to be perhaps his greatest friend,

Life

Debussy. The two were strongly drawn to each other, but it was not a simple relationship. Debussy was prepared to make his superiority felt; Satie became the jester to hide his humiliation.

In doing so Satie could be said to be adopting his most characteristic role. He knew his technique was severely limited; but pride and determination, coupled with great sensitivity, led him to try to bypass his deficiencies with intricate technical systems of his own devising. It also made him allow his natural humour to develop into a protective cloak. This conflict, together with the opposing pulls of nature and upbringing, not only shaped his fascinating, complex, prickly character; it also moulded much of his music, giving it sometimes incongruous traits that are part of its individual charm.

During the Montmartre period Satie's humour was often fashionably exhibitionist. He announced his break with Péladan in 1892 in a flowery, pseudo-archaic letter to *Gil blas*. In the same year he and de Latour wrote *Uspud*, a 'Christian ballet' that they presented to the director of the Opéra (following Péladan's custom), winning an interview only by issuing a duel challenge. Three times Satie applied for the supreme honour of a seat in the Academy. He had a stormy love affair with Utrillo's mother, the painter and one-time circus performer Suzanne Valadon. He formed his own 'Eglise Métropolitaine d'Art de Jésus Conducteur' and, with the help of a legacy of 7000 francs, published a broadsheet, *Le cartulaire*, a mixture of ecclesiastical fantasy and Péladan-style polemics against such figures as Colette's husband Willy, with whom he finally came to blows at one of the Colonne Concerts. With the same legacy he bought his famous 12 identical grey velvet suits. But his

131

generosity was as marked as his appearance and he was soon as poor as before. Two *Gymnopédies* were published in 1895, seemingly on the recommendation of Debussy, who also orchestrated a pair in the following year (not, as Cocteau and others have claimed, misunderstanding and blurring them, but closely following Satie's own orchestral practice of the time).

By now Montmartre was changing. It was losing its rustic, village character and a new generation was coming in. In 1898 Satie packed his belongings into a handcart and moved to his last home, in the southern suburb of Arcueil-Cachan. He cut his long hair, dropped his bohemian trappings and reverted to his respectable, gentlemanly self. It was the start of his most unhappy period. He was forced to earn a living as a *café-concert* pianist, which he considered 'a great lowering', and as a composer of music-hall songs and incidental music. He walked the several kilometres to Montmartre to work each day and walked back in the middle of the night. The main monument to these 15 sad years is the set of *Trois morceaux en forme de poire*, written between 1890 and 1903 and consisting for the most part of arrangements of cabaret melodies.

From 1905 to 1908 Satie became a student again and studied counterpoint, fugue and orchestration under d'Indy and Roussel at the Schola Cantorum. He won a diploma, but his surviving exercises show that he was not by any means exceptional. Nor did this step bear any quick fruit. His output remained low and much of it was a series of attempts to fuse his new contrapuntal skill into a personal style.

When the tide finally turned at the beginning of 1911, it was because Ravel played the Sarabandes at a concert of the Société Musicale Indépendante. It is clear from the programme note that the chief attraction was their prophetic nature and Satie's position as a 'precursor'. Two months later Debussy conducted a performance of his *Gymnopédie* orchestrations and was woundingly surprised at their success. The following years saw the first performances of Roland-Manuel's orchestration of the *Prélude de la porte héroïque du ciel*, and of Ravel's of an excerpt from *Le fils des étoiles*. Articles were published by Jules Ecorcheville, Calvocoressi and Roland-Manuel. In 1913 Ricardo Viñes, one of Satie's most faithful and persistent interpreters, first included his music in a recital, and for once it was a recent composition, the *Quatre préludes flasques*. This attention meant that publishers suddenly began to demand his music. Several of his old pieces were brought out and printed, and he quickly responded with a whole series of 'humorous' piano pieces, with eccentric titles and bizarre commentaries (rewards for the player and on no account to be read out).

Though the outbreak of war interrupted the steadily increasing number of Satie performances, in April 1915 he had his greatest single stroke of fortune when a performance he gave with Viñes of the *Trois morceaux* was heard by the young Cocteau. Satie's meteoric rise to fame after the war was entirely Cocteau's doing. He used his entrée in élite and wealthy circles to win commissions, he persuaded virtuosos – such as the pianist and concert promoter Jean Wiener – to give Satie performances, he wrote and lectured about Satie (particularly in *Le coq et l'arlequin*, March 1918, and *La jeunesse et le scandale*, c1920) and he contributed introductory notes and talks at concert performances.

Most important of all, he collaborated with Satie, notably in the Dyagilev–Massin–Picasso ballet *Parade*.

The opening of *Parade* in May 1917 caused a scandal, and established Satie once and for all. The authors were called 'boches' (a legal offence at the time), and Satie was given an eight-day prison sentence and a heavy fine for sending a rude postcard to a critic, but the penalty was suspended, thanks to Roland-Manuel's father-in-law. In the wake of all this, a group of young composers formed around Satie under the banner 'Les Nouveaux Jeunes'. The personnel was finally fixed in 1920 when the journalist Henri Collet somewhat arbitrarily defined Les Six.

Meanwhile, early in 1917 or possibly even before, Satie had started to work on what is often considered his masterpiece, the cantata *Socrate*. He prepared the text himself by drastically pruning Victor Cousin's translation of Plato's *Dialogues*. He was intent from the outset on writing a work that should be 'white and pure like antiquity'. The result was a creation in which his restricted means came into perfect focus and balance. It was not publicly performed until 1920, but after a private hearing in mid-1919 Stravinsky is reputed to have remarked 'French music is Bizet, Chabrier and Satie'. Satie was now enjoying fame and success and the social life they brought. In 1920 there were two festivals of his music, and in this final period his output was far more varied than before. With Milhaud he produced *Musique d'ameublement* ('furniture music') as a background for the intervals in a concert. He also wrote songs, piano music and ballet scores, culminating, in 1924, in *Mercure* (Massin and Picasso) and *Relâche* (designed by Picabia with a filmed entr'acte by René

13. *Erik Satie*

Clair). Both were scandals, *Relâche* living up to its title ('theatre closed') on the opening night, owing to the illness of the principal dancer, Jean Borlin.

In 1923, prompted by Milhaud, another group of young composers formed around him. They took the title 'L'Ecole d'Arcueil' and consisted of Cliquet-Pleyel, Desormière, Jacob and Sauguet. But Satie's health was beginning to deteriorate. For some years he had drunk quite heavily and become more and more unsociable. After *Relâche* he declined rapidly. He lost what had once been a prodigious appetite, and when he went into Paris to visit, he would sit for hours silently in front of the fire in his hat and coat, with the inevitable umbrella. His friends set him up in hotels to spare him the journey to Arcueil, and he spent his days, still dressed up, sitting in an armchair staring at his reflection, working the light and the door from where he sat with an elaborate string device. Eventually he had to move to hospital, and on 1 July 1925 he died of sclerosis of the liver. When his brother, Milhaud and one or two others went to Arcueil and finally entered the room he had lived in for nearly 30 years without admitting even the concierge, they were astounded by its bareness: a bed, chair and table, a half-empty cupboard with the 12 velvet suits piled on top, an old unused piano whose pedals worked by string, and little else. But he had kept most of his manuscript notebooks, dating back to the early 1890s, and a large quantity of documents. Most of the latter were destroyed in a fire, but thanks to Milhaud the music was saved.

Works

Satie's output of works divides itself conveniently into the decades of his life. In his 20s he wrote first the early piano works then the Rose + Croix music, in his 30s mainly cabaret music, in his 40s – after his time at the Schola – the 'humorous' piano music and in his 50s a suddenly far more varied output including the three main ballets, *Socrate*, songs and piano music.

Satie's earliest surviving piece is a ten-bar Allegro of 1884 pointing ahead to the idiom of the more tender *café-concert* melodies. The first published works, the *Valse-ballet* and *Fantaisie-valse* of 1885, bear the hallmarks of his stepmother and are probably not his unaided work. His first significant pieces were the *Ogives* of 1886. They have quasi-plainsong melodies and triadic harmonies (related, typically, by the logic of the top part rather than the bass), and they form the seed from which the remarkable Rose + Croix works blossomed. But before that he wrote his five early songs, said by de Latour to be inspired by Massenet. They again look forward to the tender cabaret melodies, but with unexpected and delightful twists that clearly show the harmonic ear that was one of his chief gifts.

The Sarabandes of 1887 became famous for their prophetic harmony, particularly their unresolved 9th chords. Though probably stimulated by Chabrier, Satie went considerably further. These pieces also contain the first hint of buffoonery in the form of awkward enharmonic chord spellings. The *Gymnopédies* are in a different world: the textures are simple, with monodies riding over plain, delicately modal accompaniments. They are gentle but stately, calm but just lilting. These pieces are said to have been suggested by Flaubert's *Salammbô*, which Satie particularly admired, and one can detect something of the spirit of *Socrate* in them. The *Gnossiennes* are somewhat similar, but their mode and melodic ornamentation give them an oriental flavour. Bizarre annotations appear for the first time, at this stage only to replace the normal Italian ones.

The Rose + Croix works of 1891–5 form, with the *Ogives*, a fascinating collection. Underlying them is an intense search for a compositional system or method, whose details are at times immensely intricate. On the surface they share a quality of quasi-mystical detachment, sometimes larded over with a buffoonery that finds its peak in *Uspud* and the 840-times repeated passage of *Vexations*. The frequent use of the term 'impressionistic' to describe the harmony of this music is totally mistaken. Satie's use of parallel 9ths and higher extensions is no more like Debussy's than that of a swing band. Some of the Rose + Croix pieces were more successful than others; few reveal their merits casually. Perhaps the most perfect miniature is the *Prélude d'Eginhard*, and the most eccentric *Salut drapeau!* in which a melody in the ancient Greek chromatic mode is accompanied by a non-tonal series of 6-3 chords.

Satie's second creative decade started with a return to the *Gnossienne* style. This he developed, through a series of transitional sketches, into the idiom of the first and third 'Airs à faire fuir' from *Pièces froides*. The 'Danses de travers' introduce a broken-chord left-hand figuration that points ahead to his clearest and most economical piano style. This decade was spent mainly in writing *café-concert* music, much of it of a high quality. The most considerable pieces were *Jack-in-the-box* and *Geneviève de Brabant*, both thought lost but found behind his piano after his death; also the *Angora Ox* (part of which found its way into the *Redite* of the *Trois morceaux*; incomplete versions also exist for piano and orchestra), *California Legend* (which was incorporated into *La belle excentrique*) and *The Dreamy Fish* (music for a story by 'Lord Cheminot', alias de Latour).

The best-known work of this period is the set of *Trois morceaux en forme de poire*. Of the seven sections only the first and the first page of the third appear to have been specially composed; the rest is an anthology of music written between 1890 and 1903. The story that Debussy criticized Satie's form and Satie replied with the *Trois morceaux* three weeks later is disproved by their correspondence. The music in the *café-concert* idiom is not idealized as has been claimed; it is in fact the real thing.

In his output of the Schola period, at the start of his next decade, he appears to have been groping for a new serious style, something that had eluded him for ten years or so. It may be regretted that several pieces from this period have recently been published, since Satie, when he had the opportunity, understandably chose not to release them. Even the *Aperçus désagréables* and *En habit de cheval*, which he did have published, are concerned with rather literal ways of assimilating his new contrapuntal skills. They are full of fugues and chorales (about which he was to say: 'My chorales equal those of Bach with the difference that they are more rare and less pretentious').

Success, when it came, stimulated him far more than study. In his late 40s he produced not only over a dozen sets of humorous piano pieces, but also his notorious play and self-portrait *Le piège de Méduse*, with its incidental music, and *Cinq grimaces* for a projected production by Cocteau of *A Midsummer Night's Dream*. With the piano pieces his style suddenly crystallized. The writing tends to be lean, often in two parts. The form is usually like a string of beads, each a bar or two of some sharply defined texture, a technique that harks back to the Rose + Croix works. Sharp contrasts between one of these 'motifs', to use his own word, and the next, suggest orchestral colours, and in a sense this style culminates in some of the movements of *Parade*. In another sense its apotheosis is in the *Sports et divertissements*, published in a de luxe facsimile with illustrations by Charles Martin. In these 20 miniatures Satie's eccentric annotations, which he had often written apart from the music before, and his beautiful calligraphy, are finally fused into the conception of the work. No element can be left out, and the result is a private art that tends to resist public performance.

Satie's last decade started with *Parade*, famous for the typewriter, siren etc called for in the score. In fact the writing is an orchestral translation of his current piano styles, including a tiny fugato prelude and epilogue. He said of these: 'I like this genre, slightly pompous and feignedly naive'.

Socrate broaches very different territory. For once there are no defences, which has been ascribed to the

14. *Picasso's design for the French Manager in Satie's 'Parade', first performed by the Ballets Russes in 1917*

141

fact that Debussy was no longer alive, although Satie started work on it at least 15 months before his friend's death and probably even before their final estrangement. In a sense the music harks back to the ideals of the Rose + Croix days, providing again a 'static sound décor' against which the words, unforced and uninflated, can emerge in their own time and create their own effect. By stripping the music of all rhetoric Satie forces the listener to sharpen his responses, to concentrate and focus his sensitivity until the slightest shift becomes significant. And to those who can meet this challenge, the death of Socrates, set to what now becomes an actual plainsong line with a bare ostinato accompaniment, is intensely moving.

There are three sets of songs from the last decade. Their contents vary from a bitter *Elégie* in memory of Debussy to an *allegretto* ('genre Gounod') setting of a poem about the Mad Hatter. To some extent they are less individual than the earlier *Trois poèmes d'amour* (1914) in which Satie's own tiny poems poke fun at the vocalized mute 'e' in sung French. (Singers who attempted to play this down infuriated him.)

Of the piano pieces, the *Sonatine bureaucratique* is interesting in that it paraphrases Clementi, thereby anticipating (and possibly influencing) Stravinsky's use of old material. But undoubtedly the most significant are the five Nocturnes. In their way some of his most serious and successful compositions, these pieces are once again the fruit of a highly calculated system. No.2, for instance, is an exercise in harmony in 2nds, 4ths, 5ths and 7ths; no.5, by contrast, is all in 3rds and 6ths. The final ballets, *Mercure* and *Relâche*, return to his music-hall idiom in varying degrees of stylization.

Satie has three main claims to fame: his possible influence on Debussy, who was certainly not above 'borrowing', and his acknowledged influence on Ravel; his more interesting and far-reaching influence on the current avant garde, via Varèse and particularly Cage; and his intrinsic merit. The last is the most important, and although the initial dispute has passed into history, it has remained a source of considerable disagreement. The reason for this is that Satie represents an extreme – an important special case in music aesthetics. The hallmark of a certain type of sophistication, of what might be called the connoisseur mentality, is to prefer small, exquisitely wrought nuances to anything more effusive which, by contrast, seems tasteless and gross. Satie's most eminent and discriminating admirers have always tended to praise, above all, his clarity, restraint, purity of style and lack of rhetoric or frills. This clearly denies many of music's most potent resources, and while some can accept it readily, many others find the sacrifices too great. More interestingly, because it is essentially a cultivated taste, still others can be educated to it, either directly or through the cultural ethos. The taste for Satie is therefore particularly susceptible to fashion.

It has also been argued that Satie's particular extreme suits some other arts better than it does music. It is no coincidence that Cocteau's description of his own role as a poet exactly parallels his views on Satie. 'True tears', he wrote, 'are not shed over a sad page, but over the miracle of a word in exactly the right place. Few are worthy to weep such tears.' Painters too, at about the time of World War I, were led to see Satie as a 'Picasso of music' who would lead it away from impressionism. *Parade* has often been described as 'Cubist'. So it is not

143

surprising that most of Satie's last works are concerned with some sort of programme, whether it be a song lyric, or a ballet scenario, or the intricate amalgam of *Sports et divertissements*. Even *Socrate* owes its effect essentially to the relationship between words and music, and few works would suffer more from one's not being able to hear or understand the text.

There was a considerable revival of interest in Satie during the early 1970s, especially in the USA, partly, perhaps, a matter of fashion. But it could well be that the man Ravel called a 'precursor both brilliant and clumsy' will eventually be seen to have been far further ahead of his time and of greater genius than his illustrious disciple ever imagined.

Numbers in right-hand margins denote references in the text.

The published output falls into three categories: works published during Satie's lifetime; works issued shortly after his death under the direction of Milhaud, and works printed much later under the direction of Robert Caby. This list includes all pieces in the first two groups as well as the more important Caby publications. Some lesser works edited by Caby are given in the appendix.

DRAMATIC

Le fils des étoiles (pastorale kaldéenne, Sâr Péladan), 3 préludes ? for fls and harps, 1891; pf score survives — 137

Deux préludes du Nazaréen (incidental music, H. Mazel), pf, 1892 — 130, 133

Uspud (ballet chrétien, 3, J. P. Contamine de Latour), 1892; pf score survives with annotations for fls, harps and str — 131, 138

Prélude d'Eginhard (incidental music), pf, 1893 — 138

Prélude de la porte héroïque du ciel (drame ésotérique, J. Bois), pf, 1894 — 133

Jack-in-the-box (pantomime, J. Depaquit), pf, 1899; as ballet (Balanchin), Paris, Sarah Bernhardt, 3 July 1926 — 139

Geneviève de Brabant (miniature marionette opera), vv, pf, 1899 — 139

Pousse l'amour (Coco chéri) (parts of operetta), c1905; Monte Carlo, 1913; lost

Le piège de Méduse (play with music, Satie), 7 dances, pf/insts, 1913 — 140

Cinq grimaces pour 'Le songe d'une nuit d'été' (incidental music, Shakespeare), orch, 1914 — 140

Parade (ballet réaliste, Cocteau, Massin), orch, 1917; Paris, Châtelet, 18 May 1917 — 134, 140, 141, 143

La belle excentrique (fantaisie sérieuse for dance) [incl. California Legend, c1902], music-hall orch, pf 2/4 hands, c1902–1920 — 139

Recitatives for Gounod: Le médecin malgré lui, 1923; Monte Carlo, 1924

Mercure (ballet, Massin), orch, 1924; Paris, La Cigale, 15 June 1924 — 134, 142

Relâche (ballet, Picabia, Börlin), orch, 1924; Paris, Champs-Elysées, 6 Dec 1924 — 134, 136, 142

VOCAL

(large-scale works)

Messe des pauvres (Lat. Mass and psalms), chorus, org/pf, c1893–5 — 134, 137, 138,

Socrate (drame symphonique, Plato, trans. V. Cousin), 1 or more vv, pf/chamber orch, 1918 — 140, 142, 144

(songs)

Elégie (Contamine de Latour), 1887; 3 mélodies (Contamine de Latour), 1887; Chanson (Contamine de Latour), 1887; Salut drapeau! (Hymne au drapeau) (Sâr Péladan), 1891; Bonjour Biqui!, 1893; 3 poèmes d'amour (Satie), 1914; 3 mélodies (Fargue, M. Godebska, Chalupt), 1916; 4 petites mélodies (Lamartine, Cocteau, 18th century, Radiguet), 1920; Ludions (Fargue), 1923 — 130, 137; 138; 142

Café-concert songs, c1900, incl. Tendrement (V. Hyspa), Je te veux (H. Pacory), La diva de l'empire (D. Bonnaud, N. Blès) — 137

INSTRUMENTAL

(other than for pf solo)

Danse, fl, ob, 2 cl, bn, timp, harp, 1890; arr. pf 4 hands in 3 morceaux en forme de poire; 3 sonneries de la Rose + Croix, tpts, harps, 1892, pf score survives; 3 morceaux en forme de poire, pf 4 hands, 1890–1903; En habit de cheval, pf 4 hands/orch, 1911; Aperçus désagréables, pf 4 hands, 1908–12; Choses vues à droite et à gauche (sans lunettes), vn, pf, 1914; 3 petites pièces montées, orch/pf 4 hands, c1920; Musique d'ameublement, pf, 3 cl, trbn, 1920, collab. Milhaud; Sonnerie pour réveiller le bon gros Roi des Singes, 2 tpt, 1921 — 132, 133, 139; 139–40; 134

(pf solo)

Allegro, 1884; Valse-ballet, 1885; Fantaisie-valse, 1885; 4 ogives, 1886; 3 sarabandes, 1887; 3 gymnopédies, 1888; 3 gnossiennes, 1890; Première pensée Rose + Croix, 1891; Fête donnée par des Chevaliers Normands en l'honneur d'une jeune demoiselle, 1892; Vexations, c1893; Danses gothiques, 1893; Modéré, 1893; Pièces froides, 1897; Poudre d'or, c1901; Le Piccadilly, c1904; Prélude en tapisserie, 1906; Passacaille, 1906; Nouvelles pièces froides, 1906–10; 4 préludes flasques (pour un chien), 1912; 3 véritables préludes flasques (pour un chien), 1912; Descriptions automatiques, 1913 — 137, 138; 130, 132, 133; 137–8; 138, 139; 133

Embryons desséchés, 1913; Croquis et agaceries d'un gros bonhomme en bois, 1913; Chapitres tournés en tous sens, 1913; Vieux sequins et vieilles cuirasses, 1913; Menus propos enfantins, 1913; Enfantillages pittoresques, 1913; Peccadilles importunes, 1913; Les pantins dansent, 1913; Sports et divertissements, 1914; Heures séculaires et instantanées, 1914; Les 3 valses du précieux dégoûté, 1914; Avant- — 140, 144 dernières pensées, 1915; Sonatine bureaucratique, 1917; 5 nocturnes, 1919; Rêverie de l'enfance de Pantagruel, c1920; Premier menuet, 1920

142

APPENDIX
(lesser works ed. Caby)

Song: Chanson médiévale (Mendès)
Pf: Arrière propos, Caresse, Désespoir agréable, 2 rêveries nocturnes, 12 petits chorals, Effronterie, Exercices, The Dreamy Fish, Fâcheux exemple, Froide songerie, Gambades, Gnossiennes nos. 4–6; Le grand singe, Harmonies [2 sets], Nouvelles pièces enfantines, Petite ouverture à danser, Poésie, Prélude canin, Prélude de la mort de M Mouche, Prière, Le prisonnier moussade, Profondeur, Songe creux
Also Rêverie du pauvre, pf acc. to missing melody, probably not by Satie

139

Principal publishers: Salabert
MSS in F-Pn

WRITINGS

Many in MSS; articles in L'avenir d'Arcueil-Cachan (1909–10), Feuilles libres (1922–4), BSIM, viii–x (1912–14), 391 (1921–4).
L'esprit musical (Liège, 1950)
ed. G. Charbonnier: 'Humour poétique', La nef (1950–51), nos.71–2
Cahiers d'un mammifère (Liège, 1951)
Mémoires d'un amnésique (Liège, 1953)
Propos à propos (Liège, 1954)
Léger comme un oeuf (Paris, 1957)
Oui: lettres d'Erik Satie adressées à Pierre de Massot (Alès, 1960)
'Mémoires d'un amnésique', 'Chronique musicale', Approdo musicale (1965), nos.19–20
ed. T. Winkfield: Dried Embryos (London, 1972)
ed. N. Wilkins: 'The Writings of Erik Satie: Miscellaneous Fragments', ML, lvi (1975), 288
ed. O. Volta: D'Esoterik Satie à Satierik (textes et correspondance) (Paris, 1976)
ed. N. Wilkins: The Writings of Erik Satie (London, 1976)
ed. O. Volta: Ecrits (Paris, 1977–)

146

BIBLIOGRAPHY

MONOGRAPHS

Roland-Manuel: *Erik Satie* (Paris, 1916)

P. D. Templier: *Erik Satie* (Paris, 1932; Eng. trans., 1969)

R. Myers: *Erik Satie* (London, 1948)

ReM (1952), no.214 [special number]

Y. Gérard: *Introduction à l'oeuvre d'Erik Satie* (diss., Paris Conservatoire, 1958)

F. Lesure, ed.: *Erik Satie: exposition* (Paris, 1966)

B. Hill: *Characteristics of the Music of Erik Satie that Suggest the 'Id'* (diss., U. of Colorado, 1967)

A. Gillmor: *Erik Satie and the Concept of the Avant-garde* (diss., U. of Toronto, 1972)

A. Rey: *Erik Satie* (Paris, 1974)

G. Wehmeyer: *Erik Satie* (Regensburg, 1974)

J. Harding: *Erik Satie* (London, 1975)

OTHER LITERATURE

J. Cocteau: *Le coq et l'arlequin: notes autour de la musique* (Paris, 1918)

H. Collet: 'Un livre de Rimsky et un livre de Cocteau – les cinq russes, les six français et Erik Satie', *Comoedia* (16 and 23 Jan 1920)

W. Roberts: 'The Problem of Satie', *ML*, iv (1923), 313

C. Koechlin: 'Erik Satie', *ReM*, v/2 (1924), 193

J. Cocteau: 'Fragments d'une conférence sur Eric Satie', *ReM*, v/2 (1924), 217 [from *La jeunesse et le scandale, Oeuvres complètes de Jean Cocteau*, ix (Geneva, 1950)]

J. P. C. de Latour: 'Erik Satie intime', *Comoedia* (3, 5, 6 Aug 1925)

J. Cocteau: *Rappel à l'ordre* (Paris, 1926)

W. Danckert: 'Der Klassizismus Erik Saties und seine geistliche Stellung', *ZMw*, xii (1929–30), 105

W. Mellers: *Studies in Contemporary Music* (London, 1947), 16ff

D. Milhaud: *Notes sans musique* (Paris, 1949; Eng. trans., 1952), 176ff

R. Shattuck: *The Banquet Years* (London, 1955), 88–145

F. Poulenc: *Moi et mes amis* (Paris, 1963), 81ff

P. Gowers: *Erik Satie: his Studies, Notebooks and Critics* (diss., U. of Cambridge, 1966)

——: 'Satie's Rose Croix Music (1891–1895)', *PRMA*, xcii (1965–6), 1

P. Santi: 'Il "point de départ" di Satie', *Chigiana*, xxiii (1966), 183

P. Dickinson: 'Erik Satie (1866–1925)', *MR*, xxviii (1967), 139

G. Wehmeyer: 'Saties Instanteismus', *Musicae scientiae collectanea: Festschrift Karl Gustav Fellerer* (Cologne, 1973), 626

A. Rey: *Erik Satie* (Paris, 1974)

J. Harding: *Erik Satie* (London, 1975)

147

H. H. Stuckenschmidt: *Die Musik eines halben Jahrhunderts: 1925–1975* (Munich, 1976)

R. Belicha: 'Chronologie satiste, ou, Photocopie d'un original', *ReM* (1978), no.312

A. Guarnieri Corazzol: *Erik Satie tra ricerca e provocazione* (Venice, 1979)

O. Volta: *Erik Satie* (Paris, 1979)

Musik-Konzepte, no.11 (1980) [Satie issue]

MAURICE RAVEL

G. W. Hopkins

CHAPTER ONE

Life

Joseph Maurice Ravel was the eldest child of Pierre Joseph Ravel, an engineer of unusually cultured outlook, and Marie (née Delouart). Shortly after Maurice's birth on 7 March 1875 at his mother's aunt's home in Ciboure, his father took up work in Paris, and the family lived permanently in the capital from then on. Whereas his father's background was largely Swiss and his mother's Basque, Ravel's childhood was a thoroughly Parisian one, and when it became clear to the boy's father that Maurice's gifts suggested a possible career in music, the best instructors and, ultimately, the Conservatoire were at hand. It seems that the elder Ravel actively desired such a career for his son: certainly he encouraged it, and in 1882 placed him with a distinguished piano teacher, Henri Ghys. In 1887 Ravel began studies in harmony with the Delibes pupil Charles-René, an association that produced his earliest known essays in composition (Schumann and Grieg Variations, a piano sonatina movement); and two years later, after becoming a piano pupil of Emile Decombes, he gained admission to Eugène Anthiôme's preparatory piano class at the Conservatoire. From here, in a further two years, he graduated to the class of Charles de Bériot, studying harmony with Emile Pessard.

If, during his first years at the Conservatoire (1889–95), Ravel's record as a student of harmony and the piano was patchy and, in terms of the establishment's awards system, ultimately unsuccessful, his record as one who sought experience was very much more impressive. At the Paris World Exhibition of 1889 Ravel, like Debussy, first encountered the music of the Javanese gamelan, which exercised a lasting enchantment on him, if not the deeper influence commentators have found in Debussy's work. At the same event he attended concerts of Russian music given by Rimsky-Korsakov, again an experience that left a distinctive imprint on his own orchestral music. Ravel's early friendship with the remarkable Spanish pianist Ricardo Viñes, a fellow pupil in de Bériot's class, stimulated a mutual exploration of the contemporary arts. In music, Wagner, the Russian school, Chabrier and Satie were objects of enthusiasm; in literature (and aesthetic theory) important links were forged with Baudelaire, Poe and Mallarmé. In 1893 Ravel made personal contact with Chabrier and Satie whose influence on his early compositions (the *Sérénade grotesque* for piano, the song *Ballade de la reine morte d'aimer* etc) he himself was the first to point out.

In July 1895 Ravel left the Conservatoire; by the end of the year he had completed three works, the song *Un grand sommeil noir*, the piano piece *Menuet antique* and the *Habanera* for two pianos, in which the distinctive characteristics of his style began to be felt. It has been suggested that this was the time when he made his decision to devote himself primarily to composition. Yet 1896 saw the production of only two songs, *Sainte* and *D'Anne jouant de l'espinette*, and it was not until the next year that he decided to return to the Conservatoire as a member of Fauré's composition class, while studying counterpoint and orchestration with André Gédalge. In fact the years 1897–8 seem to have represented a fresh start in his work as a composer; he published none of the works he composed during this period (a violin sonata, *Entre cloches* for two pianos, the songs *Chanson du rouet* and *Si morne!*, the *Shéhérazade* overture) and it is easy to see in them the admixture of boldness and uncertainty that characterizes most student work of talent. Of these works the most significant are the sonata, an extended essay in which Orenstein has seen anticipations of the 1914 Piano Trio (a work Ravel dedicated to Gédalge), and the overture, the composer's first orchestral venture, associated with a projected opera.

During the next year a return to Ravel's mock-archaic manner brought a return of his more confident handling of materials; the immediate outcome could be seen in a further Marot setting (*D'Anne qui me jecta de la neige*) and the instantly popular *Pavane pour une infante défunte*. It was somewhat as an antiquary, too, that Ravel began his career in the publishers' catalogues. Chabrier's publisher, Enoch, brought out the *Menuet antique* in 1898; and this was followed by the two Marot songs (as *Deux épigrammes*) and the *Pavane*, published by Demets in 1900. More important, the first public performances of Ravel's music date from these years. *Habanera* and *Entre cloches*, yoked together as *Sites auriculaires*, were presented in March 1898; a month later Viñes introduced the *Menuet antique*; and in May 1899 Ravel himself conducted the *Shéhérazade* overture. These performances were hardly an outright success with the critics or with the public, but there were gratifying aspects, such as Debussy's interest in the

Habanera, and at *Shéhérazade* there were, by Ravel's own account, 'more applauders than protesters'.

At the Conservatoire Ravel's time was again being well spent in any but the official view. In Fauré he had a truly sympathetic teacher whose undogmatic guidance and encouragement were to be acknowledged in the dedications of Ravel's next important works, the piano piece *Jeux d'eau* and the String Quartet; but when it came to satisfying the authorities of his abilities in fugue writing he failed abysmally. In 1900 he again found himself excluded from the Conservatoire's rolls through inability to secure a prize. Henceforth, although he continued to attend Fauré's class as an 'auditeur', his main official connection with the Conservatoire consisted in his several attempts to obtain the Prix de Rome for composition. The first of these was in 1900, when he failed to qualify for the principal part of the competition, the composition of a cantata to a set text under specially supervised conditions. He entered again in each of the next three years, producing the cantatas *Myrrha* (1901), *Alcyone* (1902) and *Alyssa* (1903); these were judged inferior to the works of the respective winners, André Caplet, Aymé Kunc and Raoul Laparra. In 1903 Ravel had to leave Fauré's class altogether, having once again failed to pick up a prize for composition.

Contemporary portraits and other documents show that the young Ravel was attracted to dandyism as a way of life (as expounded, for instance, by Baudelaire): he cultivated an impeccably elegant façade, taking fashion as his style. At this period his social life included frequentation of salons. But he was also a member of a côterie known as 'Les Apaches'. Typical of many such bands of artistic allies, it was formed around the turn of the century, and its regular meetings offered its members a stimulating platform as well as a congenial milieu for aesthetic discussion. These members included Falla, Schmitt and Delage (a pupil of Ravel), Inghelbrecht, Caplet, de Sévérac, Calvocoressi and Vuillermoz, the painter Paul Sordes and the poets Fargue and Klingsor. It was Klingsor who supplied the texts for Ravel's orchestral song cycle *Shéhérazade*. By now Ravel was producing music of mature mastery. The attitude of the Conservatoire authorities towards him was partly dictated by his failure to meet the academic requirements of the time, but largely it was a consequence of irreconcilable artistic ideals. It was not long before the eruption of 'the Ravel affair' heralded the downfall of a regime deaf to the new order of post-Lisztian piano writing so confidently established in *Jeux d'eau*, to the strength and individuality (enough, indeed, to win it a permanent place in the repertory) of the 1903 Quartet, and to the orchestral brilliance and imaginative range, embracing both breadth and delicacy of effect, which made *Shéhérazade* the most satisfying portent to date of Ravel's potential greatness.

Having neglected to compete for the Prix de Rome in 1904. Ravel again entered the competition the next year (the last year in which he was eligible because of age). As in 1900 he failed to progress beyond the preliminary round. That in the statutory choral piece and fugue he had flagrantly transgressed academic rules made it virtually impossible for the jury to accept his candidature in the competition proper. Either one must attribute to Ravel an extraordinary degree of naivety or indeed of stupidity, or one must accept that at this point in his career, for one reason or another, he was coolly playing politics; for, to the outside observer, the Conservatoire's refusal to admit to the Prix de Rome a composer already adequately established in the 'outside' world seemed a grotesque blunder. Controversy rapidly ensued, dying down only after Dubois had resigned the directorship to be replaced by Fauré and a more open-minded administration. Ravel, for his part, escaped from Paris to join a yachting cruise in Holland with a party of friends, and plunged into one of the most fruitfully creative periods of his career.

Ravel's battles were now with certain sectors of critical opinion. He had every reason to feel he was making an original, totally individual contribution to French music: perhaps such a feeling helped sustain his work on a remarkable stream of pieces, the *Sonatine* and *Miroirs* for piano, the *Introduction et allegro* for harp and ensemble, the cycle *Histoires naturelles* and a number of other fine songs, the orchestral *Rapsodie espagnole* and his first opera, *L'heure espagnole*. Certainly he became irritated by the insistence of certain critics that everything worthwhile in new music must be traced back to Debussy. In 1906 he wrote to the critic Pierre Lalo, pointing out that *Jeux d'eau* could justly claim priority in the matter of a 'special type of writing for the piano' ascribed to Debussy. Whether or not Ravel's work influenced *Jardins sous la pluie* (as Orenstein has suggested), its last ripples certainly left their mark on *Pagodes*. Again in 1907 Lalo persistently found 'the unmistakable echo of Debussy's music' in the *Histoires naturelles*, and this somewhat odd opinion, together with the excessive asperity with which the work was attacked after its first performance, sparked off a further

156

15. *Maurice Ravel, 1907*

violent controversy in the Paris press. This time, the composer again chose to turn his back on the disputes, though Lalo now published Ravel's letter to him of the previous year.

L'heure espagnole followed a number of abandoned or unfinished opera projects. After his early attraction to the subject of *The Thousand and One Nights*, Ravel's next important project was an adaptation of Hauptmann's *Die versunkene Glocke*; he worked on this sporadically between 1906 and 1914, and eventually used some of the material from it in *L'enfant et les sortilèges*. Another text he seriously considered as a potential libretto was Maeterlinck's *Intérieur*. The literary stimulus behind some of his instrumental works of this period is clear too. *Gaspard de la nuit* was composed 'after Aloysius Bertrand' (his *Histoires vermoulues et poudreuses du Moyen Age*), and *Ma mère l'oye* is based on the fairy tales of Perrault, Mme d'Aulnoy and Leprince de Beaumont. The latter work, dedicated to the children of Ravel's friend Cyprien ('Cipa') Godebski, whom he had first met in 1904, was transcribed for orchestra and ultimately expanded into a ballet score; *Valses nobles et sentimentales* was similarly adapted for the stage. By this time, however, Ravel had composed his most ambitious stage work of all, the ballet *Daphnis et Chloé*, the composition of which occupied about three years (1909–12) and was the result of a commission from Dyagilev. The visit of the Ballets Russes to Paris in 1909 made a considerable impact on the work of several leading composers, some of whom were themselves to write ballets for the company. On Ravel, there was a further impact: his meeting with Stravinsky, the brilliant young composer who had orchestrated music by Grieg and Chopin for Dyagilev, and was soon to produce his own ballet *The Firebird*. (Stravinsky joined Les Apaches in 1909, the year in which Ravel was closely associated with the founding of the Société Musicale Indépendante, a group which, as its title suggests, promoted new music regardless of its aesthetic tendency.)

At this time Ravel undertook a surprising amount of ostensibly unspectacular musical work. He harmonized folksongs and made arrangements and orchestrations of his own and others' music, often for use in ballet productions. One such task, the preparation of a new performing version of Musorgsky's *Khovanshchina*, took him to Clarens (Switzerland) where he collaborated on the task with Stravinsky. This was in 1913, and not only did Ravel there see, and appreciate, the music of *The Rite of Spring*, but he acquainted himself with Stravinsky's *Three Japanese Lyrics*, the third of which is dedicated to him. This work, with its special way of combining voice and chamber ensemble, reflected the influence of Schoenberg's *Pierrot lunaire*, which Stravinsky had recently heard in Berlin; and thus Schoenberg may be said to have been the indirect stimulus behind Ravel's own *Trois poèmes de Stéphane Mallarmé* the first of which was completed in Clarens and dedicated to Stravinsky. The settings contain writing of notable complexity set off against nostalgic reminiscences of the *Shéhérazade* cycle. This work and the subsequent Piano Trio represent the culmination of Ravel's pre-war output, the piano pieces and songs completed within the next year being distinctly lesser productions. When war broke out he was at work on his Piano Trio, a composition more reminiscent (of the

String Quartet) than prophetic. But, as seen in a letter to
Roland-Manuel, many other schemes were in his head at
this time: *Zaspiak bat* (a piano concerto on Basque
themes), *Nuit romantique* (a piano work, possibly along
the lines of *Gaspard de la nuit*), the two projected
operas, *La cloche engloutie* and *Intérieur*, a symphonic
poem *Wien* and a 'French suite'. Of these, only the last
two were eventually to come to anything, as *La valse* and
Le tombeau de Couperin.

Meanwhile, however, the war itself was a shattering
influence on Ravel's life. Clearly he believed it the duty
of the artist to share his nation's experiences to the full.
To Jean Marnold he wrote: 'They tell me that Saint-
Saëns announces to the avid crowd that during the war
he has composed theatre music, songs, an elegy and a
piece for trumpets. If instead he had been servicing
howitzers, his music might have been the better for it'.
Desperately anxious to serve his country, and dis-
qualified from military service (because he was under-
weight by two kilograms), he made every endeavour to
enlist in the air force. But instead he became a driver
with the motor transport corps, an occupation he
ultimately found less rewarding than 'servicing howitzers': in summer 1916 the urge to compose and the
conviction that he was at the height of his powers welled
up and filled him with impatience. He fell ill with
dysentry, was taken to hospital, and travelled to Paris in
order to recuperate. Hardly had he arrived when his
mother died; she had been, and would continue to be,
the only true focus and sustenance of his sentient being:
children, animals, perhaps even treasured objects, but
no other adult elicited his deepest affections.

During the war years a number of French artists

turned their attention to reviving past national glories. Debussy's sonatas suggest precisely this kind of historical nationalism. In Ravel it is expressed in two works, in the archaism of his *Trois chansons* for mixed chorus (the words of which, like those of the earlier *Noël des jouets*, Ravel wrote himself), and in the Baroque dance forms of *Le tombeau de Couperin*. Each of the six movements of this suite is dedicated to the memory of a victim of the war. The work is the last in which Ravel evoked Baroque forms, and may be seen as a culmination of the tradition that embraced works by Chabrier, Chausson, Fauré, Debussy and of course Ravel himself. A number of causes – the war, sickness, but above all the emotional shock of his mother's death – slowed his creative processes so that the completion of *La valse* was delayed until 1920, and even then had only been spurred by a commission from Dyagilev.

With Debussy dead, there were many who now saw Ravel as the leading figure in French music. His success with the public had grown steadily since the early *Pavane* and *Jeux d'eau*, both of which had quickly established themselves as favourites with pianists in France and abroad. The String Quartet too was widely performed, and a broader degree of popularity with the concert-going public was won, during the year after the notoriety of the *Histoires naturelles* controversy, with his first important orchestral work, the *Rapsodie espagnole*. The next big landmark came with the production of *L'heure espagnole* at the Opéra-Comique in 1911; a year later, *Daphnis et Chloé* was staged and went into the touring repertory of the Ballets Russes. Ravel's was undoubtedly a position of eminence, and in 1920 the republic proposed to acknowledge the fact by conferring

16. *Leon Bakst's design (1912) for the first tableau of Ravel's 'Daphnis et Chloé'*

on him the order of the Légion d'honneur. But the proposal was made public before Ravel could either accept or refuse, and his subsequent refusal of the honour, as a matter of principle, created a similarly public stir. Again it seemed that ill feeling bedevilled Ravel's relations with officialdom, but here it is difficult to accuse him of calculated political manoeuvring in his dealings with authority. He must rather have viewed the establishment as a necessary evil, something from which he must find the quickest and shortest line of retreat into artistic privacy. The same need prompted him in 1920 to acquire a home outside Paris and from 1921 he lived in Montfort-l'Amaury.

Such a withdrawal had a peculiar aptness at the time when his work with Colette on *Ballet pour ma fille* (later to become *L'enfant et les sortilèges*) demanded the imaginative creation of a magical world of childhood. Here again the process of composition was slow and a work whose planning dated back to 1918 was not finished until early in 1925; and even then Ravel's work on it had been hastened by a deadline for the Monte Carlo Opera. In the meantime he had responded to three requests for commemorative pieces: a memorial to Debussy, a tribute to Fauré, and a contribution to the celebration of the quatercentenary of Ronsard's birth. The first of these, a duo for violin and cello, was expanded into a four-movement sonata. Other preoccupations of this period were some further orchestrations (including the famous version of Musorgsky's *Pictures at an Exhibition*), ill-fated projects such as that for a concertante work based on Alain-Fournier's novel *Le grand Meaulnes*, and the brilliant violin showpiece *Tzigane*; he had also started work on his Violin Sonata, though again this proved to be a considerably protracted labour. The *Chansons madécasses*, composed to meet a commission from Elizabeth Sprague Coolidge, came more swiftly from his pen; as a cycle for voice and chamber ensemble they are at once a natural continuation of his Mallarmé set and a bold advance on it.

Ravel's American tour of 1928 is important more as a personal and social experience than for any discernible creative stimulus it produced. His music had taken him abroad several times already: to Great Britain in 1909, and in 1911 and 1913; to Vienna in 1920; and during the 1920s to Holland, Italy, Spain, Scandinavia, Belgium, Germany, Switzerland and (again) Britain. These professional engagements generally happened after the composition of the work they might have seemed most likely to stimulate; *La valse*, for instance, was written before his visit to Vienna, and the 'Blues' movement of the Violin Sonata predates his tour of North America (one exception is the *Tzigane*, manifestly suggested by the playing of Jelly d'Arányi in London.) The four-month American tour had been arranged by Elie Robert Schmitz, president of the Pro-Musica Society, and in addition to a large number of concerts and recitals, it gave Ravel the opportunity to meet many noted personalities in the arts, including the cinema. Undoubtedly the experience was an exhausting one (Ravel referred to it as a 'crazy tour', and his itinerary meant spending many nights on train journeys), but it must have brought home to him the extraordinary acclaim his music had won him overseas. In the same year the conferring on him of an honorary doctorate at Oxford University reinforced the message.

From this time until 1932 Ravel was occupied with a

number of projects, some of them commissions of a rather unusual nature. Ida Rubinstein, the dancer, requiring a ballet with a Spanish flavour, first asked Ravel to orchestrate some pieces from Albéniz's *Iberia*, but the upshot was the composition of *Boléro*. The Concerto for the left hand was written for the one-armed pianist Paul Wittgenstein at the same time that Ravel was working on a Concerto in G for his own use. Ravel's collaboration was sought in a film based on Cervantes and featuring Shalyapin, resulting in the songs *Don Quichotte à Dulcinée*; this work and its subsequent orchestration represent the last music Ravel was to complete. Other projects held his interest for varying periods of time. Briefly and impulsively he planned to touch up the orchestration of Chabrier's opera *Le roi malgré lui*. An opera–oratorio on the subject of Joan of Arc was planned in 1929 and remained a serious possibility in his mind at least until 1933; although initially based on a text by Joseph Delteil, the work would undoubtedly have been coloured by Ravel's admiration for Shaw's *Saint Joan*. The last of his projects for the stage, like the first, was drawn from *The Thousand and One Nights*: an opera–ballet *Morgiane*, which seems tantalizingly to have evolved to near-completion in his mind but was not written down.

1932 marks the beginning of Ravel's tragic final period, during which he was totally at the mercy of his last illness, a progressively incapacitating Wernicke aphasia. Some commentators have traced the first warning symptoms back to the insomnia that began to assail him at the end of the war. He complained of 'cerebral anaemia' in 1926, and about a year later his doctor, Pasteur Vallery-Radot, advised him to rest for a year. A road accident in 1932 appeared to precipitate his illness, though this was later denied by the brain surgeon Clovis Vincent; certainly after this date his powers steadily declined, despite numerous efforts of sympathetic friends to stimulate and amuse him, including holidays abroad. Soon he was no longer able to sign his name, and he moved and spoke with increasing difficulty. His life revolved round occasional concert-going, visits from performers seeking advice, and above all the companionship of his brother and a small circle of friends. His death in Paris on 28 December 1937 followed an unsuccessful brain operation.

CHAPTER TWO

Creative personality, technique, works

Ravel felt an intense need for privacy. His sexual life was shrouded in secrecy; and he made a mystery of the creative process, exposing his music only when the final touch had been applied. Undoubtedly Ravel felt vulnerable. There is too little evidence for an adequate picture of his sexual relationships to be formed, although one cannot doubt that their nature would be relatable to, and hence liable to shed light on, other instances of self-expression: the music. However, where an over-zealous commentator has been compelled to eke out the slender direct evidence with assumptions deduced from the works, these deductions, in themselves incapable of fresh illumination of the music, fail to be of interest.

Ravel's vulnerability as an artist is more interesting. He felt music was his true vocation: 'It's lucky I've managed to write music, because I know perfectly well I should never have been able to do anything else'. But the peculiar nature of Ravel's creative mind imposed special conditions on the pursuit of that vocation. As Nichols has pointed out, while Debussy gave himself over to 'a search for new styles, new "musics" . . . for Ravel, the search lay not so much beyond him as inside him'. With Debussy music was in evolution; with Ravel it was in crystallization, and a quite exceptional spiritual stillness was needed for the process to be accomplished flawlessly. He worked in solitude and with intense concentration. The music took shape on 'long expeditions in the woods, whatever the weather; nightly walks across Paris'; then, abruptly, he would shut himself off from the world to transfer his work to paper.

Even to Ravel the process seemed magical, an alchemical distillation; it relied on precarious 'inspiration'. As he grew older composition became more difficult and laboured. On the one hand he matured as an artist, becoming more comprehensively aware of the complexities and contradictions in his own nature; on the other, particularly after the death of his father in 1908, he found it increasingly difficult to escape from the cares and responsibilities of mundane existence. Consequently his capacities as an artist became ever more precarious until at the last total impotence superseded. Ravel's insecurity is reflected in his music in two important ways. Firstly, 'everything had to be done – or seem to be done – by a miracle'. Ravel had extremely scrupulous ideas about professionalism in music. The finished score that came from his workshop had to be just that: finished with the highest degree of craftsmanship, in no need of further attention. It is reported that once the long and secret labour of creation was over Ravel tended to lose interest in the work he had produced. Certainly he saw the quality of that labour as all important. 'If each of you worked as I work', he said, 'you could achieve the same results.' The care expended on the smallest detail of his music, and the thoroughness that induced him, for instance, to ensure that in orchestral works the music for each family of instruments was as satisfactory in isolation as it was when considered as part of the whole, are precautions that most composers would regard as excessive, if not potentially detrimental; for Ravel they were a kind of insurance, perhaps all the more necessary after his academic failures at the Conservatoire.

The second symptom of his insecurity goes deeper, and is inseparable from his approach to composition as manifest in his technique. The idea of composition as crystallization has been suggested above; Ravel expressed it this way:

> In my own composition I judge a long period of gestation necessary. During this interval I come progressively, and with a growing precision, to see the form and the evolution that the final work will take in its totality. Thus I can be occupied for several years without writing a single note of the work, after which the composition goes relatively quickly. But one must spend time in eliminating all that could be regarded as superfluous in order to realize as completely as possible the definitive clarity so much desired.

Objective definition was an acute need. And at another level it led him, especially in his more rapidly composed works, to an unusual degree of reliance on objective treatment of his musical components – a feature to be examined more fully in the following consideration of his technique in relation to the works themselves. Here it is necessary only to note that he was aware of the bounds of his objectivity, and of the necessity of such bounds to the vitality of his art: 'If I could explain and demonstrate the value of my own works, that from my point of view at least would prove that they were constructed entirely from elements that were obvious, superficial and tangible, and therefore imperfect works of art'. The mysterious, whether seen as inspiration or as alchemy, was clearly understood to have a leading role in the process of composition.

Reference has already been made to Ravel's adoption of the dress and manners of the fin-de-siècle dandy; it is generally accepted, and certainly probable, that this guise served to compensate for his small stature which he felt to be a social disadvantage, and which did indeed prove a disadvantage when he wanted to join the armed forces. Always meticulous about his personal appearance, he was as unlikely to present himself as he was a composition to the world in an 'unfinished' state. Somewhat spoilt as a child, he retained a longing and an affinity for the pure and uncluttered emotional horizons of childhood. He remained a collector of mechanical toys and other small-scale bric-à-brac. His huge appetite for the exotic and the antique was coloured by a preference that they should be retailed through the distorting glass of a naive intermediary, as in a child's picture book: *Daphnis* was 'less concerned with archaism than with fidelity to the Greece of my dreams which is close to that imagined and painted by the French artists of the 18th century'; and Jankélévitch has expanded on this, pointing out that Verlaine and de Régnier, favourite poets of Ravel, were largely responsible for bringing the 18th century into vogue, that the composer of the *Chansons madécasses* and *Shéhérazade* turned first to the poetry of Evariste Parny and to Galland's translation of *The Thousand and One Nights*, and that *Ma mère l'oye* is reminiscent of Boucher's pictures, the *Menuet antique* of Watteau. Finally, *L'enfant et les sortilèges* shows that Ravel could still understand the child's wilful and dictatorial response to the warm security of his mother's love: and performers associated with him found that not only did he know precisely what he wanted, but also he possessed enough blind determination to settle for nothing less.

Ravel's technique relied to an unusual extent on the manipulation of musical objects. In this context the term requires explanation, particularly as here Ravel was a pioneer. A musical object suggests a musical element considered in its own right as self-sufficient (an end in itself, as it were), hence free from the functional roles expected of musical subjects. The nature of the element, like that of the physical object, will be more or less synoptic (in other words, perceivable from a single standpoint), but whereas in physical objects this quality is extenuated by extension in space, in musical objects it is extenuated by extension in time. Since the object cannot actively participate in 'subjective' functions (those normally associated with musical exposition and development), its temporal extension must be constituted either of stasis or of some form of 'objective' (i.e. mechanical, automatic) movement. Examples would be, in the former case, the exceptionally sustained or exceptionally isolated note or chord, and in the latter case rigidly patterned movement as in ostinato figures; an example of the two combined would be a repetitive pedal point. (It is worth distinguishing from an object a 'motif', a term that self-evidently expresses an active function.)

Composition has always made use of musical objects, which in certain epochs have tended to be more synoptic than in others. The tension between the active (subject) and the passive (object) has been a sustaining feature in most styles of Western music. But it would be hard to discover a composer before Ravel who devoted so much

171

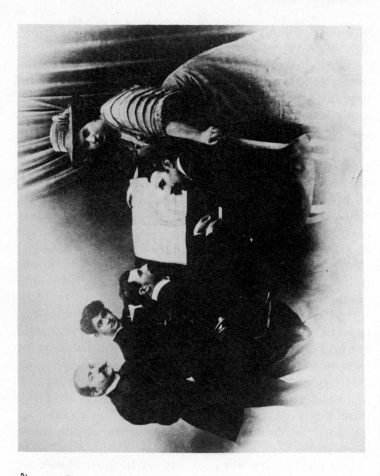

17. *Ravel with the group 'Les Apaches', c1908: (from left to right) Robert Mortier, L'Abbé Léonce Petit, Maurice Ravel, Ricardo Viñes and Jane Mortier*

172

of his imaginative passion to the minting of elaborate but virtually tangible musical complexes whose sole role is as passive stabilizer or sheet-anchor, or even as independent mechanism to fascinate the ear (commentators are apt to recall knowingly that Pierre Joseph's work as an engineer held a like fascination for his son). Ravel's consuming artistic concern was a quest for 'l'objet juste', a pursuit of striking musical imagery, which often enough was also required to correspond (in the Baudelairean sense) with some poetic or dramatic conception. The labour expended on this search was imaginatively rather than intellectually intense, and the end result varied from the exhilarating to the platitudinous. (Professionalism is by no means synonymous with artistic self-criticism.) Whether delicate or massive, however, all Ravel's objects give the feeling of beautifully sculptured solidity.

This tendency has been mentioned as being related to Ravel's feelings of insecurity: the artist who lacks confidence in his 'subjective' powers of musical discourse may be expected to take refuge in the presumed strength of impersonal artifice. Confluent tendencies in Ravel's music support this view. He required a near-absolute power of certainty with relation to his work. His frequent recourse to small-scale construction, or adherence to traditional forms, have led some observers to class him as a miniaturist or as a parasitic manipulator; and his penchant for the synoptical and the mechanical, often seen as a corollary to his weakness for figurines and clockwork toys, is also taken into account by Stravinsky's famous description of him as a 'Swiss watchmaker'. A further screen is that of stylization: the use of modes, generally to suggest antique or exotic scales; the application of characteristic gestures from Baroque or national styles (which may be taken to include jazz); and the imitation or development of a particular stylistic model, generally in homage rather than pastiche. To the extent that this stylization was 'mechanical', candidly imitative, the result would be objective; and referential musical objects, often termed 'symbols', are the materials of irony in music. Hence the link some critics have seen between the composer of the *Histoires naturelles* and Mahler. Yet another mooring, at a period when tonality was being subjected to vigorous and effective questioning, was Ravel's firm adherence to the traditional diatonic system; for all his harmonic inventiveness, his notions of the permissible and the undesirable were inflexibly dogmatic as compared, for instance, with those of Stravinsky. In all these traits, and in the very professionalism mentioned earlier, one sees Ravel's need to exercise an extraordinary degree of control over his musical output. He spoke of the work of art as a 'ripened conception where no detail has been left to chance'.

This attitude has disturbed many listeners; it is seemingly incompatible with spontaneity of utterance. Jankélévitch has pointed out that even when the style is improvisatory, the means remain strictly under control: in the capricious chromaticism of *Noctuelles* and *Oiseaux tristes*, or the rubato effects in *La valse* and *Tzigane*; to which one might add the jazz-like syncopations in the Concerto for the left hand. However, as Jankélévitch said, there is no justification for confusing calculation and stylization with lack of expressiveness. Indeed, much of the effort Ravel put into the invention of his musical objects was directed towards making them evident and adequate symbols of a wide variety of human feeling and experience. It would be fair to say that he was less anxious to depict external reality than to select those qualities of it that made it peculiarly accessible to a kind of sympathetic perception: he not so much portrayed nature as captured its effect on human sensibilities. There is no lack of expressiveness; it is merely that the sensibilities are frequently borrowed, from children or the naive, Ravel diffidently masking or suppressing his own.

Some of the many possible critical approaches to Ravel's music have been more attractive than others. Perhaps the most obvious is that which maintains that Ravel was a master of musical miniatures, and that his emotional range was correspondingly cramped. Those who find these attributes blameless applaud him most when he was being true to them: in 'gem-like' miniatures (such as the *Sonatine*, perhaps) or in re-creations of an idealized childhood (as in *Ma mère l'oye*); but those who feel shame at such innocent delights tend to prefer the Ravel of bold, large-scale forms (*La valse*, the Concerto for the left hand) and darker, maturer awarenesses (these same works). Some admire the highly sophisticated preciosity of the *Valses nobles et sentimentales*; others acclaim the broader strokes of *Daphnis et Chloé*. The automatism of *Jeux d'eau* may be weighed against the deliberative invention of the Adagio assai from the G major Concerto. A further approach might concentrate on the sheer quality of his invention, which could veer abruptly between the banal and the original from one piece to the next (*Une barque sur l'océan* to *Alborado del gracioso*, for instance). One doubts whether Ravel would have been unaware of these potential criticisms: but they are likely to be finally irrelevant, as they were seemingly irrelevant to Ravel's own purposes. For these are criticisms proper to the subjective composer. (It is, for instance, a requirement only of subjective truth that a high level of inventive quality should at all times be maintained.)

As a final precaution against insecurity, Ravel adopted a detached attitude to his art: it was for him an 'act', possibly of imitation, possibly of reportage. This left him free to disclaim intimate involvement, free, that is, to place his music beyond the bounds of traditional humanistic criticism. The decisive charge against Ravel would seem to be that of coolness: he was the somewhat disavowing type of artist who stood aside from his creation and 'pared his fingernails'. The weight of this charge will always depend on the general tendency of public and critical opinion at any time. It has been felt that anything less than the earnestness of Debussy and Schoenberg amounted to irresponsibility at a period when music was passing through the intense crisis of dissolving tonality, and it is possible in this light to view the irony, parody, imitation and other 'second-order creation' of Ravel as a facet of that fatally aimless cleverness which is a symptom of cultural decadence. (One may here aptly quote the epigraph of *Valses nobles et sentimentales*: 'le plaisir délicieux et toujours nouveau d'une occupation inutile'.) However, when cultural values are in doubt it is proper to bear in mind that the vice of one age may be the virtue of another; and that even without such clearcut idealism, the sharp, clear, refining personality of Ravel's music will exert its due attraction.

There are several strikingly recurrent features in

Ravel's technique, among the most evident being the musical objects already discussed. One of his earliest surviving manuscripts (the Verlaine setting *Le ciel est, pardessus le toit*, *c*1892) already shows heavy reliance on the hypnotic reiteration of a single accompaniment figure. In the *Habanera* (1895), however, the object in question is a pedal point on a characteristic Spanish rhythmic ostinato; and in his treatment of it Ravel transcended everything that had gone before. The reiterated note, a dominant C♯, is established as a 'solid' object, so that even a chord featuring its semitonal neighbours B♯ and D cannot quieten it; there arises what in a later age would be called a 'cluster'. But the clash is far from gratuitous; Ravel claimed that it derived from bar 16 of the first movement of Beethoven's 'Moonlight' Sonata. Although melodically Ravel was here largely working in the Phrygian mode, his harmonies are traditionally, if somewhat elliptically diatonic. The typical quasi-tonic role of the dominant in Spanish folk music provides the explanation of Ravel's cluster as a quasi-Neapolitan 6th over the ostinato pedal. (That this Phrygian melodic inflection was associated with the Spanish idiom in Ravel's mind is confirmed by the shape of the *Boléro* tune; that it may also have Basque connections is suggested by the closing passage of the reportedly Basque-flavoured first movement of the G major Concerto.)

This use of the repeated note was to become a hallmark of Ravel's style, especially in his piano music, and memorably in *Miroirs* and *Gaspard de la nuit*; but as an ostinato device on a dominant (or quasi-tonic) C♯ it was to recur with curious insistence not only in Ravel's own *Alborada del gracioso*, but also in Debussy's

177

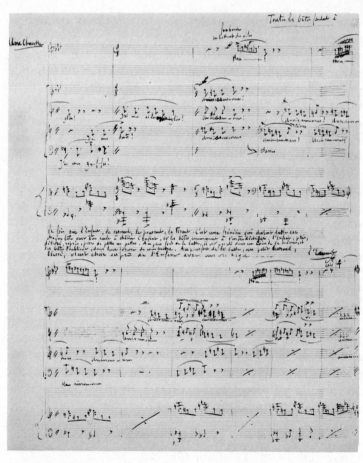

18. Part of the autograph vocal score of 'L'enfant et les sortilèges' by Ravel, composed 1920–25

Lindaraja and *Soirée dans Grenade*. Indeed, it is hardly far-fetched to find echoes of it in Messiaen's *Turangalîla* more than half a century later: such was the impact of the startlingly original *Habanera*, which Ravel incorporated in his orchestral *Rapsodie espagnole* of 1907–8. It should also be noted that such was his feeling for traditional tonality that discords like the clusters of the *Habanera* tend to be both more acute and more tonally unequivocal than comparable clashes in Debussy; only in rare cases does one find the emancipated discord in Ravel: he himself singled out the *Chansons madécasses* as a work he probably could not have composed without the example of Schoenberg. Another work of 1895, the *Menuet antique*, also features (in its opening phrase) the simultaneous use of a tonic pedal with a cadential formula, though the repeated note here, F♯, immediately discloses itself as part of a melody. Again Ravel made play with the contrast between modal melody and diatonic harmony, the latter making an unconvincing attempt to mimic the *style galant* which had already been more smoothly exploited by Fauré (*Clair de lune* op.46 no.2) and Debussy (*Suite bergamasque*), to name but two.

Another early feature of Ravel's harmony which was to persist as a conscious technique was his exploitation of parallel chords; indeed, these, with all the 'forbidden' consecutive intervals they entailed, became such a firm feature of his writing that they are to be found in his otherwise justifiably atypical Prix de Rome essay, *L'aurore* (1905). Satie and, to a lesser extent, Chabrier are the obvious influences in this respect, especially where chords of the 9th and 11th are introduced. *Entre cloches* is an interesting example, summing up Ravel's discoveries of the 1890s. The parallel chords are used as an ostinato pealing figure to support progressions of quite sophisticated chords (for instance the natural 11th of the final plagal cadence) which verge on bitonality. The harmonies are so unrestrained as to suggest the naivety that Ravel later more carefully planned in the parallel triads of *Noël des jouets* (1905), which anticipates a similar device in Stravinsky's *Petrushka.*

Ravel constantly found varied uses both for bare organum-like 4ths and 5ths and for consecutive triads. In addition to *Entre cloches*, the song *Ronsard à son âme* (1924) uses the former for a particular 'programmatic' effect; more subtle is the extract from *L'enfant et les sortilèges* shown in ex.1, where an effect of wistful aimlessness is achieved by combining bare 4ths with irregular metrical groupings. (An interesting comparison may be made with 'Petit Poucet' from *Ma mère l'oye*, where 'bare' 3rds are used in a similar situation.)

Ex.1

Sometimes parallel intervals are designed to yield a purely timbral effect, in imitation of an organ stop ('Fanfare' for *L'éventail de Jeanne*, 1927; *Boléro*).

The use of triads is somewhat more complex. At its simplest there is again the suggestion of mere reinforcement, as in scalic passages in the 'Danse générale' of *Daphnis et Chloé* and at the end of the first movement of the G major Concerto. The same principle applies in more elaborate and thematic patterns, where 'automatic' block harmonization suggests timbre rather than tonality (see ex.2, from the finale of the Piano Trio). Sometimes, however, a specifically harmonic direction is introduced by admitting irregularities, both in chord position and in mode. Thus a certain harmonic pull (without resolution) is present in the repeated five-chord figure which closes *Frontispice* (1918). An example from the 'Musette' of *Le tombeau de Couperin* (ex.3) demonstrates the flexible use of parallel harmonies in a typical confrontation between modal and diatonic elements (the use of a pedal point is not peculiar to this example, and indeed accompanies parallel harmonies quite frequently in Ravel's music).

Before proceeding to more elaborate chords, mention may be made here of Ravel's early use of parallel octaves (or, more typically, 15ths or 22nds). Where treble and bass are thus coupled (*Habanera*, *Pavane pour une infante défunte*, the first movement of the *Sonatine*) it is fair to remark the influence of Chabrier, although, as Cooper has pointed out, it often appears to be Puccini who is invoked (the Quartet's first movement, the *Introduction et allegro, Petit poucet* etc). Of parallel dissonant chords, the most obvious use is again timbral. Perhaps the most typical in Ravel is the diminished octave, which appears in all manner of conjunctions. The consecutives that open *Alborada del gracioso* are particularly striking in that they also illustrate a characteristic harmonic progression, which may be summarized as tonic–dominant–flattened leading note–subdominant. The same progression underlies the chromatically sliding added-note chords of *Le martin-pêcheur* (*Histoires naturelles*), but here Ravel was thinking rather of passing notes and their resolution than of timbres. But a lengthy progression may itself become a mechanical gesture, a mere procession, so that the repeated sequence of dominant chords in the introduction to *L'heure espagnole* once again expresses ironic detachment (and it is again difficult to avoid the thought that the quality of Ravel's musical ideas is often beyond, or beneath, criticism).

Much of Ravel's harmonic language is indeed to be understood in terms of chromatic passing notes and appoggiaturas, often resolving on to further discords or in the 'wrong' octave. There is frequently considerable freedom in the treatment of dissonance and of abrupt juxtaposition of conflicting harmonies. Tritonal contrasts of common chords are evident throughout, from the *Shéhérazade* overture and *Jeux d'eau* to the Concerto for the left hand; there is an instance in ex.2. Ravel was clearly drawn to bitonality, and an effect of distinct and independent tonalities is particularly noticeable in certain postwar works (*Frontispice*, the Sonata for violin and cello, *L'enfant et les sortilèges*). Yet, by a superb paradox, the 'masculine' asperity of key clashes often belies their origins in (unresolved) conventional feminine closes. In a letter to René Lenormand, Ravel showed the monotonal basis of the trio section of the seventh of the *Valses nobles et sentimentales*; and the same principle is applicable to superficially bitonal passages in, for example, the Violin Sonata and the G major Concerto. In Ravel's sensibility there is every justification for analysis in terms of 'yearning' appoggiaturas, whereas one would hardly adopt this approach to a composer like Milhaud.

A similar affective quality, characterized by prominent use of the falling 4th – whether on to, or leading to, resolution (*Sonatine*, first movement, second-time bar), or unresolved (close of *L'enfant et les sortilèges*) – has been noted as a feature of Ravel's melodic thought. His friend and interpreter Jacques Février, in teaching this movement of the *Sonatine*, insisted the falling 4th should echo the opera's close in evoking the word 'maman'. The opening bars of the *Valses nobles et sentimentales* (ex.4) show this feature as a motif related to the harmonic progression remarked on in *Alborada del gracioso*: as a

Ex.4

melody it is transposed to different degrees (mediant–leading note–supertonic–submediant); it is subjected to octave displacements (though the altered form in its reappearance in the eighth waltz, tonic–dominant–

183

flattened leading note–dominant, respects the 'true' registers); and chromatic appoggiaturas and passing notes appear in the harmonization (upward-tending in bar 1, downward in bar 2). Such sequences may be classed as 'melodic objects'; so may the pentatonic and modal motifs used for ironic evocation in 'Asie' (*Shéhérazade*), 'Laideronnette' (*Ma mère l'oye*) and the cup's aria in *L'enfant et les sortilèges* and found also in *Sainte*, *Jeux d'eau* and the Concerto for the left hand. In addition, gapped scales and modes form the basis of many more extended and shapely melodies, a particular favourite being a Dorian lacking second and seventh notes (found by Roland-Manuel in *Menuet antique*, *D'Anne jouant de l'espinette*, *Daphnis et Chloé* and the G major Concerto). Ravel liked to give interest to his melodies by building them on irregular metrical schemes: the Piano Trio contains more than one example; and in his earliest works 5/4 (*D'Anne jouant de l'espinette*), 7/8 (Violin Sonata, 1897), 10/8 (*Entre cloches*) and mixed signatures (*Shéhérazade* overture) are to be found. Sequential writing builds up irregular phrase lengths in the *Pavane pour une infante défunte*. Where Ravel composed melodies of exceptional scope and breadth there is usually a sense of deliberate effort. Notable examples may be found in the 'Rigaudon' from *Le tombeau de Couperin*, the central movement of the G major Concerto (castigated by Constant Lambert as 'artificial melody') and the fine opening passage of the Concerto for the left hand.

Three distinct influences marked Ravel's treatment of the piano. Chabrier's is especially prominent in the 'Spanish' pieces: *Habanera* owes something to Chabrier's piano piece of the same name; but *Alborada del gracioso*

19. *Maurice Ravel*

is far more redolent of the orchestral *España*. When Ravel came to write his *Valses nobles et sentimentales* it is clear that he was frequently mindful of the *Trois valses romantiques* (there are echoes of the second in particular). There is more than a trace of the piano accompaniments to Chabrier's animal songs in *Histoires naturelles*. And, though it is hard to endorse Jankélévitch's description of *Menuet antique* as 'the twin of the *Menuet pompeux*' (a work orchestrated by Ravel in 1918), it is possible that Chabrier's *Bourrée fantasque* figured in Ravel's mind (alongside Balakirev's *Islamey*) as a precursor of *Scarbo*. Another precursor, and always a significant influence, was Liszt, Ravel's admiration for whom counterbalanced his mature distaste for Wagner. Apart from their shared taste for virtuoso fireworks. Ravel adopted a Lisztian point of view in many of his paintings from nature (*Jeux d'eau, Noctuelles, Une barque sur l'océan* and the song *Les grands vents venus d'outremer*, 1907). Finally the Baroque keyboard composers provided models for the more archaic pieces, and it is notable that preparatory to composing *Le tombeau de Couperin* Ravel transcribed a *forlane* by Couperin.

In 1889 Ravel heard Rimsky-Korsakov conduct the *Capriccio espagnol*, and in his own works he combined the Russian's skill in blending and balancing with a personal appreciation of individual timbres. His acute awareness of the expressive potential of each instrument gives high definition to his instrumentation and leads to effects of striking originality. His love of timbral eventfulness could result in moments of trite vulgarity; but the complex crowding of densities which has offended some in *La valse* and elsewhere is, on the other hand, surely aesthetically justifiable. Ravel took a keen interest in instrumental technique; it must, however, be admitted that it was a composer's interest in what was even barely possible rather than a performer's interest in what was, in terms of instrument design, natural.

On the whole Ravel retained formal models well tested as suitable to diatonic language (a notable exception is his imitation of the Malayan *pantoum* form in the second movement of the Piano Trio); the use of ternary and sonata forms generally satisfied his need for formal poise, and where these seemed too obvious he obscured their outlines by rudimentary camouflage or curtailment. On a broader scale, his handling of dramatic forms is ingenious and convincing, though the expansive assurance of *Daphnis et Chloé* is won at the expense of characteristic detail. The design of *La valse* is bold and simple; the *Valses nobles et sentimentales* are enriched by their retrospective finale; and in the Concerto for the left hand he slotted a variety of formal types into a single movement. Better suited to the reception of musical objects is the open-ended type of form typified by *moto perpetuo*. A fairly conventional example is the finale of the Violin Sonata; more suggestive is the brief *Frontispice*, whose closing chords in the manner of Satie are an ill-fitting stopper: Schoenberg more frankly left the third of his 1909 Orchestral Pieces unfinished.

Ravel's few pupils, of whom the most creatively noteworthy were Delage, Vaughan Williams and Roland-Manuel, were disinclined to mimic their teacher: his music was simply too finished to invite emulation, and he himself was a great imitator. His attitude as a composer, however, has been a considerable influence on 20th-century music. As a promoter of musical objectivity he paved the way for Stravinsky and the whole anti-Romantic school which flourished in the 1920s and early 1930s. And at its most extreme (perhaps in the opening of *L'heure espagnole*) his enthusiasm for mechanical precision and perfection anticipated the cogs and springs of later composers – of Ligeti, for example, and Riley. His own music continues to live; its sheer elegance to delight; its pungent 'guilt-edged' sensuousness to speak; and its wistful pursuit of innocence to fascinate.

Numbers in right-hand margins denote references in the text.

Only works published and/or performed are included; for others see Orenstein (1975), 242ff.

OPERAS

L'heure espagnole (comédie musicale, 1, Franc-Nohain), 1907–9; Paris, Opéra-Comique, 19 May 1911 — 156, 158, 161, 182, 187

L'enfant et les sortilèges (fantaisie lyrique, 2 parts, Colette), 1920–25; Monte Carlo, 21 March 1925 — 158, 163, 170, 178, 180, 182, 183, 184

BALLETS AND ORCHESTRAL

Shéhérazade, ouverture de féerie, 1898 — 153, 154, 182, 184

Une barque sur l'océan [after pf work], 1906, 2nd version perf. 1926

Rapsodie espagnole, 1907–8: Prélude à la nuit, Malagueña, Habanera [after pf work], Feria — 156, 161, 179

Pavane pour une infante défunte [after pf work], 1910

Ma mère l'oye (ballet, Ravel) [after pf work, with additional movts and interludes], 1911; Paris, Arts, 28 Jan 1912 — 158

Daphnis et Chloé (symphonie chorégraphique, 3 movts, Fokin, after Longus), 1909–12; Paris, Châtelet, 8 June 1912 — 158, 161, 162, 170, 175, 180, 184, 187

Suite no.1 from 'Daphnis et Chloé', 1911: Nocturne, Interlude, Danse guerrière

Suite no.2 from 'Daphnis et Chloé', 1913: Lever du jour, Pantomime, Danse générale — 165

Valses nobles et sentimentales [after pf work], 1912; score used for Adelaïde, ou Le langage des fleurs (ballet, Ravel), Paris, Châtelet, 22 April 1912 — 158

Alborada del gracioso [after pf work], 1918

Le tombeau de Couperin [after nos.1, 3, 5 and 4 of pf work], 1919; score, excluding no.1, used for ballet, Paris, Champs-Elysées, 8 Nov 1920 — 164, 170, 179

La valse, poème chorégraphique, 1919–20; score used for ballet, Paris, Opéra, 20 Nov 1928 — 68, 160, 161, 164, 174, 175, 186, 187

Tzigane, rapsodie de concert [after work for vn, pf], vn, orch, 1924 — 164, 174

Fanfare (for ballet L'éventail de Jeanne, Y. Franck, A. Bourgat), 1927; Paris, Opéra, 4 March 1929 — 180

Boléro (ballet), 1928: Paris, Opéra, 22 Nov 1928 — 165, 177, 180

Menuet antique [after pf work], 1929 — 165, 174, 175, 182, 184, 187

Piano Concerto for the left hand, 1929–30 — 165, 175, 180, 183, 184

Piano Concerto, G, 1929–31

VOCAL
(with orchestra)

Myrrha (F. Beissier), cantata, 3 solo vv, orch, 1901 — 154

Alcyone (E. and E. Adénis), cantata, 3 solo vv, orch, 1902 — 154

Alyssa (M. Coiffier), cantata, 3 solo vv, orch, 1903 — 154

Manteau de fleurs [after song with pf], 1v, orch

Shéhérazade (T. Klingsor), Méz, orch, 1903: Asie, La flûte enchantée, L'indifférent — 155, 159, 170, 184

Noël des jouets [after song with pf], 1v, orch, 1905, 2nd version 1913 — 161

Chanson de la mariée, Tout gai [after nos.1 and 5 of song cycle Cinq mélodies populaires grecques], 1v, orch

Deux mélodies hébraïques [after songs with pf], 1v, orch, 1919

Chanson hébraïque [after no.4 of song cycle Chants populaires], 1v, orch, 1923–4

Don Quichotte à Dulcinée (P. Morand), Bar, orch, 1932–3: Chanson romanesque, Chanson épique, Chanson à boire — 165

Ronsard à son âme [after song with pf], 1v, orch, 1935

(with ensemble)

Trois poèmes de Stéphane Mallarmé, 1v, pic, fl, cl, b cl, pf, str qt, 1913: Soupir, Placet futile, Surgi de la croupe et du bond — 159, 164

Chansons madécasses (E.-D. de Parny), 1v, fl, pf, vc, 1925–6: Nahandove, Aoua!, Il est doux … — 164, 170, 179

Les bayadères tournent légères, S, chorus, orch, 1900

Tout est lumière, S, chorus, orch, 1901

La nuit, S, chorus, orch, 1902

Matinée de Provence, S, chorus, orch, 1903

L'aurore, T, chorus, orch, 1905 — 155, 179

(choral)

Trois chansons (Ravel), SATB, 1914–15: Nicolette, Trois beaux oiseaux du paradis, Ronde — 161

A la manière de . . ., 1913: Borodine, Chabrier
Prélude, 1913
Le tombeau de Couperin, 1914–17: Prélude, Fugue, Forlane,   160, 161, 181,
Rigaudon, Menuet, Toccata   184, 186
Frontispice, 2 pf 5 hands, 1918   181, 182, 187
La valse [after orch work], 2 pf (1921)
Boléro [after orch work], 2 pf (1930)

ARRANGEMENTS, EDITION   107, 159
(orchestrations)
N. Rimsky-Korsakov: Antar: excerpts, partly reorchd for use as inciden-
tal music, c1910
M. Musorgsky: Khovanshchina, c1913, collab. Stravinsky   159
E. Satie: Le fils des étoiles: Prélude, 1913
R. Schumann: Carnaval: Préambule, Valse allemande, Paganini,
Marche des 'Davidsbündler' contre les philistins, for use as ballet,
c1914, other nos. lost
E. Chabrier: Dix pièces pittoresques: Menuet pompeux, for use as ballet,   186
1918
C. Debussy: Pour le piano: Sarabande, 1922   85
——: Tarantelle styrienne, as Danse, 1922
M. Musorgsky: Tableaux d'une exposition, 1922   163

(piano reductions)
F. Delius: Margot la rouge, vocal score, 1902
C. Debussy: Nocturnes, 2 pf, 1909
——: Prélude à 'L'après-midi d'un faune', 4 hands, 1910

F. Mendelssohn: Complete works for piano solo and piano concertos,   (edition)
1915–17
Principal publishers: Durand, Eschig

WRITINGS
'Concert Lamoureux', BSIM, viii (1912), Feb, 62
'Concerts Lamoureux', BSIM, viii (1912), March, 50
'Les "Tableaux symphoniques" de M. Fanelli', BSIM, viii (1912), April, 55
'A propos des "Images" de Claude Debussy', Cahiers d'aujourd'hui (1913), Feb, 135
'Au Théâtre des Arts', Comoedia illustré, v (5 Feb 1913), 417
'Boris Gudounoff', Comoedia illustré, v (5 June 1913)
'Fervaal – poème et musique de Vincent d'Indy', Comoedia illustré, v (20 Jan 1913), 361
'La sorcière à l'Opéra-Comique', Comoedia illustré, v (5 Jan 1913), 320
'A l'Opéra-Comique', Comoedia illustré, vi (20 Jan 1914), 390
'Les nouveaux spectacles de la saison russe – Le rossignol', Comoedia illustré, vi (June 1914), 811
'Parsifal – version française d'Alfred Ernst', Comoedia illustré, vi (20 Jan 1914), 400
'Les mélodies de Gabriel Fauré', ReM, iii/11 (1922), 22
'Contemporary Music', Rice Institute Pamphlet, xv (1928), April, 131; repr. in RdM, 1 (1964), 208
Article on the pf concs., Daily Telegraph (16 July 1931)
ed. Roland-Manuel: 'Une esquisse autobiographique de Maurice Ravel', ReM (1938), no.187, p.17
ed. R. Chalupt and M. Gerar: Ravel au miroir de ses lettres (Paris, 1956)

BIBLIOGRAPHY

CATALOGUES

Catalogue de l'oeuvre de Maurice Ravel (Paris, 1954)
Catalogue de l'exposition Ravel (Paris, 1975)

MONOGRAPHS

Roland-Manuel: *Maurice Ravel et son oeuvre* (Paris, 1914)
———: *Maurice Ravel et son oeuvre dramatique* (Paris, 1928)
W.-L. Landowsky: *Maurice Ravel, sa vie, son oeuvre* (Paris, 1938, 2/1950)
Roland-Manuel: *A la gloire de Ravel* (Paris, 1938, 2/1948; Eng. trans., 1947)
V. Jankélévitch: *Maurice Ravel* (Paris, 1939, 2/1956; Eng. trans., 2/1959)
Colette and others: *Maurice Ravel par quelques-uns de ses familiers* (Paris, 1939)
M. Goss: *Bolero: the Life of Maurice Ravel* (New York, 1940)
K. Akeret: *Studien zum Klavierwerk von Maurice Ravel* (Zurich, 1941)
T. Aubin and others: *Maurice Ravel* (Paris, 1945)
H. Jourdan-Morhange: *Ravel et nous* (Geneva, 1945)
N. Demuth: *Ravel* (London, 1947)
A. Machabey: *Maurice Ravel* (Paris, 1947)
F. Onnen: *Maurice Ravel* (Stockholm, 1947)
R. Malipiero: *Maurice Ravel* (Milan, 1948)
L.-P. Fargue: *Maurice Ravel* (Paris, 1949)
J. Bruyr: *Maurice Ravel ou Le lyrisme et les sortilèges* (Paris, 1950)
L. La Pegna: *Ravel* (Brescia, 1950)
W. Tappolet: *Maurice Ravel: Leben und Werk* (Olten, 1950)
V. Perlemuter and H. Jourdan-Morhange: *Ravel d'après Ravel* (Lausanne, 1953)
V. Seroff: *Maurice Ravel* (New York, 1953)
J. van Ackere: *Maurice Ravel* (Brussels, 1957)
J. Geraedts: *Ravel* (Haarlem, 1957)
R. de Fragny: *Maurice Ravel* (Lyons, 1960)
R. Myers: *Ravel: Life and Works* (London, 1960)
G. Léon: *Maurice Ravel* (Paris, 1964)
H. H. Stuckenschmidt: *Maurice Ravel: Variationen über Person und Werk* (Frankfurt, 1966; Eng. trans., 1969)
P. Petit: *Ravel* (Paris, 1970)
M. Long: *Au piano avec Maurice Ravel* (Paris, 1971; Eng. trans., 1973)
A. Orenstein: *Ravel: Man and Musician* (New York, 1975) [incl. full bibliography]
R. Nichols: *Ravel* (London, 1977)

191

INTERVIEWS

L. Laloy: 'Wagner et les musiciens d'aujourd'hui – opinions de MM. Florent Schmitt et Maurice Ravel', *Grande revue* (10 May 1909), 160

M. Montabré: 'Entretien avec Maurice Ravel', *L'intransigeant* (28 Jan 1923)

'Entretien avec Ravel', *ReM*, no.113 (1931)

'Tien opinies van M. Ravel', *De telegraaf* (7 April 1932)

OTHER LITERATURE

T. Klingsor: 'Les musiciens et les poètes contemporains', *Mercure de France* (1900), Nov, 430

P. Lalo: 'Encore le Debussysme: une lettre de M. Ravel', *Le temps* (9 April 1907)

Roland-Manuel: 'Maurice Ravel', *ReM*, ii/6 (1921), 1

F. Shera: *Debussy and Ravel* (Oxford, 1925)

ReM, vi/8 (1925) [Ravel issue]

ReM (1938), no.187 [Ravel issue]

ReM (1939), no.188 [articles by J.-R. Bloch, Roland-Manuel and H. Sauguet]

M. de Falla: 'Notes sur Ravel', *ReM* (1939), no.189, p.81

J. Février: 'Les exigences de Ravel', *Revue internationale de musique* (1939), April, 893

M.-D. Calvocoressi: 'Ravel's Letters to Calvocoressi', *MQ*, xxvii (1941), 1

——: 'When Ravel Composed to Order', *ML*, xxii (1941), 54

R. de Fragny: 'Les inédits de Maurice Ravel', *Concorde* (11 April 1946)

Melos, xiv/12 (1947) [Ravel issue]

T. Alajouanine: 'Aphasia and Artistic Realization', *Brain*, lxxi/3 (1948), 231

P. Boulez: 'Trajectoires: Ravel, Stravinsky, Schoenberg', *Contrepoints* (1949), no.6, p.122; repr. in *Relevés d'apprenti* (Paris, 1966; Eng. trans., 1968)

Roland-Manuel: 'Lettres de Maurice Ravel et documents inédits', *RdM*, xxxviii (1956), 49

ReM (1958), no.243 [articles by R. Chalupt, R. Dumesnil, V. Jankélévitch, T. Klingsor and A. Mirambel]

J. van der Veen: 'Problèmes structuraux chez Maurice Ravel', *IMSCR*, vii *Cologne 1958*, 289

F. Lesure: ' "L'affaire" Debussy–Ravel: lettres inédites', *Festschrift Friedrich Blume* (Kassel, 1963), 231

J. Braun: *Die Thematik in den Kammermusikwerken von Maurice Ravel* (Regensburg, 1966)

Bibliography

A. Orenstein: 'L'enfant et les sortilèges: correspondence inédite de Ravel et Colette', *RdM*, lii (1966), 215

——: 'Maurice Ravel's Creative Process', *MQ*, liii (1967), 467

——: 'Some Unpublished Music and Letters by Maurice Ravel', *Music Forum*, iii (1973), 291–334

H. Macdonald: 'Ravel and the Prix de Rome', *MT*, cxvi (1975), 332

J.-M. Nectoux: 'Ravel/Fauré et les Débuts de la Société Musicale Indépendante', *RdM*, lxi (1975), 295

B. Newbould: 'Ravel's Pantoum', *MT*, cxvi (1975), 228

G. Sannemüller: 'Die Sonate für Violine und Violoncello von Maurice Ravel', *Mf*, xxviii (1975), 408

D. Pistone, ed.: 'Maurice Ravel au XXe siècle', *Table ronde internationale* (Paris, 1976)

J.-M. Nectoux: 'Maurice Ravel et sa bibliothèque musicale', *FAM*, xxiv (1977), 199

R. Grouquist: 'Ravel's Trois poèmes de Stéphane Mallarmé', *MQ*, lxiv (1978), 507

R. Viñes: 'Journal inédit', *Revue internationale de musique française*, no.2 (1980), 153

S. Bress: 'Le scandale Ravel de 1905', *Revue internationale de musique française*, no.14 (1984), 41

A. Orenstein: 'Ravel and Falla: an Unpublished Correspondence, 1914–1933', *Music and Civilization: Essays in Honor of Paul Henry Lang* (New York, 1984), 335

193

FRANCIS POULENC

Roger Nichols

CHAPTER ONE

Life

Francis Jean Marcel Poulenc was born in Paris on 7 January 1899. His family were wealthy pharmaceutical manufacturers. Poulenc received a thorough academic training at the Lycée Condorcet and made his first musical contacts largely through his mother, herself an excellent pianist; her brother, 'Oncle Papoum', gave his nephew an early familiarity with the less prim manifestations of Parisian theatrical life. He began learning the piano with his mother at the age of five, knew some of Mallarmé's poetry by heart when he was ten, and at 14 shared in the general amazement at *The Rite of Spring*. Two years later he began taking piano lessons from Ricardo Viñes, the friend and interpreter of Debussy and Ravel, and in 1917 and 1918 met Auric, Honegger, Milhaud and Satie, to whom he dedicated his first published composition, the *Rapsodie nègre*. He went on composing during his statutory period of military service (1918–21) but began to feel the need of some formal instruction. He tried both Paul Vidal and Ravel without getting beyond the first encounter and had already been dubbed a member of Les Six before finding a sympathetic teacher in Koechlin, with whom he studied from 1921 to 1924. By mutual consent Poulenc's involvement with counterpoint went no further than Bach chorales, but it is typical of his open-mindedness that, with Milhaud, he should have travelled to Vienna in 1921 to talk to Schoenberg and his pupils, and to Italy the following year to visit Casella. His reputation spread beyond Paris with Dyagilev's triumphant production of *Les biches* in 1924, although six years earlier the *Trois mouvements perpétuels* had enjoyed a vogue among the amateur pianists of Europe. However, over the next ten years natural ebullience was barely enough to conceal uncertainties of aesthetic and of technique. He reached a new maturity around 1935, precipitated by his reacquaintance with the singer Pierre Bernac and by the death of his friend Pierre-Octave Ferroud in a car accident. This tragedy, and a consequent visit to Notre Dame de Rocamadour, restored him to his paternal Roman Catholic faith, of which the first fruits were the *Litanies à la vierge noire* (1936).

During the war Poulenc remained in occupied France and demonstrated his 'resistance' by musical means, dedicating his Violin Sonata to the memory of Lorca and setting poems by Aragon and Eluard (*'C'* and *Figure humaine*), all during the black year of 1943. After the war he was concerned to resume his place in the new musical environment of Paris, defending the 'classical' Stravinsky against the 'Messiaenistes' and achieving a brilliant success with his first opera *Les mamelles de Tirésias* in 1947. The following year he and Bernac received an enthusiastic welcome on the first of several visits to the USA. In autumn 1954 trouble over the rights of *Dialogues des carmélites* put him under great nervous strain, but he made a complete recovery and in 1960 made another successful tour of North America with Denise Duval. He was working on a fourth opera based on Cocteau's *La machine infernale* when he died

20. *Francis Poulenc*

in Paris suddenly of a heart attack on 30 January 1963, some three weeks after his 64th birthday.

Between 1945 and his death he spent most of his time composing, accompanying Bernac and making records, of the music of Satie and Chabrier as well as his own. He never married but depended greatly on the support and advice of his friends, particularly Auric. He lived either in Paris or in his spacious country house Le Grand Coteau, at Noizay in Touraine; here, resisting the attempts of the villagers to make him mayor, he sought his ideal mode of life, 'une solitude coupée de visites d'amis'.

CHAPTER TWO

Works

From Ricardo Viñes Poulenc learnt a clear but colourful style of piano playing, based on a subtle use of
the sustaining pedal, and in his own piano music he was
insistent on there being 'beaucoup de pédale'. In his
earlier pieces such a style gives body to the often ar-
rogantly 'popular' tunes that abound, softening the
ostinatos in the Sonata for piano duet (1918) and the
quasi-Alberti bass in *Trois mouvements perpétuels*
(1918). In *Promenades* (1921), written for Artur
Rubinstein, a tougher harmonic language appears based
on 4ths and 7ths, and the texture is thicker than in any
of his other works for the instrument.

The bulk of his piano music dates from the early
1930s, a time when he was reappraising the materials
of his art. He later admitted that his reliance on past
formulae (long pedal notes, arpeggios, repeated chords)
was not always free of routine and that in this regard his
familiarity with the piano could be a hindrance; his most
inventive piano writing, he claimed, was to be found in
his song accompaniments. Even so, a piece such as the
Second Nocturne, *Bal de jeunes filles*, of 1933 is charming enough not to need supporting with claims of originality; it is in the manner of Chabrier but still unmis-
takably Poulenc. His own favourite pieces were the 15
Improvisations, ranging in date from 1932 to 1959 and
in dedicatee from Marguerite Long to Edith Piaf. This

confirms that the piano was not a vehicle for his deepest thoughts; he called the *Thème varié* (1951) an 'oeuvre sérieuse' and included a retrograde version of the theme in the coda to show that he was up with the latest serial ideas, but it is hardly the best of him. Inexplicably, he loathed what many would regard as his best piano work, *Les soirées de Nazelles* (1930–36), a suite of eight variations enclosed by a 'Préambule' and a 'Final' which might be described as the fusion of eclectic ideas in a glow of friendship and nostalgia. Ex.1 is typical of the suite and of Poulenc in the use of the dominant 13th, the

Ex.1 *Les soirées de Nazelles* III

pause after the end of the first phrase, the barely disguised sequence of 4ths in the bass and the circuitous route taken in bars 3–5 between the closely related keys of E minor and G major, a characteristically impertinent blend of the preceding and succeeding harmonic areas.

Chamber music

Poulenc's modest output of chamber music falls very conveniently into three chronological groups. The four works of the first period (1918–26), each under ten minutes in length, are acidly witty, garnishing plain triadic and scalic themes with spicy dissonances. No doubt they share something of the spirit of the 18th-century divertissement, but the proprieties of harmonic and syntactical behaviour are not unfailingly observed. In the Sonata for clarinet and bassoon (1922) there are passages of jazz and bitonality, often leading to a mischievous cadence; in the Sonata for horn, trumpet and trombone (1922) the opening trumpet theme is one of Poulenc's 'folksongs', clearly a relation of many in *Les biches*, which needs the correction of only three 'wrong' notes in the first four bars for it to conform with 18th-century harmonic practice – as it were, Pergolesi with his wig awry. The central group comprises the Sextet for piano and wind (1932–9), one of his most popular works, and the Sonatas for violin and piano (1942–3) and for cello and piano (1948). Poulenc admitted to being unhappy writing for solo strings and had written and destroyed two violin sonatas (1919 and 1924) before the surviving example, dedicated to Ginette Neveu. A string quartet (1947) ended up in the Paris sewers, but Poulenc rescued three themes from it to be used later in his Sinfonietta. The final three sonatas for woodwind, like the last three chamber works of Debussy, form part of a set that Poulenc did not live to complete. They have already entered their appropriate repertories by virtue both of their technical expertise and of their profound beauties. In the Sonata for oboe and piano (1962), Poulenc's last important work, dedicated to the memory of Prokofiev, his usual fast–

slow–fast pattern of movements is altered to slow–fast–slow, in which the final 'déploration' fulfils both affective and instrumental requirements.

Poulenc's best orchestral music predates World War II. The two postwar works – the Sinfonietta (1947), commissioned to celebrate the first anniversary of the BBC Third Programme, and the Piano Concerto (1949), written for himself to play – demonstrate the dangers of sectional, 'surrealist' techniques of composition: they are garrulous, uncoordinated and unmemorable. The first of the pre-war works was the *Concert champêtre* (1927–8), inspired by the playing and character of Wanda Landowska. The countryside evoked is nothing more savage than a Parisian suburb and the fanfares in the last movement emanate from nothing more exotic than the bugles in the barracks of Vincennes, but for all that it is an enchanting work. Finer still are the two concertos commissioned by the Princesse Edmond de Polignac, for two pianos (1932) and for organ, strings and timpani (1938). The earlier of the two, first performed by the composer and his friend Jacques Février, has no aim beyond entertainment, in which it succeeds completely; written in the period of 'back to X' initiated by Stravinsky, its models range from Balinese gamelan at the end of the first movement to Mozart at the beginning of the second, but as in the case of the Sonata for horn, trumpet and trombone, Poulenc's 18th-century style affords a number of calculated inelegances before branching off in a quite different direction. The Organ Concerto is altogether more ambivalent in emotional character. Recognizably a product of 'Janus-Poulenc', it leads the solo instrument from Bach's G minor Fantasia to the fairground and back again. Poulenc placed it 'on the outskirts' of his religious music.

Some of Poulenc's dramatic works deal with the inconsequential, if not the absurd. His first was incidental music to *Le gendarme incompris* (1921), a nonsense play by Cocteau and Raymond Radiguet in which the policeman delivers himself of lines by Mallarmé; despite Milhaud's enthusiasm, Poulenc withdrew the material soon afterwards. A month later, in June 1921, came the première of the ballet *Les mariés de la Tour Eiffel* incorporating two movements by Poulenc. This joint production by all the members of Les Six except Durey achieved no more than a brief *succès de scandale*. By contrast, *Les biches*, first performed in 1924, is still one of his best-known works. The absence of deep, or even shallow, symbolism was only accentuated by a tiny passage of mock-Wagnerian brass, complete with emotive minor 9ths, in the pinks and pale blues of Marie Laurencin's décor. Apart from the ballet *Les animaux modèles* (1940–41), based on eight fables from La Fontaine, Poulenc was occupied for the next 20 years by film music and incidental music to plays, until in 1944 he happened to reread Apollinaire's *Les mamelles de Tirésias* which he then set as his first opera. Described as an *opéra bouffe*, it includes a variety of scenes both inconsequential and absurd, but Apollinaire's underlying message, the need for more French babies and a corresponding distaste for incipient 'women's lib', has been a national preoccupation since Napoleon's time. The musical tone can therefore be either noble or popular, often both as in ex.2. Poulenc himself pointed out that the vocal phrase (where Thérèse/Tirésias is reading in a newspaper of the

Ex.2 *Les mamelles de Tirésias*, Act 1 scene v

death of two characters in a duel) would not disgrace a
religious work; the three introductory bars confirm the
continuity of Stravinsky's influence. *Les mamelles* is
emphatically not an operetta – knowing winks, like
smut, were anathema to Poulenc – but accommodates a
host of musical techniques, lyrical solos, patter duets,
chorales, falsetto lines for tenor and bass babies and,

Choral works

like Denise Duval whose Folies Bergères training was invaluable in the title role, it succeeds in being both funny and beautiful.

Poulenc's last two operas treat serious subjects seriously. In *Dialogues des carmélites* (1953–6) he charted the delicate vagaries of character and emotion among a group of nuns condemned to death in the French Revolution. The text, originally a film scenario, is built up from a number of short scenes whose brevity forced the composer to discriminate painstakingly between types of vocal line, of rhythm, even of vowel sound; the immediate success of this two-and-a-half-hour opera with an almost entirely female cast reveals Poulenc as a technician of the first order. He confronted similar problems in *La voix humaine* (1958) and enriched this 40-minute solo scena, one side of the telephone conversation between a young woman and the lover who is abandoning her, with non-referential 'motifs conducteurs', with a wide range of musical language mirroring both her manic condition and the perpetual interruptions of French telephonic life, with terrifying silences (as her lover is saying what the audience never hears), and with a long-term aim for A minor as the tragic goal of the harmony. The result is a powerful study of human despair.

Several of his minor secular choral works such as the *Chansons françaises* (1945–6) continue the French tradition of Janequin and Sermisy, but Poulenc's early study of Bach chorales also left its mark. His masterpiece in the genre, *Figure humaine* (1943), is a highly complex setting of words by Eluard; although instrumental support would have reduced the performers' troubles, the composer wanted a pure choral tone in order to capture the mood of supplication.

After his return to Roman Catholicism in 1935 Poulenc produced a steady flow of religious choral works. Stretching over a quarter of a century they display a remarkable unity of tone as well as an increasing complexity in language and resources. The *Litanies à la vierge noire* (1936), written in the week after his visit to Rocamadour, are for three-part female chorus in a conventionally modal style that avoids conventional cadences, the organ punctuating the discourse with fervently chromatic chords. The difficult Mass in G (1937) is nevertheless 'more sober, more Romanesque' than his next major work in the genre, the *Stabat mater* (1950) for soprano, mixed chorus and orchestra, a powerful and profoundly moving work whose choral writing enlarges on the serious implications in that of *Les mamelles*. In the *Gloria* (1959) the choral writing is unsanctimonious to the point of wilfulness, as in the stressing of the phrase 'Gloria in *excelsis* Deo', while the ostinatos, the soaring soprano and the matchless tunes proclaim Poulenc a believer who had, in Tippett's phrase, 'contracted in to abundance'. Finally, the *Sept répons des ténèbres* (1961) pursue the same lush orchestral path but with a new concentration of thought, epitomized in the minute but spine-chilling codetta to 'Caligaverunt oculi mei' where Poulenc showed that his recognition of Webern was neither a matter of distant respect nor a piece of time-serving diplomacy.

In the *Rapsodie nègre* (1917) Poulenc showed a marked affinity with words that were less than explicit, but his setting of six poems from Apollinaire's *Le bestiaire* (1918–19) is an extraordinarily individual and competent piece of work for a young man of 20, in which he captured the mood of the tiny, elusive poems, often by simple yet surprising means such as abnormal word-setting (as with 'mélancolie', the last word of all). The scoring is at once economical and faintly 'impressionist', but in *Cocardes* (1919) he imitated the sound of a street band, and Stravinsky's *The Soldier's Tale* was also surely in his mind. There followed a period of 12 years before Poulenc again wrote songs by which he set any store, the *Trois poèmes de Louise Lalanne* (1931) – a fictitious poet born of Apollinaire's lively imagination; the second poem is by him, the others by his mistress Marie Laurencin. Apollinaire and Max Jacob provided the texts for the other vocal works of 1931–2. Poulenc's favourite was *Le bal masqué*, a nostalgic romp in which the 'côté paysan' of his nature is uncluttered by any kind of chic.

On 3 April 1935 Poulenc and Bernac gave their first public recital, including the first performance of the *Cinq poèmes d'Eluard*. Poulenc had been attracted by Eluard's poetry since adolescence but there was 'a stillness about it which I did not understand'. In the *Cinq poèmes* 'for the first time, the key is grating in the lock', and the door opened wide the following year in the cycle of love-songs *Tel jour, telle nuit*, a masterpiece worthy to stand beside Fauré's *La bonne chanson*. It lacks the common touch of some other Poulenc songs, the sentimentality of *Hôtel* or the earthiness of the *Chansons villageoises*, but otherwise it is highly characteristic. Where a single song contains more than one tempo, Poulenc followed Satie's lead in making them 'successive' rather than 'progressive'; there is only one rallentando in the whole cycle; five of the nine songs move at a single, inexorable speed. However, Poulenc planned at least three of them (nos.3, 5 and 8) as transitions between their more important neighbours; in particular he intended the final climax of no.8, *Figure de force*, 'to make more keenly perceptible the kind of silence that marks the beginning of "Nous avons fait la nuit" '. Often piano and voice work on independent dynamic levels, a dimension of songwriting not widely explored before his time. The texture of the accompaniment is never complex but there must always be 'beaucoup de pédale'.

From this point there was little change in the technique of his songwriting, rather a continual refinement of means, an attempt to say more and more with less and less, a search for the pure line he admired so much in Matisse. This tendency reached its utmost point with *La fraîcheur et le feu* (1950), 'the most carefully wrought' of his songs, being a setting of a single Eluard poem in seven sections, in which two contrasted tempos (mostly crotchet = 120 and crotchet = 66–9) are treated as structural elements. Poulenc's last important setting of Eluard was of texts he commissioned from the poet to form *Le travail du peintre* (1956), a homage to seven contemporary painters. His last set of songs was *La courte paille* (1960), written for Denise Duval to sing to her young son and containing the hilarious patter song 'Ba, be, bi, bo, bu', but his last significant work for solo voice, *La dame de Monte Carlo* (1961), a monologue for soprano and orchestra to words by Cocteau, shows, like *La voix humaine*, that Poulenc understood all too well the terrors of mental depression.

In general, the sections that make up a Poulenc song are quite short and often built of two- or four-bar phrases. His technique has much in common with the 'surrealist' poets whom he set, in the value he placed on the resonance of the individual elements. He rarely began his songs with the beginning. Usually a line or two would come at a time, and in the case of *Montparnasse* (a song of 20 lines) the process was spread over a period of four years. Furthermore, ideas always came to him in particular keys and he never transposed them; for example, D♭ major seems to have been a key of relaxation and in it the fourth degree tends to be sharpened. Towards the end of the compositional process, therefore, he might be confronted with a collection of quite disparate tonal areas which he then had to combine to reach the listener as a single experience. Much though it annoyed him, the legend of Poulenc the rich playboy of music, from whom *mélodies* flowed with every exhalation of breath, is the perfect compliment to this most scrupulous of craftsmen.

At no stage did Poulenc ever question the supremacy of the tonal–modal system. Chromaticism in his music is never more than passing, even if he used the diminished 7th more than any leading composer since Verdi. Texturally, rhythmically, harmonically, he was not particularly inventive. For him the most important element of all was melody and he found his way to a vast treasury of undiscovered tunes within an area that had, according to the most up-to-date musical maps, been surveyed, worked and exhausted. His standing in the world of contemporary music mattered to him and he kept alive to the best around him; in 1961 he wrote 'I'm truly sorry to miss [Boulez's] *Pli selon pli*, because I'm sure it's well worth hearing [plus que valable]'. His definitive statement came perhaps in a letter of 1942: 'I know perfectly well that I'm not one of those composers who have made harmonic innovations like Igor [Stravinsky], Ravel or Debussy, but I think there's room for *new* music which doesn't mind using other people's chords. Wasn't that the case with Mozart–Schubert?' And if Poulenc was not quite a Schubert, he is so far the 20th century's most eligible candidate for the succession.

Numbers in right-hand margins denote references in the text.

DRAMATIC

(operas)

Les mamelles de Tirésias (opéra bouffe, prol, 2, Apollinaire), 1944; Paris, Opéra-Comique, 3 June 1947 — 198, 205–7, 208

Dialogues des carmélites (opera, 3, Bernanos), 1953–6; Milan, La Scala, 26 Jan 1957 — 198, 207

La voix humaine (tragédie lyrique, 1, Cocteau), 1958; Paris, Opéra-Comique, 6 Feb 1959 — 207, 210

Recits for Gounod: La colombe, 1923, unpubd

Amphitryon (Molière), 1947, unpubd; Paris, Marigny, 5 Dec 1947 — 205–7

Renaud et Armide (Cocteau), 1962, unpubd

(film scores)

La belle au bois dormant, 1935

La duchesse de Langeais (Baroncelli), 1942

Le voyageur sans bagages (Anouilh), 1944

Ce siècle a 50 ans, 1950, collab. Auric

Le voyage en Amérique (Lavorel), 1951; Cannes, Etoiles, 14 Aug 1951

(ballets)

La baigneuse de Trouville and Discours du général for 'Les mariés de la Tour Eiffel' (1, Cocteau), 1921, unpubd, other nos. by Auric, Honegger, Milhaud and Tailleferre; Paris, Champs-Elysées, 18 June 1921 — 205

Les biches (1, 17th-century text), chorus, orch, 1923; Monte Carlo, 6 Jan 1924 — 198, 203, 205

Pastourelle for L'éventail de Jeanne (1, Y. Franck, A. Bourgat), 1927; Paris, 16 June 1927

Aubade (choreographic conc.), pf, 18 insts, 1929; Paris, 18 June 1929

Les animaux modèles (ballet, after La Fontaine), 1940–41; Paris, Opéra, 8 Aug 1942 — 205

(incidental music)

Le gendarme incompris (Cocteau, Radiguet), 1921, unpubd; Paris, Mathurins, May 1921 — 205

Esquisse d'un fanfare, ov. for Act 5 of Romeo and Juliet (Shakespeare), 1921

Intermezzo (Giraudoux), 1933, unpubd; Paris, Comédie des Champs-Elysées, March 1933

La reine Margot (Bourdet), 1935, unpubd, collab. Auric

Léocadia (Anouilh), 1940, unpubd except for song Les chemins de l'amour

La fille du jardinier (Exbrayat), 1941, unpubd

Le voyageur sans bagages (Anouilh), 1944, unpubd

La nuit de la Saint-Jean (Barrie), 1944, unpubd

Le soldat et la sorcière (A. Salacrou), 1945, unpubd

ORCHESTRAL

Trois mouvements perpétuels [arr. of pf work], before 1927, unpubd — 204–5

Concert champêtre, hpd, orch, 1927–8 — 204

Concerto, d, 2 pf, orch, 1932 — 204

Deux marches et un intermède, chamber orch, 1937; composed for entertainment at the Paris Exhibition, other nos. by Auric — 204

Concerto, g, org, str, timp, 1938

Suite from 'Les biches', 1939–40

Suite from 'Les animaux modèles', 1942

Sinfonietta, 1947 — 203, 204

Piano Concerto, 1949

Matelote provençale for 'La guirlande de Campra', 1952

Bucolique for 'Variations sur le nom de Marguerite Long', 1954

Orchestration of Satie: Deux préludes posthumes et une gnossienne, 1939 — 207–8

CHORAL

Chanson à boire (17th-century), TTBB, 1922

Sept chansons, unacc., 1936: Blanche neige (Apollinaire), A peine défigurée (Eluard), Pour une nuit nouvelle (Eluard), Tous les droits (Eluard), Belle et ressemblante (Eluard), Marie (Apollinaire), Luire (Eluard) [Blanche neige replaced La reine de Saba (J. Legrand), sung at 1st perf. but later rejected]

Litanies à la vierge noire, SSA, org, 1936 — 198, 208

Petites voix (M. Ley), SSA, 1936: La petite fille sage, Le chien perdu, En rentrant de l'école, Le petit garçon malade, Le hérisson

Mass, G, SATB, 1937 — 208

1934; no.4, c, 1934; no.5, d, 1934; no.6, G, 1934; no.7, E♭, 1935; no.8, 1938
Caprice [after finale of Le bal masqué], 1932
Valse-improvisation sur le nom de Bach, 1932
Improvisations nos.1–6, b, A♭, b, A♭, a, B♭, 1932; no.7, C, 1933; no.8, a, 1934; no.9, D, 1934; no.10 (Eloge des gammes), F, 1934; no.11, g, 1941; no.12 (Hommage à Schubert), E♭, 1941; no.13, a, 1958; no.14, D♭, 1958; no.15 (Hommage à Edith Piaf), c, 1959   *201*
Villageoises, 1933: Valse tyrolienne, Staccato, Rustique, Polka, Petite ronde, Coda
Feuillets d'album, 1933: Ariette, Rêve, Gigue
Presto, 1934
Intermezzi, C, D♭, 1934
Badinage, 1934
Humoresque, 1934
Suite française [after chamber work], 1936
Les soirées de Nazelles, 1930–36: Préambule, Variations, Cadence, Final   *202*
Bourrée au pavillon d'Auvergne, 1937
Mélancolie, 1940
Intermezzo, A♭, 1943
L'embarquement pour Cythère, valse-musette, 2 pf, 1951
Thème varié, 1951
Capriccio [after Le bal masqué], 2 pf, 1952   *202*
Sonata, 2 pf, 1952–3
Elégie, 2 pf, 1959
Novelette sur un thème de M. de Falla, e, 1959
Principal publishers: Chester, Durand, Eschig, Heugel, Ricordi, Rouart-Lerolle, Salabert

WRITINGS
BOOKS

Emmanuel Chabrier (Paris, 1961)
Moi et mes amis, ed. S. Audel (Paris, 1963)
Journal de mes mélodies (Paris, 1964; Eng. trans., 1985, incl. discography)
Correspondance, 1915–1963, ed. H. de Wendel (Paris, 1967)
Pisma [Letters], ed. G. Filenko (Leningrad, 1970)
Journal de vacances (Boulogne, 1979) [(extracts)] – Luchon (Aug 1911), Biarritz (April 1912); incl. 'Poulenc dans ses jeunes années: souvenirs par Jacques Soulié']

ARTICLES AND INTERVIEWS

'Paris Notes', *Fanfare*, i (1921)
'Entretien avec Francis Poulenc', *Guide du concert* (1929), April–May
'A propos de Mavra', *Feuilles libres* (1932), June–July
'Igor Stravinsky', *Information musicale* (3 Jan 1941), 195
'Le coeur de Maurice Ravel', *Nouvelle revue française* (1941), no.323, p.237
'Centenaire de Chabrier', *Nouvelle revue française* (1941), no.329, p.110
'La leçon de Claude Debussy', *Catalogue de l'exposition Claude Debussy*, ed. A. Martin (Paris, 1942), p.xii
'Oeuvres récentes de Darius Milhaud', *Contrepoints* (1946), no.1, p.59
'Francis Poulenc on his Ballets', *Ballet* (1946), Sept, 57
'Mes mélodies et leurs poètes', *Les annales* (1947)
Tribute to Christian Berard, *Ballet* (1949), April, 30
Contribution to 'Opera Forum', *Music Today* (London, 1949), 137
'Extrait d'un journal de voyage aux USA', *Table ronde* (1950), no.30, p.66
'La musique de piano d'Erik Satie', *ReM* (1952), no.214, p.23
'La musique de piano de Prokofieff', *Musique russe*, ii (Paris, 1953), 269
'Souvenirs: à propos de la musique de scène d'Intermezzo de Jean Giraudoux', *Jean Giraudoux et 'Pour Lucrèce'* (Paris, 1953)
Francis Poulenc: entretiens avec Claude Rostand (Paris, 1954)
'Hommage à Béla Bartók', *ReM* (1955), no.224, p.18
'Lorsque je suis mélancolique', *Mercure de France* (1 Jan 1956)
'Inventur der modernen französischen Musik', *Melos*, xxiii (1956), 35
Preface to G. Laplane: *Albéniz: sa vie, son oeuvre* (Paris, 1956)
'Comment j'ai composé les Dialogues des carmélites', *Opéra de Paris* (1957)
'Commémoration de la mort d'Apollinaire', "La mélancolie de son sourire"; entretien avec Hélène Jourdan-Morhange', *Les lettres françaises* (13–19 Nov 1958)
'La musique et les Ballets Russes de Serge de Diaghilev', *Histoire de la musique*, ed. Roland-Manuel (Paris, 1960), 985
'Opera in the Cinema Era', *Opera*, xiii (1961), 11
'A propos d'une lettre d'Arthur Honegger', *SMz*, cii (1962), 160
'Hommage à Benjamin Britten', *Tribute to Benjamin Britten on his Fiftieth Birthday* (London, 1963), 13

BIBLIOGRAPHY

MONOGRAPHS AND CATALOGUES

H. Hell: *Francis Poulenc, musicien français* (Paris, 1958, 2/1978; Eng. trans., 1959)

Discographie des oeuvres de Francis Poulenc (Paris, 1963)

M. Allard: *The Songs of Claude Debussy and Francis Poulenc* (diss., U. of S. Calif., 1964)

J. Roy: *Francis Poulenc* (Paris, 1964)

W. K. Werner: *The Harmonic Style of Francis Poulenc* (diss., U. of Michigan, Ann Arbor, 1966)

I. Medvedeva: *Fransis Pulank* (Moscow, 1970)

Catalogue de l'exposition à Tours: Georges Bernanos, Francis Poulenc et les 'Dialogues des carmélites' (Paris, 1970)

P. Bernac: *Francis Poulenc* (Paris, 1977; Eng. trans., 1977)

K. W. Daniel: *Francis Poulenc, his Artistic Development and Musical Style* (diss., U. of Michigan, Ann Arbor, 1982)

OTHER LITERATURE

L. Durey: 'Francis Poulenc', *The Chesterian* (1922), no.25, p.1

J. Cocteau: 'Les biches . . . notes de Monte Carlo', *Nouvelle revue française* (1924), no.126, p.275

D. Milhaud: 'Francis Poulenc et Les biches', *Etudes* (Paris, 1927), 61

R. H. Myers: 'Francis Poulenc', *MMR*, lx (1931), 129

G. Pitteluga: 'Francis Poulenc and the Praise of Paradox in Art', *The Chesterian* (1935), no.124, p.37

E. Lockspeiser: 'Francis Poulenc and Modern French Poets', *MMR*, lxx (1940), 29

A. Schaeffner: 'Francis Poulenc, musicien français', *Contrepoints* (1946), no.1, p.50

C. Rostand: *La musique française contemporaine* (Paris, 1952)

H. Jourdan-Morhange: *Mes amis musiciens* (Paris, 1955)

G. Favre: 'Francis Poulenc: Sécheresses', *Musiciens français contemporains*, ii (Paris, 1956), 122

D. Drew: 'The Simplicity of Poulenc', *The Listener* (16 Jan 1958), 137

P. Bernac: 'Notes sur l'interprétation des mélodies de Francis Poulenc', *Feuilles musicales* (1961), May–June, 68

H. Jourdan-Morhange: 'Francis Poulenc et ses poètes', *Feuilles musicales* (Lausanne, 1961), May–June, 76

D. Cox: 'Poulenc and Surrealism', *The Listener* (11 July 1963), 69

R. H. Myers: 'Hommage à Poulenc', *Music and Musicians*, xi/7 (1963), 8

A. Payne: 'Tribute to Poulenc', *Music and Musicians*, xi/10 (1963), 44

N. Rorem: 'Poulenc: a Memoir', *Tempo* (1963), no.64, p.28

J. Bellas: 'Francis Poulenc ou le "son de voix de Guillaume" ', *Guillaume Apollinaire*, iii (1964), 130

217

M. Houdin: 'La jeunesse nogentaise de Francis Poulenc', *Bulletin de la Société historique et archéologique de Nogent-sur-Marne*, iv (1964)

J. Bellas: 'Apollinaire et Poulenc: peut-on mettre "Alcools" en musique?', *Journées Apollinaire: Stavelot, 1965*

——: 'Les mamelles de Tirésias en habit d'Arlequin', *Guillaume Apollinaire*, iv (1965), 30

G. Auric: 'A propos du Gendarme Incompris', *Cahiers Jean Cocteau*, ii (Paris, 1971), 39

J. Amis: 'In Search of Poulenc', *Music and Musicians*, xxii/3 (1973), 44

Y. Gouverné and others: *Poulenc et Rocamadour* (Paris, 1974)

A. Schaeffner: 'Francis Poulenc, musicien français', in *Essais de musicologie et autres fantaisies* (Paris, 1980), 317

OLIVIER MESSIAEN

Paul Griffiths

CHAPTER ONE

Life

Olivier Eugène Prosper Charles Messiaen was born in Avignon on 10 December 1908. Partly because his father was called up for war service during four crucial years of his childhood, Messiaen was brought up largely by his mother, the poet Cécile Sauvage, who wrote a cycle of poems about him during her pregnancy. His early years were spent at Avignon, at Ambert (Chabrier's birthplace) and, during the war years, at Grenoble, where he was lastingly impressed by the nearby mountains. There he also began to learn music. According to his own account, he had begun to play the piano and to compose at the age of eight, before having lessons. Then, once he had learnt to read music, his favourite presents were operatic vocal scores: he devoured Mozart, Gluck, Berlioz and Wagner in imagination, while at the same time gaining an acquaintance with the newest French music, that of Debussy and Ravel. When these twin influences had come together and a teacher gave him the score of *Pelléas et Mélisande*, his determination to be a composer was set.

Messiaen started at the Paris Conservatoire in 1919 (the family was by now reunited in the capital) and remained there for a full decade. Among his teachers were Georges Falkenberg for the piano, Jean Gallon for harmony (second prize, 1924), Georges Caussade for counterpoint and fugue (first prize, 1926), C. A. Estyle for piano accompaniment (first prize, 1927), Marcel Dupré for the organ and improvisation (first prize, 1928), Maurice Emmanuel for music history (first prize, 1928), Paul Dukas for composition (first prize, 1929) and Joseph Baggers for timpani and percussion, this last an unusual study suggesting that Messiaen was already – perhaps prompted by Stravinsky's *The Wedding*, which he saw at this time – looking beyond the norms of Western musical presentation. Certainly his other teachers would have encouraged him in this direction. Emmanuel was an expert on the metres of Greek verse and the modes of Greek, liturgical and Eastern use, all of which he applied in his own compositions: Messiaen has recalled how, after a hearing of his *Trente chansons bourguignonnes*, he was 'at once converted to modal music'. Dupré and Dukas were also modal composers, and models for their pupil in other ways: Dupré showed that organ music could be flamboyantly virtuoso, and Dukas, fiercely self-critical, provided an example of artistic conscientiousness.

Messiaen left the Conservatoire in 1930 to take the post of organist at La Trinité in Paris, which houses one of Cavaillé-Coll's great instruments. He had already begun to make a mark as a composer (his earliest acknowledged piece, the organ meditation *Le banquet céleste* dates from 1928) and during the 1930s he confirmed his position as one of the outstanding organist–composers of his generation, especially with his hour-long cycle *La nativité du Seigneur* (1935). At the same time he was expounding theology through the orchestra, in a sequence of works crowned by *L'ascension* (1932–3), which he also adapted for the organ. Yet other works grew out of his passionate Christian vision of family life. He married the violinist Claire Delbos in 1931 and dedicated to her his *Poèmes pour Mi* (1936), a song cycle on marital union. The birth of their son Pascal in 1937 stimulated another cycle, *Chants de terre et de ciel* (1938), in which all three members of the family are portrayed.

On a more public stage, Messiaen was active as teacher and propagandist. He began teaching at the Ecole Normale de Musique and the Schola Cantorum in 1936 and in that year, with André Jolivet, Daniel-Lesur and Yves Baudrier, he founded the group La Jeune France. All four young composers were concerned to rediscover passion and sensuality in music, in reaction to the prevailing clipped neo-classicism of Parisian music in the 1930s (Messiaen remained a great admirer of the Stravinsky of *The Rite of Spring*, while his opinion of the Symphony of Psalms, as expressed in an article of the period, was distinctly less enthusiastic). There were several Jeune France concerts in Paris between 1936 and 1939 and it is possible that Messiaen learnt from Jolivet in the use of irrational values to loosen his rhythm. However, the group did not outlast the opening of World War II.

Messiaen was immediately called up for military service and in May 1940 he was captured and taken to a prisoner-of-war camp at Görlitz in Silesia. There, during the winter of 1940–41, he composed his *Quatuor pour la fin du temps* for himself to play as pianist with three other musicians he found among the inmates: a violinist, a cellist and a clarinettist. This was his most ambitious and fully, variously achieved work to date, cast in eight movements as images of a music of eternity: non-developmental, sometimes based on rhythmic pro-

223

cesses of long duration, sometimes exceedingly slow. It had its first performance at the camp, before a huge audience of prisoners.

After his release in spring 1941 Messiaen was appointed to teach harmony at the Conservatoire. Paris was now an occupied city, and perhaps the becalmed condition of musical life there contributed to rendering him almost musically silent for two years. But during this time he wrote an outline of his compositional methods, *Technique de mon langage musical*, and gathered an extraordinarily gifted circle of students, including the composers Pierre Boulez and Serge Nigg and the pianist Yvonne Loriod. His wife had by now succumbed to illness and entered a sanatorium, where she remained in steadily diminishing health until her death in 1959. Meanwhile Loriod became the focus for an erotic impulse that could be expressed only musically before their marriage in 1962: he wrote the *Visions de l'Amen* (1943) for the two of them to play, the *Trois petites liturgies* (1943–4) with her as soloist, the two-hour *Vingt regards sur l'enfant Jésus* (1944) for her, and another song cycle, *Harawi* (1945), as a celebration of sexual love, which became the first 'act' in a trilogy of works on the Tristan legend, the others being the ten-movement *Turangalîla-symphonie* (1946–8) and the *Cinq rechants* for small chorus (1948).

Messiaen's other pupils were scarcely less important in provoking this exuberant flood of music. Between 1943 and 1947 he gave private lessons in composition outside the walls of the Conservatoire and introduced his pupils not only to his own methods but also to those of the Second Viennese School (Berg's Lyric Suite had been among a small portable library of scores he took with him to Görlitz). The atmosphere was that of a revolutionary cadre, and the pupils called themselves 'les flèches' (the arrows) to indicate their questing fervour. Boulez and Nigg produced the first French serial compositions and Messiaen began in parts of the *Turangalîla-symphonie* to apply 12-note methods to rhythmic values. Teacher and pupils stimulated each other, and for a short time, around 1950, it seemed that Messiaen was about to join his younger contemporaries on the road to and through total serialism. In this, however, he remained an encourager and astute observer. He never entirely deserted his old modal practice, and his works from *Réveil des oiseaux* (1953) onwards began a process of integration, drawing on all the discoveries he had catalogued in *Technique de mon langage musical* and on those he had made since.

Messiaen needed such a diversity of techniques – tonal and atonal, key-centred and modal, irregular and repetitive – to deal with the material that interested him, for most of his works of the 1950s are based on the songs of birds. The piano concerto *Réveil des oiseaux* used them exclusively to present a sound portrait of the period from midnight through the dawn chorus to mid-morning silence. *Oiseaux exotiques* (1955–6), a much more compact work for piano and orchestra, is loud with the cries of American and Asian birds, and the immense *Catalogue d'oiseaux* (1956–8) is a collection of creative recordings of different French birds in their habitats. In all these works and others (since birdsongs appear in all Messiaen's subsequent compositions) the songs are based on notation made by the composer, usually in the field, though occasionally from recordings, and Messiaen used the journeys he made as a revered musical figure (to the USA many times, to Japan in 1962 and to Argentina in 1964) to add to his ornithological repertory.

Messiaen was also adding to his store of pupils. His clandestine classes were brought into the Conservatoire in 1947 when he was given an analysis class, but he was not granted a composition class until 1966. He has also taught abroad, notably at the Darmstadt summer school (1949–51). In Paris his pupils have included nearly all the important French composers of two generations (Barraqué, Amy and Murail as well as Boulez and Nigg) besides a great number of foreign students, among them Stockhausen and Goehr. Perhaps only Haydn, Sechter and Schoenberg can compare with him in the stature of their pupils, and in the range: few of his students have adopted much of his style, though all have been marked by the clarity of his thought and by his separation of the constituents of music (pitch, duration, instrumentation etc). He in turn enjoyed the stimulus of teaching and was saddened when he was obliged to retire from the Conservatoire on reaching the age of 70.

However, the period of his closest creative alliance with his younger contemporaries had come to an end in the early 1960s. *Chronochromie* for orchestra (1959–60) was written for the Donaueschingen Festival, which had become the principal showcase of the avant garde, and two works for piano and small orchestra were composed for Boulez's Domaine Musical concerts: the *Sept haïkaï* (1962) and *Couleurs de la cité celeste* (1963), a transitional work in that it returns to theological subject matter after a dozen years of secular birdsong works and in that it includes elements of a monumental style. This was further developed in *Et exspecto resurrec-*

21. *Olivier Messiaen at Rocamadour in 1961*

tionem mortuorum for large wind ensemble and percussion (1964), commissioned by the French government for performances in the Sainte-Chapelle and in Chartres Cathedral, and still more so in *La transfiguration de Notre-Seigneur Jésus-Christ* (1965–9), an oratorio for seven instrumental soloists, chanting chorus and large orchestra.

With the exception of *La fauvette des jardins*, a pendant to the *Catalogue d'oiseaux*, all Messiaen's later works have been of similar proportions to *La transfiguration*. They also complete the process of resumption and integration begun in the 1950s. The *Méditation sur le mystère de la Sainte Trinité* (1969) bring together all the elements of Messiaen's organ style – the slowness, the converse character of hectic virtuosity, the unusual timbres (often occasioned by birdsong imitations) and the verse-refrain forms – while adding the ciphering of theological messages by means of a 'communicable language' translating letters as pitches. This also appears in *Des canyons aux étoiles . . .* (1971–4), a 12-movement work for piano and small orchestra which looks back over the composer's orchestral output from the *Turangalîla-symphonie* onwards. His most complete summa, however, is the opera *Saint François d'Assise* (1975–83), commissioned by the Paris Opéra and first performed there 12 days before his 75th birthday.

228

CHAPTER TWO

Style, works

Messiaen is the first great composer whose works exist
entirely after, and to a large degree in ignorance of, the
great Western tradition. For though he has spoken
warmly of his regard for composers central to that
tradition – for Mozart's rhythm, for Chopin's piano
writing – his music is sublimely indifferent to its principal axioms: diatonic harmony, forward motion expressed as development, and the interdependence of
rhythm and pitch structure. Diatonic chords constitute
a very large part of his harmonic vocabulary but their
normal functions are annulled by their use within the
symmetrical frameworks of his modes. This deprives his
music of harmonic impetus and hence of the necessary
force for development (nothing shows this better than
his few early attempts at sonata form, in, for example,
the last of the Preludes). The energy for forward motion
therefore has to come from rhythm, and in particular
from an emphatic pulsing enlivened by syncopation, if
the music is not left in stasis, and the strongly directed
forms of developing music are replaced by essentially
symmetrical structures: palindromes and verse-refrain
sequences. Lack of development is also responsible for
a loosening of the need for a particular melodic-harmonic idea to have a particular rhythm. Messiaen's
stasis has provided the opportunity for a profuse elaboration of rhythm as a decorative element, while his

dependence on rhythmic dynamism elsewhere has brought an intensive study of pulse and irregularity in *The Rite of Spring*, variously applied in most of his works.

Stravinsky is indeed his most obvious ancestor as a master of rhythmic propulsion and formal discontinuity, while it is equally clear that the unresolved diatonic discords of his harmonic style come out of earlier French music: Debussy, Ravel and his teacher Dukas. His combination of these strands, however, is entirely original and opens his music to a third area of influence: that of non-Western music. In 1931 he heard Balinese music at the Exposition Coloniale in Paris, and though this had no immediate effect, the sound of the gamelan evidently prompted the tuned percussion ensembles characteristic of his orchestra from the *Trois petites liturgies* (1943–4) onwards. Indian music, too, has been important – not directly, but through the pages of the Lavignac encyclopedia. There he discovered the *jātis* and *deçi-tâlas* (melodic shapes and rhythmic formulae) catalogued in Sanskrit treatises, which have provided basic elements of his compositions since *La nativité du Seigneur* (1935). Another correspondence with Eastern music is in quality of mind. Because it abandons the logic and development of Western tradition, Messiaen's music does not ask to be followed as consistent, continuous thought. Instead it creates conditions for mental excitation or reflection. If conventional Western music is narrative in its integrated, goal-oriented planning, Messiaen's is by contrast liturgical: structured in self-contained blocks, proceeding by statement rather than development, by exposition rather than argument. This fits it very naturally for the theological purposes to which Messiaen has applied his art from the first, but it has also provided paradigms of a conception of time little valued in Western music since the Renaissance: a notion of time not as a thread to be observed but as an element to be inhabited. Where other music uses metre to measure the speed of the thread, Messiaen uses rhythm to 'colour' his medium, as he has himself expressed it.

All these essential divergences from the Western tradition are expressed in his first published composition, *Le banquet céleste* (1928), an organ piece consisting of only 25 bars but lasting for six minutes at the tempo of the second edition (1960). The first chord in ex.1 should last for seven seconds: it becomes an atmosphere rather than an element in a musical discourse. At this speed there can be no sensation of metre, even though the phrasing is so square (a mark of the young Messiaen, soon to be eradicated). Similarly, there can be no sensation of tonal movement, particularly when Messiaen uses chords on the notes of a diminished 7th (C♯–

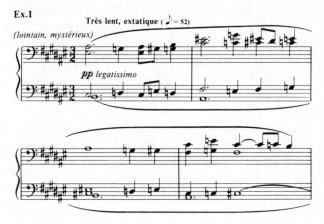

Ex.1

Très lent, extatique (♪ = 52)

(lointain, mystérieux)

pp legatissimo

231

E–G–A$\sharp$ in the first bar). Such usage is eminently characteristic and is associated with his 'second mode of limited transpositions', which consists of alternating major
and minor 2nds and which provides triads on a diminished
7th: C$\sharp$–D–E–E$\sharp$–G–G$\sharp$–A$\sharp$–B is its form in the first bar
of the example; the second bar uses one of its possible
transpositions and the only other transposition appears
later in the piece.

The mode is 'of limited transpositions', in Messiaen's
terms, because of its symmetry: transposition of any
form by a minor 3rd, tritone or major 6th will generate
the same notes, and so there are only three different
forms. Of the 'first mode' there are only two different
forms, for this is the whole-tone scale, so much a feature
of Debussy's music that Messiaen has avoided em-
phasizing it. Instead he has preferred the 'second mode'
and the 'third mode', where the symmetry is that of the
augmented triad instead of the diminished-7th chord:
one form is C–C$\sharp$–D–E–F–F$\sharp$–G$\sharp$–A–A$\sharp$. Like the
'second mode', this creates a framework on which diatonic
chords can be used in a symmetrical fashion inimical to
diatonic progression. In ex.1, for instance, the harmonic
movement is within diminished-7th areas, and the end
of the piece is concerned with establishing a resolution
not on to an F$\sharp$ major triad but on to a dominant 7th.

If *Le banquet céleste* is about the denial of movement,
there are many other works in which Messiaen uses
rhythmic means to create a definite propulsion, though
usually with his symmetrical modes strongly present in
order to prevent any diatonic participation in the
activity. An example is the 'Danse de la fureur' from
the *Quatuor*, a vigorous melody played by the four instruments in unison or at the octave below (ex.2). This

is an instance of the 'third mode', with F♯ strongly felt as modal final (the tritone cadence is exceedingly common in Messiaen, a symmetrical replacement for the diatonic fall by a perfect 5th). And quite by contrast with ex.1, there is a hectic energy here that comes not only from the rudeness of the scoring but also from the rhythm, and in particular from the insertion of what Messiaen calls 'added values' (the C in the first bar etc) into the regular crotchet pulse.

Ex.2

Exx.1 and 2 are instances of purely homophonic and monodic textures respectively. The main, and much more common, alternative in Messiaen's music is heterophony: not polyphony, which would imply an ordering of the parts to some progressive end, but instead a heterophony of independent lines, which may be dynamic in its pulsing and small-scale melodic-harmonic movement and at the same time static in its profusion of unrelated material. The first of the *Trois petites liturgies* is typical (ex.3). The vocal line shows again, within a smoother style than that of the 'Danse de la fureur', some common traits of Messiaen's melody: rhythmic regularity occasionally dislocated, modality of a symmetrical sort (the first phrase is in a 'truncated' form of the 'second mode', the second in the 'fifth mode', both replete with tritones) and tritone

Ex.3

cadencing. In the piano there is what Messiaen terms a 'rhythmic canon': the left hand, doubled by strings and maracas, plays the rhythmic sequence of the right hand,

234

doubled by vibraphone, in a 3:2 ratio. Also highly characteristic is the chordal colouring of these durational lines. The right hand fits a sequence of 13 chords in the 'sixth mode' on to a sequence of 18 values, while the left hand covers a similar rhythmic sequence with repetitions of a flow of nine chords in the 'third mode'. There is no logic in this, only a delight in regularities and irregularities of patterning similar to that which sustains the combination of color and talea in a medieval motet (and it is significant that Messiaen's closest contact with Western music should be with its pre-Renaissance, pre-diatonic history). Similarly on a larger scale there is no logic to the simultaneous placement of the choral chant, the orchestral 'canon' and the brilliant decorations of solo violin and ondes martenot: the richness is essentially static and ornamental.

Many of the stylistic features described above – in particular the 'modes of limited transpositions', the rhythmic activity and the heterophony – are to be found throughout Messiaen's output, but nevertheless one can distinguish five broad phases in his creative life. First, the music he wrote up to the age of 30, up to and including the organ cycle *Les corps glorieux* (1939), shows a gradual development and sophistication of the basically homophonic style of *Le banquet céleste* and of a contrasting rhythmic exuberance that came partly out of *The Rite of Spring*, partly out of Dupré's toccatas and partly, from 1935 onwards, out of the Indian rhythms Messiaen discovered in Lavignac (the orchestral talea of ex.3 is compounded of these rhythms). The second phase, covering the great works of the 1940s from the *Quatuor* to *Turangalîla*, brought everything in Messiaen's early style to a climax of achievement. Then, between 1949 and 1952, came a brief period when he experimented with new techniques: electronic music, strict system and the serialization of durations, dynamic levels and (on the piano) varieties of touch. After this came the years of birdsong re-creation, blending into a late period when most of the works have been of monumental character and all-embracing scope.

During his early years Messiaen was very much an organist–composer and his most important works were those he wrote or adapted for his own instrument: *Le banquet céleste*, *L'ascension* (originally an orchestral score, the culmination of a series of bold and colourful meditations for orchestra), *La nativité du Seigneur* and *Les corps glorieux*. All these are typical in dwelling on the awesomeness of God's presence (whether in the person of Jesus or in the eucharist) or else on the wonder of resurrected existence. These were to remain Messiaen's favourite, indeed almost his only subjects, according with a musical style in which the art of time is opened to glimpses of the eternal, which in this early period is most often achieved by extreme slowness (*Le banquet céleste*, finales of *Les offrandes oubliées* and *L'ascension*, much of *Les corps glorieux*). But balancing and often commingled with the spiritual in Messiaen's art there is also the sensual (as in the poetry of the Song of Solomon or the temple buildings of India), and in the 1930s this aspect was most fully expressed in two song cycles: the *Poèmes pour Mi* and *Chants de terre et de ciel*. Both set the composer's own words, in which marital and parental relationships are glossed with a mixture of biblical imagery and language derived from the surrealist poets he admired at the time (especially Pierre Reverdy). Both, like the organ cycles, also contain diverse, strongly characterized movements: this

236

is particularly true of the later work, with its range from the pentatonic to the virtually atonal and with its imaginative variety of keyboard textures, contrasting with the pianistically much simpler *Poèmes pour Mi*, which only attain their full splendour and strangeness in the later orchestral transcription.

The *Quatuor* is another cycle of sharply divergent movements, but now conceived with still more inventive resource and virtuosity. This is Messiaen's nearest approach to chamber music, yet even so it contains nothing of intimate discourse: its subject is the end of time, which it evokes once more in extraordinary slowness (the two 'Louanges', for cello and for violin with piano), in seemingly endless reiterations of un-synchronized ostinatos (the 'Liturgie de cristal') or else in violent, quasi-orchestral images sparked off by texts from the Apocalypse (e.g. the 'Danse de la fureur'). In its startling contrasts and its new ways of conceiving music, the work is one of Messiaen's most radical, individual and powerful creations, and though all the elements of its style had been present before, they are now handled with decisiveness.

This is true also of the other works of the next few years which are all (an unimportant piano *Rondeau* excepted) on an ample scale. The *Visions de l'Amen* (1943) and the *Trois petites liturgies* (1943–4) share a grounding in pentatonic A major, which is for Messiaen a key of serene joy (it is also, according to the corre-spondences he finds between harmony and colour, a blue key). Both works, too, are impressed by exotic music as much in sonority as in harmony: the *Visions de l'Amen* in their percussion effects and their quasi-Balinesse heterophonies of speeds, the *Trois petites liturgies* in their ostinatos and metallic percussion. The brilliance of their piano writing, stimulated by Loriod's virtuosity, is also central to the *Vingt regards* (1944), which circle round F♯ major, Messiaen's key of ecstatic adoration. There is room here for a vast range of manners, including massive, pounding fugato ('Par lui tout a été fait'), warm and sweet contemplation ('Le baiser de l'enfant Jésus'), severely automatic system (L'échange') and surrealist vision ('Regard de l'onction terrible').

Just as the spiritual in these three works of 1943–4 welcomes the sensual, so the sensual subject matter of the next, Tristan trilogy is seen as a mirror of divine love. The three compositions are quite separate in most respects except that of subject, and there is no narrative continuity among them. *Harawi* (1945) is another song cycle for soprano and piano, alluding in music and text to Peruvian love-songs, and presenting discontinuous moments from a story of physical passion and death. The *Turangalîla-symphonie* (1946–8) uses a large orchestra, with solo ondes martenot as a 'vox humana' stop and solo piano to lead a tuned percussion ensemble, in a sequence that interleaves flamboyant love music with alarming images and rhythmic speculations. *Cinq rechants*, more compact than the other two, is a sequence of verse-refrain forms in which meaningful phrases are delivered in a forest of onomatopoeic noises and freshly imagined choral textures. Neither here nor in *Harawi* (both works have words by the composer) is there any explicit mention of the divinity, but the love that both celebrate is seen on a cosmic scale and the great central dance of the symphony has the title 'Joie du sang des étoiles'. 'Turangalîla' itself is a Sanskrit word, used to name one of the rhythmic formulae reproduced in Lavignac and having connotations approximating to those of Bergson's 'élan vital': its musical expression is a symphony which once more centres on the suprapersonal exultation of F♯ major.

The thematic links among the three Tristan works are carried over into the piano piece *Cantéyodjâya* (1949), whose mosaic form also includes elements that look forward – particularly the section marked 'mode de durées, de hauteurs et d'intensités', which is a triple heterophony of lines using 12-note sets not only of pitches but also of durational values. The application of serialism to rhythm and other parameters is something that Messiaen had been contemplating since the early 1940s, and which he began to explore in parts of the *Turangalîla-symphonie*, where the percussion patter out sequences of arithmetical values (demisemiquaver, semiquaver, dotted semiquaver, quaver etc). *Cantéyodjâya* establishes a 12-note rhythmic grouping in the set of arithmetical values from a demisemiquaver to a dotted crotchet; another piano piece, *Mode de valeurs et d'intensités* (1949), is composed entirely in the austere three-line style of the earlier work's episode, with distinct categories of loudness and timbre as well as pitch and duration. The piece was a powerful stimulus to younger composers: Boulez based his first book of *Structures* on a 12-note series from it, and Stockhausen was immediately set on the road to the abstractness of his *Kreuzspiel*. However, the *Mode* is, as its title declares, a modal and not a serial composition: it works not with defined sequences but with repertories of notes, and the categorization of the elements is used not to ensure circulation but rather the better to identify each

22. Part of the autograph MS of Messiaen's 'Chronochromie', composed 1959–60

240

sound, since each pitch has the same durational value, dynamic and attack symbol throughout.

This high degree of systematization gives the *Mode* an impersonal character only partly prefigured in earlier movements from the *Chants de terre et de ciel*, *Les corps glorieux*, the *Quatuor* and the *Vingt regards*. It was a *ne plus ultra*: an experiment repeated only to atmospheric ends in 'La chouette hulotte' from the *Catalogue d'oiseaux*. Even so, it did bring into relief an objective, speculative element in Messiaen's creativity that remained of determining importance in his *Livre d'orgue* (1951) and the orchestral *Chronochromie* (1959–60). On another level, the *Livre d'orgue* was, with the contemporary *Messe de la Pentecôte* (a homage to Tournemire in its liturgical form), a permanent memento of Messiaen's discoveries as an improviser: apart from a test piece for the Conservatoire, *Verset pour la fête de la dédicace* (1960), it was his farewell to the organ until the Trinity meditations of nearly 20 years later.

On yet another level, the *Livre d'orgue* announces the next period, since its last movement is an enormous architecture of durations filled with birdcalls. Another Conservatoire test piece, *Le merle noir* for flute and piano (1951), was made as a bird portrait, and then for the next few years Messiaen based all his music around birdsongs. He himself has insisted on the accuracy of his transcriptions from nature, allowing only that he decelerates and transposes down the very fast, high ululations of his models. However, in doing so he also adds features of his own musical style, notably a strong pulse and often his favoured motif of a tritone plus a perfect 4th or 5th. Certainly his bird music is immediately identifiable as his, whether in the fresh, bright

23. *Scene from Act 3 of Messiaen's opera 'Saint François d'Assise' (completed 1983), first performed at the Paris Opéra, 28 November 1983*

242

heterophonies of *Réveil des oiseaux*, the gaudy block structures of *Oiseaux exotiques* or the brilliant piano textures of the *Catalogue d'oiseaux*. It also, characteristically, has a symbolic function since birds are for him earthly avatars of the angels: creatures of joy and praise which, after the nature-study works of the 1950s, he has caused to sing in all his later and more theologically inclined works.

The last of Messiaen's non-religious compositions were *Chronochromie* and the *Sept haïkaï*, the first largely a birdsong work while including, like the *Catalogue*, symbols of other natural phenomena (alpine rocks and cascades especially), the second a set of Japanese sketches. These again include birdsong transcriptions alongside impressions of landscape and a movement that transposes gagaku music into Messiaen's world. In its scoring, for piano and a small orchestra with prominent wind, the work is similar to its immediate successor, *Couleurs de la cité céleste*, but otherwise the works are quite unalike. In the *Sept haïkaï* Messiaen worked with complex, irrational rhythms nearer to Boulez or Stockhausen than to anything else in his own music, whereas *Couleurs* generally restores the reiterative pulse. The later work is also (unusually for Messiaen) cast as a single sequence of repetitions, decorations and new departures (Stravinsky's Symphonies of Wind Instruments provide the nearest prototype) rather than as a group of more regular forms. The 'colours' of the title are those of the semi-precious stones used in the building of the celestial city, and Messiaen marks in the score the colours his harmonies are meant to represent.

This connection of sound and colour is also for him

important in *Et exspecto resurrectionem mortuorum*, which was why he was pleased its early performances were in churches lit by medieval stained glass. He has said, however, that these massive wind chants and chorales would be suited to performance on mountain tops, and it was to a story of mountain splendour from the Gospels that he turned for his next work, the immense *La transfiguration*. Cast in two 'septenaries' of seven movements each, this, as much as the *Trois petites liturgies*, is an essay in making the concert hall a place of worship. The story of the Transfiguration is intoned by the chorus in four relatively short narrative sections, each followed by a pair of meditations for chorus and orchestra, with the instrumental soloists often splashing over the surface in birdsong figuration. Each part then ends with a huge chorale. The words, except in the Gospel narratives, come largely from St Thomas Aquinas, but the range of musical reference is to Messiaen's own output: to the sugared modal styles of his earliest pieces as much as to the less concordant language of such works as *Chronochromie*.

As a summa, *La transfiguration* is outdone only by the two similarly enormous works that followed it. *Des canyons aux étoiles . . .* is not colossal in its material resources – it is for solo piano (a part written, like nearly all Messiaen's piano music, for Loriod) with an orchestra of full wind and percussion but modest string complement – but its 12 movements make up a complete concert programme and comprise a cycle of contemplations on the majesty of God revealed in the depths of the earth (the canyons of Utah) and in the far distances of the heavens. *Saint François d'Assise*, by contrast, is gigantic both in its scoring and its length. The opera is a set of tableaux from the life of St Francis, acted out by a small cast but musically commented on by a choir of 150 and an orchestra of over 100, including as ever large ensembles of woodwind and tuned percussion and three ondes martenot, which return to Messiaen's music from the *Trois petites liturgies* and the *Turangalîla-symphonie*; the work lasts for about four and a half hours, discounting intervals.

The appearance of an opera from Messiaen was unexpected since his music is innocent of precisely those narrative elements that made opera possible throughout the diatonic era. But his musical style is eminently right for ceremony and meditation, and it is in these terms that *Saint François* is conducted, with repetitive actions and much space for contemplation on a vast and colourful scale: there is little of Franciscan simplicity here, for Messiaen has been concerned to project 'the progress of grace in a soul', which he sees as a subject of immeasurable wonder. The vocal lines look back to the modal arioso of his song cycles, but the orchestral music profits from all his imaginative uses of that medium, right from the wild fast movements of his earliest scores to the magical birdsong heterophonies, the awesome, cold 12-note inventions and the towering chorales of later compositions. The work is the culmination to a creative life spanning more than half a century.

Numbers in right-hand margins denote references in the text.

OPERA

Saint François d'Assise: scènes franciscaines (Messiaen), 1975–9, orchd 1979–83; Paris, Opéra, 28 Nov 1983 — 228, *242*, 244–5

ORCHESTRAL

Fugue, d, 1928, unpubd
Le banquet eucharistique, 1928–9, unpubd, related to Le banquet céleste [see 'Organ']
Simple chant d'une âme, 1930, unpubd
Les offrandes oubliées: méditation symphonique, 1930, red. pf, 1930 — 236
Le tombeau resplendissant, 1931, unpubd
Hymne au Saint Sacrement, 1932
L'ascension: méditations symphoniques, 1932–3; movts 1, 2 and 4 arr. org, 1933–4 — 222, 236
Turangalîla-symphonie, pf, ondes martenot, orch, 1946–8 — 179, 224, 225, 228, 235, 238–9, 243

Réveil des oiseaux, pf, orch, 1953 — 225, 243
Oiseaux exotiques, pf, 11 wind, 7 perc, 1955–6 — 225, 243
Chronochromie, 1959–60 — 226, 240, 241, 243, 244

Sept haïkaï, pf, 13 wind, 6 perc, 8 vn, 1962 — 226, 243
Couleurs de la cité céleste, pf, 13 wind, 6 perc, 1963 — 226, 243
Et exspecto resurrectionem mortuorum, 34 wind, 3 perc, 1964 — 226, 228, 244, 260

Des canyons aux étoiles . . ., pf, 23 wind, 7 perc, 13 str, 1971–4 — 228, 244

VOCAL

Deux ballades de Villon, 1v, pf, 1921, unpubd
Trois mélodies, 1v, pf, 1930: Pourquoi? (Messiaen), Le sourire (Sauvage), La fiancée perdue (Messiaen)
La mort du nombre (Messiaen), S, T, vn, pf, 1930
Mass, 8 S, 8vn, 1933
Vocalise, S, pf, 1935
Poèmes pour Mi (Messiaen), S, pf, 1936, arr. S, orch, 1937: Action de grâces, Paysage, La maison, Epouvante, L'épouse, Ta voix, Les deux guerriers, Le collier, Prière exaucée — 223, 236–7
O sacrum convivium!, SATB/S, org, 1937

Chants de terre et de ciel (Messiaen), S, pf, 1938: Bail avec Mi (pour ma femme), Antienne du silence (pour la jour des anges gardiens), Danse du bébé-Pilule (pour mon petit Pascal), Arc-en-ciel d'innocence (pour mon petit Pascal), Minuit pile et Face (pour la mort), Résurrection (pour la jour de Pâques) — 223, 236–7, 241
Choeurs pour une Jeanne d'Arc, chorus, 1941, unpubd
Trois petites liturgies de la Présence Divine (Messiaen), 36 female vv, pf, ondes martenot, 5 perc, str, 1943–4 — 224, 230, 233–5, 237–8, 244, 245
Harawi: chant d'amour et de la mort (Messiaen), S, pf, 1945: La ville qui dormait, toi; Bonjour toi, colombe verte; Montagnes; Doundou tchil; L'amour de Piroutcha; Répétition planétaire; Adieu; Syllabes; L'escalier redit, gestes du soleil; Amour oiseau d'étoile; Katchikatchi les étoiles; Dans le noir — 224, 238
Cinq rechants (Messiaen), 3 S, 3 A, 3 T, 3 B, 1948 — 228, 244
La transfiguration de Notre-Seigneur Jésus-Christ (Bible, Missal, Aquinas), SSMezAATTBarBB (100vv), pf, vc, fl, cl, vib, mar, xylorimba, orch, 1965–9

CHAMBER AND INSTRUMENTAL

Thème et variations, vn, pf, 1932
Fantaisie, vn, pf, 1933, unpubd
Quatuor pour la fin du temps, cl, vn, vc, pf, 1940–41 — 223–4, 232–3, 235, 237, 241

Le merle noir, fl, pf, 1951 — 241

ORGAN

Esquisse modale, 1927, unpubd
Le banquet céleste, 1928 — 222, 231–3, 235, 236

L'hôte aimable des âmes, 1928, unpubd
Variations écossaises, 1928, unpubd
Diptyque: essai sur la vie terrestre et l'éternité bienheureuse, 1930
Apparition de l'église éternelle, 1932
L'ascension [after orch work], 1933–4: Majesté du Christ demandant sa gloire à son Père, Alléluias sereins d'une âme qui désire le ciel, Transports de joie d'une âme devant la gloire du Christ qui est la sienne, Prière du Christ montant vers son Père — 222, 236

La nativité du Seigneur: neuf méditations, 1935: La vierge et l'enfant, Les bergers, Desseins éternels, Le verbe, Les enfants de Dieu, Les anges, Jésus accepte la souffrance, Les mages, Dieu parmi nous   222, 230, 236

Les corps glorieux: sept visions brèves de la vie des resuscités, 1939: Subtilité des corps glorieux, Les eaux de la grâce, L'ange aux parfums, Combat de la mort et de la vie, Force et agilité des corps glorieux, Joie et clarté des corps glorieux, Le mystère de la Sainte Trinité   235, 236, 241

Messe de la Pentecôte, 1949–50: Entrée (Les langues de feu), Offertoire (Les choses visibles et invisibles), Consécration (Le don de sagesse), Communion (Les oiseaux et les sources), Sortie (Le vent de l'Esprit)   241

Livre d'orgue, 1951: Reprises par interversion, Pièce en trio, Les mains de l'abîme, Chants d'oiseaux, Pièce en trio, Les yeux dans les roues, Soixante-quatre durées   241

Verset pour la fête de la dédicace, 1960   241

Méditations sur le mystère de la Sainte Trinité, 9 movts, 1969   228, 241

PIANO

La dame de Shalott, 1917, unpubd

La tristesse d'un grand ciel blanc, 1925, unpubd

Preludes, 1928–9: La colombe, Chant d'extase dans un paysage triste, Le nombre léger, Instants défunts, Les sons impalpables du rêve, Cloches d'angoisses et larmes d'adieu, Plainte calme, Un reflet dans le vent   229

Fantaisie burlesque, 1932

Pièce pour le tombeau de Paul Dukas, 1935   237

Rondeau, 1943   224, 237

Visions de l'Amen, 2 pf, 1943: Amen de la création, Amen des étoiles, de la planète à l'anneau, Amen de l'agonie de Jésus, Amen du désir, Amen des anges, des saints, du chant des oiseaux, Amen du jugement, Amen de la consommation   224, 238, 241

Vingt regards sur l'enfant Jésus, 1944: Regard du Père, Regard de l'étoile, L'échange, Regard de la vierge, Regard du Fils sur le Fils, Par lui tout a été fait, Regard de la croix, Regard des hauteurs, Regard du temps, Regard de l'esprit de joie, Première communion de la vierge, La parole toute-puissante, Noël, Regard des anges, Le baiser de l'enfant Jésus, Regard des prophètes, des bergers et des mages, Regard du silence, Regard de l'onction terrible, Je dors, mais mon coeur veille, Regard de l'église d'amour

Cantéyodjâya, 1949   239

Quatre études de rythme: Ile de feu 1, 1950, Mode de valeurs et d'intensités, 1949, Neumes rythmiques, 1949, Ile de feu 2, 1950   239, 241, 254, 272

Catalogue d'oiseaux, 1956–8: Le chocard des alpes, Le loriot, Le merle bleu, Le traquet stapazin, La chouette hulotte, L'alouette lulu, La rousserolle effarvatte, L'alouette calandrelle, La bouscarle, Le merle de roche, La buse variable, Le traquet rieur, Le courlis cendré   225, 228, 241, 243

La fauvette des jardins, 1970   228

ELECTRONIC

Fête des belles eaux, 6 ondes martenot, 1937, unpubd

Deux monodies en quart de ton, ondes martenot, 1938, unpubd

Musique de scène pour un Oedipe, ondes martenot, 1942, unpubd

Timbres-durées, tape, 1952, unpubd, withdrawn

Principal publishers: Leduc, Durand, Universal

WRITINGS

with others: *Vingt leçons de solfège moderne* (Paris, 1933)

'Ariane et Barbe-bleue de Paul Dukas', *ReM* (1936), no.166, p.79

'Le rythme chez Igor Strawinsky', *ReM* (1939), no.191, p.91

Vingt leçons d'harmonie (Paris, 1939)

Technique de mon langage musical (Paris, 1944; Eng. trans., 1957)

Preface to A. Jolivet: *Mana* (Paris, 1946)

'Maurice Emmanuel: ses "trente chansons bourguignonnes"', *ReM* (1947), no.206, p.108   223

Conférence de Bruxelles (Paris, 1958)

Conférence de Notre Dame (Paris, 1978)

Traité du rythme (Paris, in preparation)   224, 225

BIBLIOGRAPHY

BOOKS

C. Rostand: *Olivier Messiaen* (Paris, 1957)

A. Goléa: *Rencontres avec Olivier Messiaen* (Paris, 1960)

P. Mari: *Olivier Messiaen* (Paris, 1965)

C. Samuel: *Entretiens avec Olivier Messiaen* (Paris, 1967; Eng. trans., 1976)

S. Waumsley: *The Organ Music of Olivier Messiaen* (Paris, 1968, 2/1975)

R. S. Johnson: *Messiaen* (London, 1974)

R. Nichols: *Messiaen* (London, 1975, 2/1986)

S. Ahrens, H.-D. Möller and A. Rössler: *Des Orgelwerk Messiaens* (Duisburg, 1976)

P. Borum and E. Christensen: *Messiaen: en handbog* (Copenhagen, 1977)

I. Hohlfeld-Ufer: *Die musikalische Sprache Olivier Messiaens, dargestellt an dem Orgelzyklus 'Die Pfingstmesse'*, with A. Rössler: *Zur Interpretation der Orgelwerke Messiaens* (Duisburg, 1978)

M. Reverdy: *L'oeuvre pour piano d'Olivier Messiaen* (Paris, 1978)

A. Perier: *Messiaen* (Paris, 1979)

H. Halbreich: *Olivier Messiaen* (Paris, 1980)

P. Griffiths: *Olivier Messiaen and the Music of Time* (London, 1985)

OTHER LITERATURE

J. Barraqué: 'Rythme et développement', *Polyphonie*, nos.9–10 (1954), 47–73

D. Drew: 'Messiaen: a Provisional Study', *The Score* (1954), no.10, p.33; (1955), no.13, p.59; (1955), no.14, p.41

Melos, xxv/12 (1958) [Messiaen issue]

R. Smalley: 'Debussy and Messiaen', *MT*, cix (1968), 128

H. Heiss: 'Struktur und Symbolik in "Reprises par interversion" und "Les mains de l'abîme" aus Olivier Messiaens "Livre d'orgue" ', *Zeitschrift für Musiktheorie*, i/2 (1970), 32

T. Hold: 'Messiaen's Birds', *ML*, lii (1971), 113

K. Hochreither: 'Olivier Messiaen: La nativité du Seigneur', *Festschrift für Michael Schneider* (Berlin, 1974), 64

P. Boulez: 'Olivier Messiaen', *Anhaltspunkte* (Stuttgart and Zurich, 1975), 154

Musik-Konzepte, no.28 (1982) [Messiaen issue]

PIERRE BOULEZ

G. W. Hopkins

CHAPTER ONE

Career

Pierre Boulez was born at Montbrison, Loire, on 26
March 1925. As a boy he first divided his attention between music and mathematics. He sang in the choir of his
Catholic school at St Etienne, he enjoyed playing the
piano; but his early aptitude for mathematics marked
him out – at least in the eyes of his father, a steel
industrialist – for a career in engineering. On leaving
school in 1941, he spent a year attending a course in
higher mathematics at Lyons with a view to gaining
admission to the Ecole Polytechnique in Paris. During
that year he made what progress he could with music,
cultivating his proficiency as a pianist and acquiring a
groundwork of theory.

It was the latter which stood him in good stead when
he moved to Paris in 1942 and, against his father's
wishes, opted for the Paris Conservatoire rather than
the Ecole Polytechnique; he had failed the pianists'
entrance examination. After three years he took a
premier prix in harmony, having attended Messiaen's
famous harmony class. Along with some of his contemporaries in Messiaen's class, he took exception to the
hidebound curriculum of the Conservatoire and looked
beyond its walls for instruction in counterpoint. This he
studied privately with Andrée Vaurabourg, the wife of
Arthur Honegger.

It was in Messiaen's class that Boulez, respected as

well as encouraged by his teacher, first gave proof of exceptional abilities as a musical analyst. Quick to detect genuine originality of craftsmanship, he equally quickly lost patience with music whose renown rested on anything less substantial. He viewed composition as a form of aesthetic research and demanded that it be conducted on stringently scientific (that is, logical) lines; in this light, the cult of personal stylistic development – a hangover from Romanticism – counted for nothing. Infected by a common zeal, Boulez and a number of his fellow pupils demonstrated their protest vocally at performances of works whose modernity they considered a facile and arbitrary disguise; not even the personal reputation of a Stravinsky was sacrosanct, and many a lesser one was mercilessly deflated.

Boulez's aesthetic research at the time had led him to 'a very clear awareness of the necessity for atonality'. His *Trois psalmodies* for piano (1945) were marked, not only by Messiaen's influence, but by that of the pre-serial Schoenberg too. When Schoenberg's pupil Leibowitz began to introduce dodecaphonic music to the French public, Boulez readily applied to him for instruction in serial techniques. Within a year his earliest published compositions (the Sonatine for flute and piano, the First Piano Sonata, *Le visage nuptial*) had taken shape; his inventive energies had taken the route suggested by Schoenberg's Wind Quintet op.26 (which he had heard in 1945) and by the later works of Webern. Again, Boulez was subsequently to write: 'Any musician who has not felt . . . the necessity of the dodecaphonic language is OF NO USE ('Eventuellement . . .', 1952, in *Relevés d'apprenti*, 1966).

On the recommendation of Honegger, Boulez was appointed musical director of the new Compagnie Renaud–Barrault in 1946. He thus laid the solid foundations of his career as a conductor with performances of theatre music, including specially composed scores by Auric, Poulenc and Honegger himself. (Roger Desormière, from whom he received guidance, could be considered his one 'teacher' of conducting.) Boulez was in charge of Milhaud's music for Claudel's *Christophe Colomb* when the company's production of the play was recorded on disc, and in 1955, the penultimate year of his association with the company, Boulez himself wrote the incidental music for their production of the *Oresteia* at the Bordeaux Festival.

The first works to bring Boulez before the public as a composer were not those of 1946, but the Second Piano Sonata and *Le soleil des eaux*, both dating from 1948. The latter, first given as a cantata in Paris in July 1950, grew out of some incidental music Boulez wrote for a radio production of Char's work of the same name, broadcast in April 1948. The music of the original version, reworked, became 'Complainte du lézard amoureux', and Boulez added to this a second movement, 'La sorgue'. The scoring of the cantata, both impressionistically delicate and violent, has a hallucinatory clarity which accords well with Boulez's surrealist aims in this work.

In contrast with the one-movement Sonatine and the two-movement First Sonata, Boulez's Second Sonata is a monumental work in four movements. Avowedly modelled on Beethoven, its movements follow a sufficiently Classical pattern for the many facets of Boulez's style to be systematically deployed. The work's reputa-

tion grew less from relatively obscure early performances by Yvette Grimaud and Yvonne Loriod than
from circulation of the score, which was published in
1950. This composition, more than any other, first
spread Boulez's fame abroad: its first performance in
Darmstadt (by Loriod in 1952) was one of the most
eagerly awaited musical events of the postwar years, and
through the advocacy of Tudor it reached the ears of the
American avant garde.

Also in 1948 work was begun on the *Livre pour
quatuor*, which foreshadows much of the later development of Boulez's musical thinking. The work is in the
form of a collection of movements, and it is left to the
performers to select which will be given at any one
performance. Thus the *Livre* anticipates those works of
the late 1950s in which the performer is allowed to
choose his own path through the music. Its immediate
significance, however, was as a pointer towards the
technique of 'total serialization'. Stimulated by the last
works of Webern and by Messiaen's *Quatre études de
rythme* (1949–50), Boulez sought to develop a technique whereby the principles of serialism could be made
to govern the timbre, duration and intensity of each
sound, as well as its pitch. Some of the movements of the
Livre pour quatuor may be considered as first sketches
towards such a technique.

By 1951 Boulez had arrived at a stage where he could
commit his first essays in the new technique to paper –
and to magnetic tape. The resources of the studio for
musique concrète run by Schaeffer under the auspices of
French radio enabled Boulez to compose two *Etudes* in
which the precise organization of timbres, durations and
intensities could remain immune from the hazards of

human performance. These hazards proved to be a real stumbling-block in *Polyphonie X* for 18 soloists (1951), which was composed for and performed at the Donaueschingen Festival of that year. The last, and most successful, of Boulez's essays in total serialization was *Structures I* for two pianos, written in 1952. Organization of timbres was here replaced by that of 'modes of attack', and the treatment of durations in particular became more flexible in the last two of the work's three sections. The first section was performed at a Paris concert in 1952 by Messiaen and the composer.

At the same time Boulez completed a revised version of his early cantata, *Le visage nuptial*. Originally written for two vocal soloists and a chamber ensemble, the work was reorchestrated for very much larger forces including a women's chorus. Densely orchestrated and richly polyphonic, the work reaches towards lyrical paroxysm and its style shares certain features with both Messiaen and the expressionism of Berg. In two of its five movements (each a setting of a poem by Char) Boulez freely used quarter-tones. It was not until December 1957 that the work was given its first performance, under the composer's direction, in Cologne.

The next five years saw a marked slowing down in Boulez's production as a composer. It was a period in which much of his musical thinking found expression in articles on technique and aesthetics, many of which are to be found in the collection *Relevés d'apprenti*. Perhaps the most notorious of all his writings was his 'obituary' in *Score* (1952) 'Schönberg est mort', in which he continued his protest against what he considered the inadequate working-out of musical discoveries. But this was also a period during which Boulez won wide and

255

even popular acclaim for a work which very soon came to be thought of as a keystone of 20th-century music, a worthy companion to *The Rite of Spring* and *Pierrot Lunaire*: *Le marteau sans maître* (1953–5, revised 1957).

Unlike Boulez's earlier settings of Char's poetry, *Le marteau sans maître* is scored for a small ensemble; its contralto soloist is complemented only by alto flute, xylorimba, vibraphone, percussion, guitar and viola. Char's three poems are embedded in a nine-movement structure of interlacing settings and related instrumental movements. Recalling the cellular style of late Webern, Boulez cultivated a certain rhythmic monotony, emphasized by his use of the percussion in some of the movements. This is offset by abrupt tempo transitions, passages of broadly improvisatory melodic style, and – not least of all – the fascination of exotic instrumental colouring, underlining the work's basically static conception.

In 1954, supported by the Compagnie Renaud–Barrault and by the patronage of Suzanne Tézenas, Boulez was able to found the Domaine Musical series of concerts. New works were given carefully prepared performances in programmes which included only those works of the past thought to be of special relevance to contemporary music. These 'composers' concerts' found an enthusiastic following in Paris, and set a pattern which has since been widely and successfully imitated. The Domaine Musical gave European premières of works by Stravinsky, Messiaen and many younger composers of different nationalities. Its concerts became a regular feature of Parisian musical life, and in 1967 Boulez was succeeded as musical director by Amy.

Following the success of *Le marteau sans maître*,

Boulez began to be in considerable demand as a teacher of composition. In 1955, and for 12 years thereafter, he visited Darmstadt in that capacity; between 1960 and 1963 he was professor of composition at the Basle Musikakademie, in 1963 he was visiting lecturer at Harvard University, and in addition he found time for private teaching. It was at Darmstadt that he gave the series of lectures which were to become *Musikdenken heute*. The book outlines in systematic fashion the developments of serial technique which followed Boulez's preoccupation with total serialization; in particular, it relates to the group of works (the Third Piano Sonata, *Poésie pour pouvoir*, *Doubles*, *Structures II*, *Pli selon pli*) he composed between 1957 and 1962.

By now the broadening of his serial techniques had led Boulez to an interest in the possibilities of open form. At one level, individual works were increasingly to be seen as parts of a greater whole, a 'work in progress', to be taken up again and reworked as the larger entity came to assume its own shape. The two *Improvisations sur Mallarmé* for soprano and chamber ensemble and the orchestral *Strophes*, all of 1957, in this way became parts of *Pli selon pli* (1962); and *Doubles*, commissioned by the Lamoureux Orchestra for performance in 1958, was later expanded into *Figures–Doubles–Prismes* (1966). But more far-reaching was the freedom Boulez now tended to give the performer. There are, for example, passages in *Improvisation sur Mallarmé II* that are marked 'senza tempo', leaving the soloist and conductor free to judge durations for themselves.

In the Third Sonata the performer has considerably more freedom of choice. Within certain limits, the order of the work's five movements may be freely selected; within movements themselves, the performer is offered a number of alternative routes, and must choose which passages to perform and which to omit. However, the composer's planned scheme of options represents a much firmer control over the work's identity than is to be found in such aleatory music as Stockhausen's *Klavierstück XI*. Only two of the sonata's movements have so far been published, the remainder having been withdrawn into the category of 'work in progress'. Completed works of the period include *Poésie pour pouvoir* for orchestra and tape, and *Structures II* for two pianos. The former, based on a text by Michaux, continues the spatial exploitation of orchestral sound which Stockhausen inaugurated with his *Gruppen*. *Structures II* (1956–61) added a further volume to the studies in serialism of 1952, supplementing them with examples of a more developed and freer serial technique.

The extent of Boulez's new freedom is perhaps most amply demonstrated in *Pli selon pli*, a work for soprano and large orchestra in five movements, sub-titled 'portrait de Mallarmé'. Extended passages in which the registers of notes remain fixed make for a new simplicity of style, particularly in the vocal writing of the three *Improvisations* which form the work's central core. The density of instrumental textures varies from the use of the full orchestra in the outer movements to the delicate chamber ensemble which accompanies the second *Improvisation*. The frequently ornate vocal style of the work does not preclude a somewhat expressionistic treatment of Mallarmé's text, but Boulez's real homage to the poet lies deeper, in the formal correspondences between his music and Mallarmé's poetic syntax.

Eclat for 15 instruments (1965) heralded a group of compositions in which Boulez turned his attention to variously constituted chamber ensembles of moderate size. This work, featuring an important solo piano part among the nine non-sustaining instruments of its original version, finally grew into *Eclat/Multiples* for orchestra. In *Cummings ist der Dichter* for 16 solo voices and 24 instruments (1970–), Boulez invented a new type of chamber cantata; more concise than *Pli selon pli*, the work is another portrait of a poet, and is again built round a central 'improvisatory' section in which sustained notes alternate with violent vocal ejaculations.

The possibilities of open forms continued to exercise his imagination. In *Domaines*, for clarinet alone or with 21 instruments (1968), as in *Poésie pour pouvoir* and *Figures–Doubles–Prismes*, Boulez emphasized the role of spatial location in the distribution of the ensemble; the solo clarinettist moves among the work's six instrumental groups. The freedom given to the performers in determining the work's form is allotted alternately to the soloist and to the ensemble, under the leadership of the conductor. In '. . . *explosante-fixe* . . .' (1971), a wide range of possible forms can be decided on by the players involved, whose number and instruments Boulez does not prescribe. He returned in 1968 to his 'work in progress' of longest standing, the *Livre pour quatuor* he had embarked on 20 years previously; he prepared a new version (*Livre pour cordes*) for full string orchestra.

This is just one instance of how Boulez's music has continued for him to be mutable, constantly challenging him to further consideration. Even *Pli selon pli* was not

259

immune from this, though twice recorded by him in a version that had appeared to have become stable in 1962, for 20 years later he revised the third *Improvisation* to remove its options and at the same time make the orchestration more subtle, with sprinklings of cello figuration added to the percussion cadenzas. And even *Notations*, the earliest work he acknowledges, became the subject of second thoughts in 1977 when he embarked on a vast orchestral amplification of its minuscule ideas. He has further announced his intention to make new versions of *Polyphonie X*, *Poésie pour pouvoir*, *Domaines* and '. . . *explosante-fixe* . . .', besides leaving himself further work to do on such long-standing projects as the Third Piano Sonata and *Figures–Doubles–Prismes*.

Within this unsettled oeuvre *Rituel* (1974–5) was a curious appearance. Created as a memorial to Boulez's friend and colleague Bruno Maderna, it is a severe litany of verses and refrains for eight orchestral groups of different sizes, each operating with a percussionist timekeeper. The verses are heterophonies in which the groups go their separate ways in elaboration of a melodic formula played at first by a solo oboe, while the refrains are based on slow tutti chords built from the same formula. The effect, enhanced by the predominance of tritones, is of a throwback to Messiaen's *Et exspecto resurrectionem mortuorum*, and of a gigantism that eradicates the possibility of the extreme virtuosity of colouring to be found in the orchestral *Notations*.

The search for a similar fine control of timbre, and for ways of making electronics essential to musical thought, has occupied Boulez in his work at the Institut de Recherche et de Coordination Acoustique/Musique (IRCAM) in Paris, where he was founder-director, and where he spent much of his time from the mid-1970s. At first planned as a meeting-place for scientists, instrumentalists, technicians and composers, IRCAM swiftly became, less ambitiously but more usefully, a studio for computer music, and Boulez made use of digital techniques developed there in his *Répons* (1980–). The scoring of this work, for six tuned percussion soloists with a small orchestra, has obvious parallels with that of *Eclat*, and there is a similar antagonism between percussive and sustaining instruments that fuels vigorous toccata movements and ampler passages of flamboyant ornamentation. The electronic manipulations – applied only to the soloists – provide the composer with the means to transport sounds through the concert hall, to open clangorous artificial spaces, to alter timbres with finesse and to set up processes of varied repetition.

Boulez's conducting career began with the Domaine Musical concerts, where he conducted many new works by young composers as well as his own *Le marteau sans maître*. In 1957, at the invitation of Scherchen, he conducted the first performance of *Le visage nuptial* in Cologne; during the next year, he not only conducted the première of *Doubles* in Paris, but participated with Rosbaud and the South-west German RSO in the first performance of *Poésie pour pouvoir*. He was again invited to conduct the same orchestra when an early version of *Pli selon pli* was introduced in Cologne in 1960; meanwhile, he had become a guest conductor with the orchestra, and had taken up residence in Baden-Baden. Although always primarily concerned with the performance of 20th-century music, and notably that of Debussy, Stravinsky, Webern and Messiaen, he extended his repertory during this time to include a number of earlier works (by Haydn, Beethoven, Schubert and others) with which he felt a special affinity.

After some years of alienation from the official musical world in Paris, Boulez returned there triumphantly in 1963 to conduct the first French performance of *Wozzeck* at the Paris Opéra. Very quickly he came to be in demand for a wide variety of occasions in many different countries. In 1964 he conducted a special concert performance of *Hippolyte et Aricie* for the Rameau bicentenary celebrations in Paris, in 1965 he was at the Edinburgh Festival to conduct *Pli selon pli* and in 1966 he was entrusted with *Parsifal* at the Bayreuth Festival. In 1967 he became a guest conductor with the Cleveland Orchestra, with whom he made a number of recordings, and four years later he was appointed principal conductor of both the BBC SO and the New York PO. He relinquished the former post in 1974 to take up the direction of IRCAM, and in 1978 he gave up the latter. In 1976 he conducted the *Ring* at Bayreuth, in Patrice Chéreau's controversial production, and in 1979 at the Paris Opéra he had charge of the first production of Berg's *Lulu* in complete form.

Boulez's performances are primarily noted for their analytical clarity of sound: every note, even in complex scores, makes its point as a contribution to the whole. This proved an invaluable feature of Boulez's pioneering performances of new music, even though at first they were often hampered by some aridity in orchestral sonority. Given superior orchestras, the freshness of his approach gave particularly successful results in his per-

24. *Pierre Boulez, 1979*

formances of Debussy's scores, presenting a stark contrast with a long-standing tradition of impressionist cloudiness. A certain deliberacy of forward propulsion, admirably suited to many of the modern scores he performs (*The Rite of Spring*, for instance), can at other times impede the flow or overload the beat: the sensitivity of his musical ear is widely and justly renowned; the suppleness of his 'muscle' is less likely to claim such regard. He brings a composer's insight to the shaping of structure and form, and imagination to his interpretation of a work's aesthetic. This insight and imagination

263

is also displayed in his verbal introductions to many of the works he performs, for he has continued, both in the concert hall and through the mass media, to be a most active propagandist and spokesman for the music of the 20th century.

CHAPTER TWO

Compositional style

Boulez's famous phrase about 'organized delirium' ('Son et verbe', 1958, in *Relevés d'apprenti*, 1966) is a most useful starting-point for examining his style and aesthetics. 'Delirium' situates the music's essential poetics: it points to the post-expressionist colouring of individualist subjectivism in which the humanism of Boulez's music has its deepest roots; and it directs the listener's attention to the unique inflections of the composer's voice. 'Organization', on the other hand, speaks of the effort to exteriorize expression in universal terms: it indicates the nature of the Platonic model to which Boulez relates his work, and instructs one to seek out the logic in its workings. Composers of Boulez's generation have commonly seen the inseparability of style and logic as a criterion of musical excellence; and it is within such terms as theirs that critical analysis of Boulez's music has most often been conducted.

With rare exceptions (notably in the Third Piano Sonata), Boulez's music displays its firmest foundations in linear, melodic thinking. In adopting and imaginatively developing the principles of Schoenbergian serialism in his organization of pitches, Boulez rapidly evolved a melodic manner of wide-ranging flexibility. The freedom with which he uses every possible tempered melodic interval is restrained only by a recurrent tendency of these intervals to fall into 'characteristic'

265

Ex.1

(a) Rapide

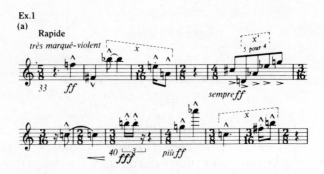

(b) [Rapide] Ralentir   Plus large

(c)

(d) Très large

266

Compositional style

aggregations, somewhat in the manner of Webern. This gives rise to melodic 'cells', which can be used in an overtly thematic manner, as in the early sonatas and in the Sonatine, whose form is modelled on that of Schoenberg's First Chamber Symphony op.9, and from which the following examples are taken. Ex.1 shows a principal theme of the work and some of its later appearances. The figure x, taken from a characteristic opening flourish (ex.2), is later used, together with its inversion (x'), retrograde (x'') and retrograde inversion (x''') forms, as the basis of an extended development section (ex.3). The use of repeated notes in this example anticipates their appearance in the first movement of the Second Piano Sonata, where they help to articulate the motivic content.

Ex.2

In the works with orchestra of the late 1940s, instrumental overlapping tends to create a more obvious continuity of melodic line and there is correspondingly less emphasis on chiselled melodic–rhythmic cells. Even in those works of 1951–2 where Boulez was applying a technique of total serialization, there is not the marked discontinuity of horizontal line which characterizes the 'point' (isolated note) composition of Stockhausen's contemporary works (e.g. *Punkte* for orchestra). Melodic passages are given to individual instruments in *Polyphonie X*; indeed, in the first piece of *Structures I*,

267

Ex.3

the use of constant dynamic levels and modes of attack does much to emphasize the continuous conception of each polyphonic strand. (The wide leaps in register between notes do not affect this fundamental continuity: they had been part of Boulez's melodic thinking for the piano since the time of the First Piano Sonata, as that work's second movement clearly shows.)

The broader serial thinking of subsequent years produced a distinctly more improvisatory melodic style – sometimes highly embellished, sometimes circling round a central note or group of notes. As an example of

268

this, the writing for solo clarinet in *Domaines* is interesting – often a single note is decorated in a manner
suggesting, in Boulez's own phrase, 'a polyphony which
remains latent' (*Boulez on Music Today*, p.137). The
opening of *Improvisation sur Mallarmé I* (ex.4) demon-

Ex.4   Pas trop lent (58 ♩ ♩ ♪ 66)

strates the effect of a fixed 'constellation' of registers in
melodic writing of this kind. Another, more incidental,
feature of certain works of this period is the use of
preponderant intervals, usually by means of a careful
shaping of the registral scheme in an appropriate way;
thus, much of *Le marteau sans maître* shows a prepon-
derance of minor 3rds (see ex.5), and *Improvisation sur
Mallarmé II* is likewise marked by major 9ths.

The fixing of a field of pitch registers over a compar-
atively long stretch of music is a rather sporadic phenomenon in Boulez, though he continues to resort to this

269

Ex.5
(a) Third movt.

Modéré sans rigueur (♩ = 52)

La   rou - lot -te   rou - ge   au

bord   *10*   du

♩. = 70

etc

clou

(b) Second movt.

Plus rapide, irrégulier et heurté (♩. = 120 / ♩. = 80)

technique in '... *explosante-fixe* ...'. The static, decorative effect to which it gives rise is particularly evident in certain passages of Boulez's writing for the piano (in *Structures II* and *Eclat*, for instance); and in *Don*, the opening section of *Pli selon pli*, it notably draws the attention from the pitch structure to details of instrumental timbre. By contrast, Boulez went to the other extreme in his early works. Here he consistently avoided fixity of register by maintaining a steady flow of transpositions, even in the slower passages of orchestral writing occurring in *Le visage nuptial* and *Le soleil des eaux*. Sometimes, indeed, the flow is so fast as blatantly to contravene the Schoenbergian guiding principle of octave-avoidance (see exx.1*d*, 3).

Boulez's polyphonic thinking, unlike Webern's, is allied to a harmonic style of some density which has its roots not only in Schoenberg but in Messiaen too. This is evident in Boulez's richly sounding vertical aggregates and instrumental voicing, in his cluster effects, in his treatment of the extreme registers of the piano, and in his occasional use of organum-like parallel chord movement (see ex.1*d*; more complex examples are to be found in later works such as *Eclat*). Less obvious, although no less effective than parallel homophonic movement, are those passages dominated by preponderant harmonic intervals. The third movement of the Second Piano Sonata is haunted by major 2nds; and the character of *Le marteau sans maître* owes much to the deployment, both melodically and harmonically, of 3rds and 6ths (ex.5).

This example demonstrates one of the methods most commonly used by the serialists in their attempts to bring about a fusion between horizontal and vertical pitch structures. The melodic line in ex.5*a* contains a full range of intervals, yet for the most part it is developed from the sort of chordal spacing suggested in ex.5*b*, which is exclusively occupied with the minor 3rd and its inversion. (In the transcription of this example, certain details are omitted, notably the part for percussion.) It should be noted, however, that this type of fusion leaves the typical melodic and harmonic textures unaltered. The harmonic writing here is obstinately in four parts; and only the slight hint of 'latent polyphony' in the vocal line shows Boulez moving towards the textural fusion which marks the Third Piano Sonata.

The procedures Boulez came to use in order to produce suitably mobile pitch structures from serial premises are described in *Musikdenken heute*. In the example he gives there, a melodic series is broken up into polyphonic segments (one- to three-part writing), each of which is thickened by 'multiplication' with a vertical aggregate. It is this technique of multiplication that represents the true 'diagonal' between melody and harmony. It is possible that Boulez had been consciously seeking this path from the very start; rapid flourishes using equal durational values (e.g. ex.2) frequently appear in the early works and may have been conceived, if naively so, as a fusion between vertical and horizontal writing. But it is only the later technique that represents a truly serial approach to textural density, offering a solution which had eluded Boulez at the time of his research into the possibilities of total serialization.

The serialization of durations was first attempted by Messiaen in *Mode de valeurs et d'intensités* (the second of his *Quatre études de rythme*), in which an alphabetical series of durational values is used. The same approach was also favoured by Boulez (see *Structures Ia*), and his subsequent conception of musical time owes much to it. However, the 'global' organization of time and the performance of rhythms within time require greater differentiation than the exclusive use of such durational series offers. In *Structures Ib*, Boulez introduced regular subdivisions of the larger temporal units, and soon (see 'Eventuellement . . .', 1952) he was finding ways of incorporating a flexibility of rhythmical movement commensurate with that of his early works.

These works were firmly founded on a form of cellular rhythmic motivicism which derived from the practice of Messiaen. Small rhythmic groups could be varied and developed by using simple procedures of permutation, augmentation, diminution, extension and elision; in this way, a very small number of rhythmic ideas could engender enough rhythmic forms to sustain an extended composition. There are some simple examples of this in the Sonatine. The values marked x' in ex.1b are a regular diminution of the first three notes of ex.1a; and the first four values of ex.1b appear in a reversed form in ex.3 (x and x'; retrograde in x'' and x'''). As a means of articulating the thematic content of sonata forms, the technique has many advantages, and it corresponds admirably to the use of recurrent pitch aggregates.

A similar correspondence can be found in non-thematic music, where passages of varying rhythmic regularity can be set off against highly regular or highly irregular passages; this parallels the musical characterization that can be achieved by the control of pitch structures. The extreme regularity of the subdivisions in *Structures Ib* continues to represent one type of charac-

273

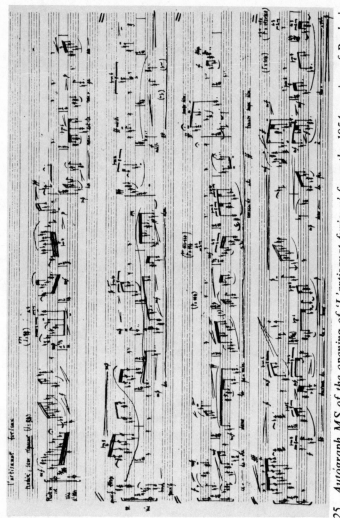

25. *Autograph MS of the opening of 'L'artisanat furieux' from the 1954 version of Boulez's 'Le marteau sans maître'*

terization, as, for example, in *Domaines* (see the writing for trombones in their 'Miroir' section). The harmonic example from *Le marteau sans maître* (ex.5*b*) shows how regularity of values can link up with motivic thinking. Irregular durations are generally formed by introducing 'irrational' subdivisions (a technique Boulez took over from Varèse and Jolivet) or by adding fractional values in the manner of Messiaen (ex.1 contains simple instances of both techniques). From the first, these rhythmic techniques were an important factor in the suppleness of Boulez's melodic style, especially in his writing for the voice. Ex.5*a* is a typical example of the masterly way in which he welds together rational and irrational, regular and irregular elements.

In many of his works, Boulez's approach to problems of musical form has been guided by a poetic text. In *Le visage nuptial* the relationship between text and musical form is particularly transparent: it is a curiosity of the final version of this work that, for all the vast orchestral resources Boulez could call upon, there are amazingly few bars of vocal inactivity. The text very closely determines the form of the music, even when (as in the fourth movement, 'Evadné') it is merely declaimed relentlessly in unpitched semiquavers. *Le soleil des eaux* shows a marked advance on this, and its instrumental interludes and wordless vocalise anticipate the commentary movements in *Le marteau sans maître*. In the later vocal works, the texts become 'sources of irrigation', the 'centre and absence' of the musical conceptions Boulez builds around them ('Poésie – centre et absence – musique', 1963). They continue to suggest forms, without dominating them.

The instrumental forms preferred by Boulez in the

late 1940s are only superficially affiliated with the neo-classical movement. Sonata forms provided the merest skeleton, a pretext for thematic presentation and development at a time when Boulez's serial language was superbly equipped to follow those lines. His later forms are both more freely conceived and more sectional. Serial organization on a broad scale stimulates the invention of forms whose constituent parts are related only to one another, rather than to a pre-existing model. It also provides general criteria for linking structures in a number of alternative ways, thus clearing the way for the open forms Boulez used in, for example, the Third Piano Sonata and *Domaines*. In the Sonata the five movements, or 'formants', can be played in a number of different orders, always grouped round the central 'Constellation'; the order and choice of sections within formants is similarly variable. In *Domaines* there are 12 sections to be played through in two groups of six, the order being chosen once by the soloist, once by the conductor.

To have gained a perspective in which serialism implies, and even logically entails such freedom, is one of the triumphs of Boulez's imagination. Yet the earlier works are far too convincing in themselves to be dismissed as preparatory exercises. Some critics have shown concern at the vast difference in character between early Boulez and post-1952 Boulez. The 'musical scientist' may indeed have satisfied his thirst for a system; but, so long as that system remains an open one, he is still free to go on making discoveries.

Numbers in right-hand margins denote references in the text.

277

Mon Faust (incidental music, Valéry), 1962; unpubd

Pli selon pli, 1957–62, consists of Don, Improvisations sur Mallarmé I–III, Tombeau — 109, 211, 257, 258, 259–60, 261, 262, 271

Marges, perc ens, 1962–4; sketches only

Éclat, 15 insts, 1965; cond. Boulez, Los Angeles, 26 March 1965; expanded as Éclat/Multiples, orch, BBC SO, cond. Boulez, London, 21 Oct 1970; work in progress — 109, 259, 261, 271

Domaines (cl, 21 insts)/cl, 1961–8; solo part, Deinzer, Ulm, 20 Sept 1968; complete, Boeykens, Belgian RSO, cond. Boulez, Brussels, 20 Dec 1968; rev. 1969: only cl solo pubd — 259, 260, 269, 275, 276

Livre pour cordes, str orch, 1968–; Ia, NPO, cond. Boulez, London, 1 Dec 1968; Ib, NPO, cond. Boulez, Brighton, 8 Dec 1968; work in progress — 259

Untitled contribution to A Garland for Dr K, fl, cl, va, vc, pf, 1969; unpubd

Cummings ist der Dichter, Chamber chorus, small orch, 1970; Schola Cantorum Stuttgart, South German RSO, cond. Boulez, Gottwald, Stuttgart, 25 Sept 1970 — 259

'... explosante-fixe ...', unspecified forces, 1971; realization for fl, cl, tpt, London Sinfonietta, London, 17 June 1972; realization for fl, cl, tpt, harp, vib, vn, va, vc, elec, New York PO, New York, 5 Jan 1973; rev., BBC SO, Rome, 13 May 1973; rev., Musique Vivante, La Rochelle, 6 July 1974 — 259, 260, 271

Ainsi parla Zarathoustra (incidental music, Barrault, after Nietzsche), 1974; Paris, Oct 1974

Rituel: in memoriam Maderna, orch in 8 groups, 1974–5; BBC SO, cond. Boulez, London, 2 April 1975 — 260

Messagesquisse, vc, 6 vc, 1976; members of the jury of the Rostropovich Competition, La Rochelle, 1977

Notations [after pf pieces of 1945], orch, 1977–; I–IV, Paris Orch, cond. Barenboim, Paris, 18 June 1980; work in progress — 260

Répons, 6 tuned perc soloists, small orch, elec, 1980–; Ensemble InterContemporain, IRCAM technicians, cond. Boulez, Donaueschingen, 18 Oct 1981; work in progress — 261

Dérive, fl, cl, pf, vib, vn, vc, 1984; London Sinfonietta, cond. Knussen, London, 31 Jan 1985

Also reconstruction of cel part of Debussy: Chansons de Bilitis, speaker, 2 fl, 2 harp, cel, c1964

WRITINGS

(only uncollected articles listed)

'Probabilités critiques du compositeur', Domaine musical (1954), no.1, p.3

'Der Vogel Strauss im Labor', Melos, xxiii (1956), 65

'Zu meiner III. Sonate', Darmstädter Beiträge zur neuen Musik, iii (1960), 27; Eng. trans. as 'Sonate, que me veux-tu?', PNM, i/2 (1963), 32

'Disziplin und Kommunikation', Darmstädter Beiträge zur neuen Musik, iv (1961), 25

'Le goût et la fonction', Tel quel (1963), nos.14–15

'Wie arbeitet die Avantgarde?', Melos, xxviii (1961), 301 [on Improvisation sur Mallarmé II] — 257, 272

'L'esthétique et les fétiches', Panorama de l'art contemporain, ed. C. Samuel (Paris, 1962); Ger. trans. in Melos, xxxiv (1967), 229

'Dire, jouer, chanter', La musique et ses problèmes contemporains 1953–1963 (Paris, 1963), 300

Musikdenken heute [= Darmstädter Beiträge zur neuen Musik, v] (1963); Fr. orig. as Penser la musique aujourd'hui (Paris, 1964); Eng. trans. as Boulez on Music Today (London, 1971) — 269

'Poésie – centre et absence – musique', Melos, xxx (1963), 33 — 275

'Situation et interprétation de "Wozzeck"', CBS 3003 [disc notes]

'Hommage à Varèse', Nouvel observateur (17 Nov 1965); repr. in ReM (1969), nos.265–6, p.30

'J'ai horreur du souvenir!', Roger Desormière et son temps, ed. D. Mayer and P. Souvtchinsky (Monaco, 1966), 134

'Der Raum wird hier zur Zeit', Melos, xxxiii (1966), 400 [on work with Wieland Wagner]

Relevés d'apprenti (Paris, 1966; Eng. trans. as *Notes of an Apprenticeship*, 1968; It. trans., 1968) [essays of 1948–62]   252, 255, 265, 273

'en marge de là, d'une disparition (th.w. adorno – 6.8.1969)', *Melos*, xxxvi (1969), 370

'Chemins vers "Parsifal"', Bayreuth Festival programme book (Bayreuth, 1970); repr. with DGG 2720034 [disc notes]

'Miroirs pour "Pelléas et Mélisande"', CBS 77324 [disc notes]

'Music and Invention', *The Listener*, lxxxiii (1970), 101

'Style ou idée?', *Musique en jeu* (1971), no.4, p.5 [on Stravinsky]

Werkstatt-Texte (Frankfurt and Berlin, 1972)

'Mobile-musique', *Cahiers Renaud-Barrault*, no.87 (1974), 36

'Donc on remet en question', *La musique en projet*, ed. B. Marger and S. Benmussa (Paris, 1975), 11

'Perspective-Prospective', *La musique en projet*, 23

'Invention/Recherche', *Passage du XXe siècle: 1er partie* (Paris, 1976), 85 [IRCAM programme book]

'Technology and the Composer', *Times Literary Supplement* (6 May 1977), 570 [repr. in S. Emmerson, ed., *The Language of Electro-acoustic Music* (London, 1986)]; orig. in *Passage du XXe siècle*, i (Paris, 1977), Jan–July [see also reply by A. Goehr, *Times Literary Supplement* (10 June 1977), 703]

with P. Chéreau and others: *Histoire d'un 'Ring': Bayreuth 1976–1980* (Paris, 1980)

ed. J.-J. Nattiez: *Points de repère* (Paris, 1981/R1985; Eng. trans., 1986)

BIBLIOGRAPHY

INTERVIEWS
M. D. Hastings: 'M. Boulez' Press-conference', *MO*, lxxxix (1965), 21

J. Buzga: 'Interview mit Pierre Boulez in Prag', *Melos*, xxxiv (1967), 162

'Sprengt die Opernhäuser in die Luft!', *Der Spiegel* (1967), no.40; Eng. trans. in *Opera*, xix (1968), 440

G. Harewood: 'Whither Opera?', *Opera*, xx (1969), 922

J. Häusler: 'Gespräch mit Pierre Boulez', Donaueschingen Festival programme book (Amriswil, 1969), 9 [on *Domaines*]

M. Cotta and S. de Nussac: 'L'express va plus loin avec Pierre Boulez', *L'express* (1970), no.979, p.144

H. Pousseur: 'Pierre Boulez', *VH 101* (1970–71), no.4, p.6

M. Kendergi: 'Pierre Boulez interrogé', *Cahiers canadiens de musique* (1971), no.2, p.31

J. Bornoff: 'Music, Musicians and Communication: 2. Pierre Boulez', *Cultures*, i/1 (1973), 123

J. Häusler: 'Gespräch mit Pierre Boulez', Donaueschingen Festival programme book (Munich, 1973), 27 [on '. . . *explosante-fixe* . . .']

Z. Peskó: 'Gespräch mit Pierre Boulez', *Melos*, lx (1973), 274

L. Pinzauti: 'A colloquio con Pierre Boulez', *NRMI*, vii (1973), 226

D. Jameux: 'Pierre Boulez: sur *Polyphonie X* et *Poésie pour pouvoir*', *Musique en jeu* (1974), no.16, p.33

G. Liebert: 'Entretien avec Pierre Boulez', *Avant-scène opéra*, nos. 6–7 (1976), 144

Par volonté et par hasard: entretiens avec Célestin Deliège (Paris, 1975; Eng. trans., 1977)

R. Emerson: 'An Impromptu Discussion', *Records and Recording*, xxii/3 (1978), 16

ARTICLES AND BOOKS
M. Scriabine: 'Pierre Boulez et la musique concrète', *ReM* (1952), no.215, p.14

J. Barraqué: 'Rythme et développement', *Polyphonie* (1954), nos.9–10, p.47

R. Craft: 'Boulez and Stockhausen', *The Score* (1958), no.24, p.54

A. Goléa: *Rencontres avec Pierre Boulez* (Paris, 1958)

G. Ligeti: 'Pierre Boulez: Entscheidung und Automatik in der Structure Ia', *Die Reihe* (1958), no.4, p.33; Eng. trans. in *Die Reihe* (1960), no.4, p.36

H. Michaux: 'Genèse des trois "Poésies pour pouvoir" ', *Melos*, xxv (1958), 308

M. Wilkinson: 'Pierre Boulez' Structure Ia: some Thoughts on Twelve-tone Method', *Gravesaner Blätter* (1958), no.10, p.23

Bibliography

K. Stockhausen: 'Musik und Sprache', *Die Reihe* (1960), no.6, p.36; Eng. trans. in *Die Reihe* (1964), no.6, p.40

M. Butor: 'Mallarmé selon Boulez', *Melos*, xxviii (1961), 356

A. Hodeir: *La musique depuis Debussy* (Paris, 1961; Eng. trans., 1961), 106

S. Bradshaw and R. R. Bennett: 'In Search of Boulez', *Music and Musicians*, xi (1963), no.5, p.10; no.12, p.14

G. W. Hopkins: 'Le soleil des eaux', *Tempo* (1964), no.68, p.35

H. U. Lehmann: 'Figures–Doubles–Prismes', *Tempo* (1964), no.68, p.34

R. Henderson: 'Le soleil des eaux', *MT*, cvi (1965), 367

K. Boehmer: *Zur Theorie der offenen Form in der neuen Musik* (Darmstadt, 1967), 84ff

G. W. Hopkins: 'Debussy and Boulez', *MT*, cix (1968), 710

B. Canino: 'Boulez prima e dopo', *NRMI*, iii (1969), 672

J.-P. Derrien: 'Dossier: Pierre Boulez', *Musique en jeu* (1970), no.1, p.103

M. Fink: 'Pierre Boulez: a Selective Bibliography', *CMc* (1972), no.13, p.135

J. Grimm: 'Formaspekte der 2. Klaviersonate van Boulez', *SMz*, cxii (1972), 201

I. Stoïanowa: 'Pli selon pli: portrait de Mallarmé', *Musique en jeu* (1973), no.11, p.75

R. Gehrlach: 'Pierre Boulez und Stéphane Mallarmé: ein Fragment über das Artifizielle', *Über Musik und Sprache*, ed. R. Stephan (Mainz, 1974)

T. Hirsbrunner: 'Die surrealistische Komponente in Pierre Boulez: *Le marteau sans maître*', *NZM*, cxxxv (1974), 420

R. Stephan: 'Bemerkungen zu Pierre Boulez: Komposition von Rene Chars *Klage der verliebten Eidechse*', *Zur musikalische Analyse*, ed. G. Schuhmacher (Darmstadt, 1974), 441

I. Stoianowa: 'La *Troisième sonate* de Boulez et le projet mallarméen du Livre', *Musique en jeu* (1974), no.16, p.9

——: 'Verbe et son "centre et absence" ', *Musique en jeu* (1974), no.16, p.79 [partly on *e. e. cummings ist der Dichter*]

A. Cross: 'Form and Expression in Boulez' *Don*', *MR*, xxxvi (1975), 215

G. Levin: *An Analysis of Movements III and IX from Le marteau sans maître by Pierre Boulez* (diss., Brandeis U., 1975)

J. Peyser: *Boulez: Composer, Conductor, Enigma* (New York, 1976; London, 1977) [reviewed by S. Lipman, *Times Literary Supplement* (11 March 1977), 277]

A. Trenkamp: 'The Concept of "Aléa" in Boulez's "Constellation-Miroir" ', *ML*, lvii (1976), 1

281

Boulez

L. Koblyakov: 'Pierre Boulez "Le marteau sans maître": Analysis of Pitch Structure', *Zeitschrift für Musiktheorie*, vii/1 (1977), 24

P. Griffiths: *Boulez* (London, 1978)

M. Stahnke: *Struktur und Ästhetik bei Boulez: Untersuchungen zum Formanten 'Trope' der Dritten Klaviersonate*, Hamburger Beiträge zur Musikwissenschaft 21 (Hamburg, 1979)

D. Jameux: 'Boulez and the "Machine": Some Thoughts on the Composer's Use of Various Electro-acoustic Media', *Contemporary Music Review*, i (1984), 11

J. Häusler, ed., *Pierre Boulez: eine Festschrift zum 60. Geburtstag* (Vienna, 1985)

T. Hirsbrunner: *Pierre Boulez und sein Werk* (Laaber, 1985)

Index

283

Index

285

Index

Index

Picabia, Francis, 134
Picasso, Pablo, 134, *141*, 143
Pierné, (Henri Constant) Gabriel, 104
Plato: *Dialogues*, 134
Pleyel [instrument makers], 65
Poe, Edgar Allan, 47, 55, 152
Polignac, Princesse Edmond de [Princess of Scey-Montbéliard], 7, 8, 204
Poulenc, Francis Jean Marcel, 197–218, 253
Poulenc (née Royer), Jenny [mother], 197
——, uncle of, 197
Pourville, 47, 95
Prokofiev, Sergey, 203
Pro-Musica Society [based in New York], 164
Proust, Marcel, 8
Prudhomme, René-François-Armand: *see* Sully-Prudhomme
Puccini, Giacomo, 182

Radics, Béla, 103–4
Radiguet, Raymond, 205
Rakhul'sky, *43*
Rambouillet, 4
Rameau, Jean-Philippe, 17, 103
——, *Hippolyte et Aricie*, 262
Ravel, Edovard [brother], 166
Ravel (neé Delouart), Marie [mother], 151, 160, 161, 170
——, aunt of, 151
Ravel, (Joseph) Maurice, 8, *10*, 20, 85, 86, 89, 102, 106–7, 108, 132, 133, 143, 144, 151–93, 197, 212, 221, 230
——, projected works, 158, 160, 163, 165
Ravel, Pierre Joseph [father], 151, 168, 173
Regnier, Henri de, 170
René, Charles, 151
Rennes, 3
——, St Sauveur, 3
Reverdy, Pierre, 236

Revue blanche, La, 44
Revue musicale, 107
Reyer, Ernest, 11
Riley, Terry, 187
Rimsky-Korsakov, Nikolay Andreyevich, 49, 107, 152
——, *Capriccio espagnol* op.34, 186
Rocamadour, *227*
——, Notre Dame, 198, 208
Roger, Thérèse, 44
Roger-Ducasse, Jean, 8, *10*, 11
Roland-Manuel [pseud. of Roland Alexis Manuel Lévy], 133, 134, 160, 184, 187
——, father-in-law, of, 134
Rolland, Romain, 102, 106
Rome, 42, 57, 73, 100
——, Villa Medici, 42
Ronsard, Pierre de, 163
Rosbaud, Hans, 261
Ross, Earls of, 98
Rossetti, Dante-Gabriel: *The Blessed Damozel*, 58
Roussel, Albert, 132
Rubinstein, Artur, 201
Rubinstein, Ida, 56, 165
Russia, 42, 45, 107

St Etienne, Loire, 251
St Germain-en-Laye, 41
St Jean-de-Luz, 48
Saint-Marceaux, Mme Marguerite de, 8
St Petersburg (now Leningrad), 12
Saint-Saëns, Camille, 3, 4, 6, 9, 17, 21, 23, 24, 58, 59, 62, 104, 160
——, *Samson et Dalila*, 5
Salis, Rudolph, 130
Samain, Albert, 7
Sargent, John, 9
Satie, Alfred [father], 129, 130
Satie, Conrad [brother], 136
Satie, Erik (Eric) Alfred Leslie, 104, 129–49, 152, 179, 187, 197, 200, 209
Satie (née Barnetsche), Eugénie [stepmother], 129, 137

289

Index